Conversations with Paule Marshall

Literary Conversations Series
Peggy Whitman Prenshaw
General Editor

Conversations with Paule Marshall

Edited by James C. Hall and Heather Hathaway

University Press of Mississippi   Jackson

Books by Paule Marshall

Brown Girl, Brownstones, Random House, 1959
Soul Clap Hands and Sing, Atheneum Publishers, 1961
The Chosen Place, the Timeless People, Harcourt, Brace, 1969
Reena and Other Stories, Feminist Press, 1983
Praisesong for the Widow, Putnam, 1983
Daughters, Atheneum Publishers, 1991
The Fisher King, Scribner, 2000
Triangular Road: A Memoir, Basic Civitas Books, 2009

www.upress.state.ms.us

The University Press of Mississippi is a member of the Association of American University Presses.

Copyright © 2010 by University Press of Mississippi
All rights reserved
Manufactured in the United States of America

First printing 2010   ∞

Library of Congress Cataloging-in-Publication Data
Marshall, Paule, 1929–
  Conversations with Paule Marshall / edited by James C. Hall and Heather Hathaway.
  p. cm. — (Literary conversations series)
  Includes index.
  ISBN 978-1-60473-743-1 (cloth : alk. paper) 1. Marshall, Paule, 1929—Interviews. 2. Authors, American—20th century—Interviews. 3. African American women authors—Biography. I. Hall, James C., 1960– II. Hathaway, Heather. III. Title.
  PS3563.A7223Z46 2010
  813'.54—dc22
  [B]   2010018387
British Library Cataloging-in-Publication Data available

Contents

Introduction   vii

Chronology   xvii

A Discussion with Dr. Hiram Haydn and Others on *The Chosen Place, the Timeless People*   *Hiram Haydn*   3

Re-creating Ourselves All Over the World: A Conversation with Paule Marshall   *'Molara Ogundipe-Leslie*   31

In Celebration of Our Triumph   *Alexis De Veaux*   40

A Talk with Mary Helen Washington   *Mary Helen Washington*   54

Talk as a Form of Action: An Interview with Paule Marshall   *Sabine Bröck*   59

PW Interviews Paule Marshall   *Sally Lodge*   72

Interview with Paule Marshall   *Sandi Russell*   77

A *MELUS* Interview: Paule Marshall   *Joyce Pettis*   84

An Interview with Paule Marshall   *Daryl Cumber Dance*   96

Holding onto the Vision: Sylvia Baer Interviews Paule Marshall   *Sylvia Baer*   116

The *Booklist* Interview: Paule Marshall   *Donna Seaman*   124

Meditations on Language and the Self: A Conversation with Paule Marshall
Melody Graulich and Lisa Sisco 130

To Be in the World: An Interview with Paule Marshall *Angela Elam* 151

The Art and Politics of Paule Marshall: An Interview
James Hall and Heather Hathaway 157

Paule Marshall on Race and Memory *Dawn Raffel* 189

Index 193

Introduction

On a sunny September morning in 2001, we sat down with Paule Marshall to discuss her work. Our primary interest lay in her then-latest novel, *The Fisher King* (2000), but thanks to her patience and graciousness, six hours later we had traveled over much broader ground ranging from her vision of her art to her role in the civil rights movement. Our 2001 conversation stands as the most recent extended interview of Marshall; her lengthy 1970 dialogue with students in the class of Professor Hiram Haydn, Marshall's original editor at Random House, marks the beginning. (Neither of these conversations has been published elsewhere.) The interviews compiled here range in form from brief pieces to more extensive conversations between the writer and scholars of her work. The latter have, for the most part, been conducted by academics shaped by second-stage feminism and feminist-influenced literary criticism and, as a result, often focus on the trajectory of her career as an important synecdoche for the emergence of women's—and especially black women's—writing. The former, while also attentive to Marshall's authorial voice and identity, allow for more personal revelations. As a whole, these conversations provide a valuable and multifaceted view of both the writer and the woman. They offer a clear sense of the things that change but also of things that remain constant in Marshall's work and in her commentaries on the world around her, providing a comprehensive glimpse of the many stages of her long career.

Several continuing threads run throughout these conversations. The first involves Marshall's descriptions of the artistic influences that shaped her conception of language and literature. She discusses in numerous interviews, as well as recounts in her oft-cited essay, "Shaping the World of My Art" (1973), how, in childhood, she entered into "the never-ending apprenticeship which is writing" by listening silently to the conversations of her Barbadian mother and her mother's friends—the women to whom Marshall has referred as the "poets in the kitchen." In her interview with Alexis De Veaux, Marshall explains:

Perhaps the most important influence in my becoming a writer is due to those fantastic women, my mother and her friends, who would gather every afternoon after work—they did day's work—and talk. We lived in an old brownstone house, which we leased. It had a huge, old-fashioned kitchen with a coal stove. An almost daily ritual for them was to gather there and talk. In that kitchen I was in the presence of art of a very high order because those women, in their talk, knew what literature was all about. . . . They *created poetry* as they sat around a table talking. It wasn't that they read. There weren't books of poetry around the house as such. . . . But their ability to recreate scene, to talk about people, to dissect a character, that was the stuff of poetry and literature. . . . There was theatre taking place in that kitchen each day. Theatre of a very high order.

In childhood and adolescence, as Marshall tells interviewer Sabine Bröck among others, she complemented this aural apprenticeship with a voracious reading appetite that introduced her to everything from Nancy Drew and Laura Ingalls Wilder to Jane Austen, Joseph Conrad, Thomas Mann, and, eventually, Ralph Ellison. But the transformative influence came in Marshall's discovery around age ten of Paul Laurence Dunbar, whom she describes to Sally Lodge (1984) as making her "aware that there was a mass body of material by black writers" and giving her "the courage to go up to the white librarian and say, 'I'd like to have some books by Negro writers.'"

One of those books turned out to be Gwendolyn Brooks's *Maud Martha*. Whereas Marshall's mother and her friends were Marshall's informal literary foremothers, Brooks proved to be her formal literary foremother thanks to the life she gave to Maud Martha, the first black female character whom Marshall considers to be fully realized in fiction. Marshall explains to Bröck: "I think she . . . was a truly . . . break-through character in American literature in the sense that Brooks took the life of a terribly ordinary young woman and made of it something of art. . . . Even though I hadn't started writing at that point, I sensed that this was the kind of thing I would attempt when I started writing: to say that there was something of worth, something to celebrate, that there was something to acknowledge about the life of women who had been simply dismissed by society."

Exploring and celebrating the lives of "ordinary" women like Maud Martha, women whom society often dismisses because of their race and gender, constitutes a second thread running through both Marshall's fiction and the interviews contained here. She is routinely considered by writers and scholars alike to be a literary pioneer in terms of her depiction of women of African ancestry, beginning with her 1959 novel, *Brown Girl, Brownstones*.

INTRODUCTION ix

The story of how Marshall went about getting a publisher for her first novel aptly illustrates the tenacity and determination that have underscored her long career. As she relayed to us,

> I had no idea how to go about it in the orthodox way, which meant even then getting yourself an agent who would shop it around for you and know what publishers might be interested in your type of manuscript. So, not knowing any of that I simply went to the Yellow Pages of the New York telephone book, then to "Publishers." There were no publishers under A, but there was one under B, Bobbs-Merrill, so I sent it to Bobbs-Merrill, which was a very reputable publishing house at that time. Bobbs-Merrill kept it for close to six months. . . . [Eventually] I learned that Bucklin Moon, who was one of the great editors at the time, had very much liked the book. But editors played musical chairs and he had gone off . . . somewhere else and left the manuscript behind, so they sent it back to me. But in the interim . . . I had heard that the editor-in-chief at Random House was interested in young writers. . . . So I said, "Interested in young writers? Okay!" I packed up my manuscript, sent it off, and they took it!

Upon its publication, *Brown Girl, Brownstones* received significant critical acclaim. As Marshall describes in her memoir, *Triangular Road* (2009), Langston Hughes was so impressed that he attended the book party intended to publicize the novel. But, as a book about the life of a young black woman in 1959, it was only modestly marketed by the press and read by the public. It took until its republication in 1981 by the Feminist Press, in fact, for *Brown Girl, Brownstones* to be recognized as a literary classic. Since 1981, Marshall has come to be seen as a vital link between the writing of Gwendolyn Brooks, Anne Petry, and Margaret Walker in the forties and fifties and the "renaissance" in African American women's writing that emerged in the seventies, featuring Toni Morrison and Alice Walker, among others. It is important to note, however, that Marshall does not merely link the two periods; rather, she *spans* them, publishing her first novel in 1959 and her memoir in 2009. She has produced critically acclaimed work consistently over a half century and these interviews chart nicely, if read chronologically, her growing recognition of the significance of that contribution over the course of her career.

Marshall continued to be highly productive following the publication of *Brown Girl, Brownstones*. In 1961 she authored a collection of novellas titled *Soul Clap Hands and Sing* (1961). This was followed by three short stories, "Return of the Native" (1964), "To Da-duh, In Memoriam" (1967), and "Some

Get Wasted" (1974), as well as several essays and magazine articles. She also wrote her second novel, *The Chosen Place, the Timeless People* (1969), embarking upon another stage of her career—one in which, like Richard Wright, she determined that words could, and should, be used as weapons in the fight for social justice. As *Triangular Road* clearly depicts, Marshall has always been keenly attentive to politics and particularly to the geo-political issues affecting members of the African diaspora. Her conception of the important relationship between art and politics constitutes a third thread running throughout these conversations. Marshall emphasizes her interest in the subject repeatedly throughout the interviews: see, for example, her early debates with the students in Haydn's class about the political and social function of the novel; her discussions about the writer as activist with both Maya Angelou and Malcolm X, as described in our conversation; her dialogue with De Veaux about the presence of the U.S. in Cambodia; and her critique of neo-colonialism in the Caribbean, which she addresses with Dance. In all these conversations Marshall makes clear that, for her, politics and storytelling go hand in hand. As she describes to us, there has never been "a separation of writing and politics; it was just always clear for me as a writer that the political was inseparable, *inseparable*, from what I felt I needed to say—what I was impelled to say—in the world. I could not avoid the political. I would always, yes, be primarily a storyteller, but a storyteller who is always telling about the social, the political, the racial, because they are my reality . . . the struggle is fought in many ways, on many fronts, and literature is certainly one of those fronts."

Marshall tackles political issues using the formal elements of plot, characterization, and setting as her tools. Consider, for instance, her second novel, *The Chosen Place, the Timeless People*, a work she describes to interviewer 'Molara Ogundipe-Leslie as "largely dramatizing political ideas." The novel explores in detail the political issues related to colonialism and white supremacy, addressing these subjects through individual portrayals of human contradiction and complexity. Again, gender and women's roles are particularly significant. Marshall explains:

> *Chosen Place* is a very political novel in that it reflects my effort to move my women characters to another level in the fiction by having them participate in social and political issues. I see them as activists, doers, agents of change. I didn't come from a passive people, you know. The mother-poets didn't just gossip—they talked about current events, politics, the economy, the world. And this has had a great impact on me. The Black woman character [Merle Kinbona] in *Chosen*

Place is trying on the one had to work through certain personal problems and to achieve personal freedom, but on another level she speaks for—she embodies— the aspirations of the have-nots of the world. I'm not a political writer—I'm a storyteller—and I try never to forget that. But if you look closely at my work, below the surface the political is always there.[1]

She has occasionally paid the price of popular acclaim as a result of this interest in rendering and reflecting upon political and social realities. For instance, part of the larger world that Marshall explored in *The Chosen Place, the Timeless People* involved an interracial relationship, something that was clearly out of sync with the political, if not necessarily the literary, climate of the late sixties and early seventies. As she comments in her interview with us, "It was vilified! . . . An interracial relationship . . . was just insupportable to [the black intelligentsia], so they didn't even deal with the real meaning of the novel."

But Marshall's solution to such marginalization has been simply to "stay the course," as she puts it, and this proves to be a fourth thread running through the interviews. In a 1966 article on "The Negro Woman in American Literature," she explains that she developed early on a means of sustaining herself as a writer in the midst of criticism or popular neglect: ". . . the writer has to remain at all times true to her personal vision, even though it might not be in fashion this season. . . . I believe—perhaps I have to in order to justify my own commitment to writing—that sound art, good writing, the long years and the pain that one has to invest to learn one's craft, cannot in the long run be ignored. Not for always, anyway."[2] Thirty-five years later, Marshall reiterates this same point to us: "You write for a readership that can appreciate it. It might not be sizeable in terms of millions, but a respectable readership out there sustains you. As one young scholar said to me, 'Your work has given us a future.' Wonderful, wonderful! So you take something like that and you let it sustain you because that's what it's about."

Marshall's third and fourth novels, *Praisesong for the Widow* (1983) and *Daughters* (1991), might be considered as marking another stage in life as a writer. She explains that *Praisesong*

grew out of something very personal: as I moved into middle age, I wanted to explore the whole question of what it means to grow older in this society. The notion that after age thirty everything is downhill—the American idea of youth— offends me deeply, because it says that after a certain age you are locked into a kind of rigidity, your life is through. What is suggested in *Praisesong* is that one has the capacity to change—to reconstitute one's life—at any age. Once can stage a kind of personal revolution and win.[3]

Daughters also recounts a "personal revolution" of sorts as it tells the story of a young woman seeking to sever the patriarchal ties that bind her to her father. But in keeping with Marshall's interest in the political, this personal tale is set within a larger context of neo-colonialism in the Caribbean. The interview in this collection conducted by Daryl Cumber Dance is especially informative about *Daughters*, as well as about the events in Marshall's own life that influenced the creation of this work.

Marshall published her fifth novel, *The Fisher King*, in 2000. Somewhat surprisingly, our interview is the only one to consider the novel in detail but from our conversation, it is clear that, while many themes and methods remain constant in each stage of her work, many also continue to change. For instance, in *The Fisher King* Marshall breaks new ground through her creation of her first male protagonist. She explained to us that she deliberately tried to write against the model of her previous "full-blown" novels, opting instead to experiment with "brevity, . . . compression, . . . implication and suggestion" rather than the detailed explication that characterized *Brown Girl, Brownstones* and *The Chosen Place, the Timeless People*. At the same time, as in her previous work, Marshall is also keenly conscious of both the surface and subsurface messages in her writing. "I wanted to challenge readers also in *The Fisher King*. I wanted readers to be involved in the book with the same intensity that I was. I wanted them not just to deal with the surface story but to unearth themes and concerns below the surface. The reader of *The Fisher King* is going to have to work almost as hard as I did." Readers must work hard to understand the unconventional forms of love that she presents in the novel. They must be attentive to the role of history as it shapes the lives of her characters. Finally, they must read carefully to discern the potential for reconciliation and unification among individuals, peoples, or nations.

It is this latter theme—the possibility of unity and reconciliation—that provides the fifth and perhaps most important thread weaving itself vibrantly through the interviews and "the work," as Marshall refers to it. In each stage of her career, regardless of whether she is writing about West Indian and African American communities in Brooklyn, class and race conflicts in the Caribbean, or challenges couples face in simply trying to sustain a relationship, Marshall strives, in the end, to bring people together. As she described to Jacqueline Trescott in a 1991 *Washington Post* interview, "In all of this, I try to express my hope for reconciliation, cooperation, love and unity between us. And respect for each other."[4]

Not surprisingly, these same threads shape Marshall's most recent work, *Triangular Road: A Memoir*. Based on a lecture series she delivered at Harvard University in 2005 related to the theme "Bodies of Water," Marshall organizes her memoir around three specific waterways—the James River, the Caribbean Sea, and the Atlantic Ocean—and reflects upon their significance to black history and culture in the Americas. At the same time, she comments more extensively on events in her own life than she has in any other public venue and in so doing, creates a rich self-portrait that complements the themes underscoring her fiction.

The role that the artist can play in political activism, for example, is a main focus of the memoir. In the opening piece, "Homage to Mr. Hughes," on whose poem "The Negro Speaks of Rivers" Marshall bases her chapter headings, Marshall chronicles for the first time her experiences traveling with Langston Hughes and William Melvin Kelly to Europe as a cultural attaché in 1965. We learn a great deal about the discussions she had with Hughes about the role of the writer as "revolutionary" during periods of political ferment—for him, during the resistance against lynchings and burnings of the 1920s and 1930s and on up to the McCarthy era, and for her, during the then-ongoing Freedom Struggle of the civil rights movement. In the second chapter, Marshall focuses on the James River and the role of Richmond in the trade of enslaved Africans. Here she examines, through both political observations and personal anecdotes, how the history of slavery in the United States continues to cripple personal relationships, local civic life, and national politics. Though the third chapter of the memoir, "I've Known Seas: The Caribbean Sea," reveals much about her personal and family history, Marshall's pursuit of social and political justice underscores each vignette, whether she is discussing colonization of the Caribbean islands or contemporary cultural rituals reclaiming history and asserting independence. The final chapter, "I've Known Oceans: The Atlantic," continues the pursuit as it depicts the cultural confrontations and political issues surrounding FESTAC '77, the Second World Festival of Black and African Arts held in Lagos, Nigeria, in 1977.

Marshall also provides more personal information about herself and her family in *Triangular Road*. She reiterates the important influence her mother's language had upon her development as a writer, but she also sheds light upon the back-story, if you will, of Deighton and Silla Boyce in *Brown Girl, Brownstones*. Though her first novel is only loosely autobiographical, the stories recounted in the memoir of her own parents' immigration to the United States and their respective patterns of adjustment clearly provide a foundation for her fiction.

But the steadiest beat throughout the memoir, as it is of the interviews, consists of Marshall's interest in reconciliation and unity. As always, she portrays this as neither a small nor simple task, particularly between blacks and whites. In the chapter on the James River, for example, which flows through Richmond, Virginia—the heart of the Confederacy and, ironically enough, Marshall's current home—she points to the crimes originally inflicted on blacks during slavery and their lingering consequences for contemporary black-white relationships. It is not clear whether she believes that these rifts are, in the end, reconcilable. In the chapter on FESTAC '77, however, she talks of forgiving Africans for "the old shameful footnote of history" in which "their forebears [had] been complicit, some of them, in the nefarious trade that had reduced our . . . [forbears] to mere articles of . . . *chattel cargo* to be bought and sold and whipped and worked for free!" (159). For this, however, she concludes that "All's forgiven." Such reconciliation among disparate wings of the African diaspora is possible in the memoir—indeed, in Marshall's life—because of the coherence she feels among the three prongs of her identity. "Africa, Barbados, Brooklyn—that's the triangle that defines me and my work," she said in a *New York Times* interview with Felicia Lee (March 12, 2009) explaining the title of *Triangular Road*. "There is so much in the West Indian culture that has that African flavor," she said. "This [memoir] is my attempt to get a fuller picture. We need to see the triangular nature of our inheritance and our place in the world."

As many of Marshall's themes have remained constant over the stages of her career, so has she, as an interviewee. As so many interviewers convey, always she is cordial and tolerant. She is most engaged when discussing the details of specific passages of her work; she is clearly delighted by those who read her fiction closely. Notable in many of the interviews is the degree to which each novel, regardless of the distance between the present and its creation, seems to be a living document that remains as fresh to Marshall as it was on the day it was published. As interviewer Joyce Pettis notes: "One gets the singular impression that the ideas and plans for all of her fiction, retained or discarded, remain vibrantly alive in her thinking and imagination to animate her conversation as she recalls planning and researching content or selecting concept and images to convey her ideas." She appears as eager to discuss her first work as her last, and part of the joy of interviewing her results from the pleasure she, herself, takes in opening old copies of her novels, finding the passage in question, and revisiting it to test her or her interviewer's interpretation of it.

Marshall is less willing, however, to share details about her personal life. These interviews clearly reflect that overall, she remains a private person. She is a self-described loner who finds the work of writing to be both exasperating and exhilarating and who finds the work of promoting her fiction to be the least desirable aspect of her profession. As De Veaux noted of her nearly thirty years ago, "Paule is not interested in 'selling the book.' Television and radio appearances, book parties, public debates, cocktail parties and the like do not appeal to her." As the number of interviews conducted in her own living room attest, "she will, more often than not, opt for the comforts of her own private environment." She seeks not to be a literary megastar, but rather to have her work be recognized for its quality and the contributions it makes to American literature. Again, to quote De Veaux, "though not wanting attention focused on herself, she does want attention given to her work, and that is the paradox Paule Marshall finds herself constantly caught up in." We hope that this collection and the rich portrait that it paints of Paule Marshall, particularly when read in conjunction with *Triangular Road*, will ensure the ongoing critical and popular attention that her oeuvre warrants.

HH
JCH

1. Kate Rushin, "Paule Marshall: Stages in a Writer's Life," *Sojourner* 10.6 (April 1985): 16–17.

2. Alice Childress, Paule Marshall, and Sarah E. Wright, "The Negro Woman in American Literature," *Freedomways* 6.1 (Winter 1966): 8–25.

3. Rushin, "Paule Marshall: Stages in a Writer's Life," *Sojourner* 10.6 (April 1985). 16.

4. Jacqueline Trescott, "The Daughter of the Mother Poets: Novelist Paule Marshall," *Washington Post*, October 8, 1991: C1–2.

Chronology

1929   Valenza Pauline Burke ("Paule") born 9 April in Stuyvesant Heights neighborhood of Brooklyn, NY to Samuel and Adriana (Clement) Burke, immigrants from Barbados.

1936   First visit to Barbados.

c.1948   First sustained writing while convalescing in an upstate New York sanatorium.

1949   Graduates from high school.

1950   Marries Kenneth E. Marshall.

1952   Ralph Ellison's *Invisible Man* is published; John O. Killens founds The Harlem Writers' Guild which Marshall occasionally attends.

1953   Earns B.A. (cum laude) from Brooklyn College and is Phi Beta Kappa; begins work at *Our World* magazine; publishes story "The Valley Between"; attends Hunter College; appearance of Gwendolyn Brooks's novel *Maud Martha* which has significant impact upon Marshall.

1957   Travels to Brazil and the Caribbean on assignment for *Our World*.

1958   Birth of her son Evan Keith; continues to write her novel from the privacy of a friend's apartment.

1959   Publishes *Brown Girl, Brownstones* with Random House.

1960   CBS Television Workshop Production of *Brown Girl, Brownstones*.

1961   Guggenheim Fellowship; publishes *Soul Clap Hands and Sing*.

1962   Rosenthal Award; moves temporarily to Grenada to work on *The Chosen Place, the Timeless People*

1963   Divorces Kenneth E. Marshall.

1964   Receives Ford Foundation Grant; participates in the June debate at New York's Town Hall, "The Black Revolution and the White Backlash"; Ellison publishes *Shadow and Act* which Marshall deeply admires.

1965   Travels with Langston Hughes and William Melvin Kelly to Europe as cultural attaché for the U.S. State Department.

1966 Receives National Endowment for the Arts Grant; groundbreaking panel presentation at New School for Social Research, "The Negro Woman and American Literature," eventually published as "The Negro Woman in American Literature" in *Freedomways*; first appearance of "Reena" in John Henrik Clarke's *American Negro Short Stories*.
1967 Publishes "To Da-duh, In Memoriam" in *New World Magazine*.
1969 Publishes *The Chosen Place, the Timeless People* with Harcourt, Brace.
1970 Marries Nourry Menard; hired as lecturer at Yale University; publishes "Fannie Lou Hamer: Hunger Has No Color Line" in June *Vogue*.
1973 Publishes "Shaping the World of My Art" in *New Letters*.
1974 Receives Creative Artists Public Service Fellowship; publishes "Some Get Wasted," in John Henrik Clarke's *Harlem, USA*.
1977 Receives National Endowment for the Arts Grant; attends FESTAC, first travel to Africa.
1979 Publishes "Return of the Native," in Roseanne Bell, et al., eds., *Sturdy Black Bridges*.
1980 Travels to Kenya and Uganda.
1981 Republication of *Brown Girl, Brownstones* by Feminist Press.
1983 Publishes *Praisesong for the Widow* with Putnam and *Reena and Other Stories* with Feminist Press; "The Making of a Writer: From the Poets in the Kitchen" in *New York Times Book Review*; faculty in residence at the Iowa Writer's Workshop; begins appointment as Professor of Creative Writing at Virginia Commonwealth University in Richmond.
1984 Receives Before Columbus Foundation Award; Regent's Professor at the University of California at Berkeley.
1985 "Rising Islanders of Bed-Stuy," in *New York Times Sunday Magazine*, 3 November.
1989 Receives John Dos Passos Award for Fiction.
1991 Publishes *Daughters* with Atheneum.
1992 Receives MacArthur Foundation Fellowship ("Genius Award"); *Daughters* nominated for *Los Angeles Times* Book Award.
1995 Publishes *Language Is the Only Homeland: Bajan Poets Abroad* with the Central Bank of Barbados.
1997 Named Helen Gould Sheppard Professor in Literature and Culture, New York University.

2000 Publishes *The Fisher King* with Scribner.
2001 Receives Black Caucus of the American Library Association Literary Award.
2009 Publishes *Triangular Road: A Memoir* with Basic Civitas Books.

Conversations with Paule Marshall

A Discussion with Dr. Hiram Haydn and Others on *The Chosen Place, the Timeless People*

Hiram Haydn/1970

From a collection of interviews with creative writers conducted by Hiram Haydn at the University of Pennsylvania. Courtesy of Department of Special Collections, Stanford University Libraries.

Part I

Students Present: Anne Bovee, Elliot Abhau, Alan Stern, Bob McCloud, Lee Eisenberg, Susan Hermann

Lee: You say that you write primarily for black people, that you wrote this book for black people.
PM: I write for black people. That was a kind of general statement, not only about this book.
Lee: Right. We had a little bit of trouble coming to grips with what we called the "mysticism" of Bournehills, the elusive quality that Saul had a great deal of trouble with in terms of finding out what made the island and the people tick. I was wondering whether you think a white audience could ever discover what that mysticism was? It was unclear to some of us. Exactly what do you mean by the elusive qualities?
PM: Hmmm. Unfortunately, a lot of black readers don't understand it either, but the elusive quality is the thing about Bournehills that makes it, indeed, the chosen place.
Dr. H: I want them to work on this more. He's asking whether you think

it's possible for a white reader to comprehend the full significance of the "myth"?

PM: Yes, I think it's possible . . . There are some black people who don't really penetrate the significance and symbolic meaning of Bournehills.

Dr. H: Let me explain a little more what I mean about this. I'm trying to see how far these students can get, unaided, into this. Let's make them work a little.

PM: Yes, right, yes. This is something, Hiram, that we discussed long before the book was finally completed and put between two covers because you were mystified and said there has to be some indication given as to just what the meaning is. So, I go back to you. Did you read, really in depth, the closing section of the chapter . . . when Saul leaves Merle after her "breakdown" because of the closing of Bournehills, when he comes to her bedroom and finds her in an almost catatonic state?

Dr. H: Yes, that was brought up yesterday. Who has the pages?

PM: The description of the room begins on page 400. It says, "Curiously now he looked around the large room." He not only is struck by what her room means, this place he's never been permitted to enter before—how she's brought together all the things that have gone into making it and has surrounded herself with all of this—but he also, for the first time, links it up to Bournehills itself. He begins to see as he leaves, the significance. From 401 to 403 pretty much explains what he finally gets to understand as a mystery of Bournehills. If you read 402 again, that shouldn't be a mystery to any reader, black or white.

Lee: Maybe the question should be more detailed in the sense that I think I understood the timelessness, the fact that tomorrow would not be different from yesterday, the solitary figure standing alone on the beach, as you mentioned at one point. Is that enough, though, for the white reader or the average reader? Is it enough to appreciate the theoretical concept, the timelessness of that mystical bind with what went before . . . or is it necessary to really feel that sort of elusiveness, that ephemeral quality? I didn't feel it. I think I cognitively appreciated it, but I didn't identify with it.

PM: Well, it has nothing to do with the fact that you're white. Perhaps for you the whole sense of the timelessness of the place and of the people was not strongly enough stated, but that would make me a different writer if I did it that way. I mean, I couldn't do it that way. It has to be a kind of a subtle, unstated thing that one senses, but one doesn't actually pick up into words. I had figures sort of standing outside of time, and I described how their eyes seemed to have that sense of looking back into the past. These are my devices of suggesting that timelessness. I can't do it in any more obvious a way.

Lee: Right. So in other words, when you say you write for black people primarily, or at least that is in the front part of your mind, you're not precluding any sort of cultural differences which would impair a reader from another race.

PM: I really think you're talking about two different things, the technical strategies of writing versus the theme. When I say I write primarily for black people, I'm thinking primarily in terms of my larger theme . . . You see, because one of the great struggles for me, especially with this book, (I really noticed it more with this book than with the other two), was the struggle to maintain it on one level—that first level—as an interesting story so that a lot of people who are not going to be concerned about other meanings can go along. My whole feeling about writing is that I am, first and foremost, a storyteller in the very African sense of a storyteller—a man who sits by the fire and tells stories. On the other hand, how could I say all that I wanted to at the same time? Letting these two things move together, be one, having my themes be an integral part of the story itself, was a battle. So I had to do it in ways like the pig-sticking.

Dr. H: That's a very effective way. Your use of symbolism throughout led us when we came to a discussion about characterization. Several people found characters very convincing and very real, and others felt they were somewhat stereotyped. It was Mr. Eisenberg who said—why don't I let you say it, Lee?

Lee: Well, very simply, I think that the people who were criticizing the book on the basis that some of the characters were stereotyped were condemning the use of stereotypes per se as not good for any book. I just raised the point that perhaps there are times, given certain themes, where an allowance should be made for more stereotyping. I'm not saying that all characters should literally be stereotypes, but stereotype characteristics are excusable and even called for in certain kinds of books. I would just submit that your book is one of those, where any tendency to see stereotypes might be an excusable one.

PM: Well, I'd be interested in pursuing what characteristics of a soul you found to be stereotyped.

Lee: I was not one of those who were criticizing the stereotype.

PM: No, no, no. I'm not talking in terms of criticizing, I'm just curious.

Dr. H: He was suggesting that the symbolic values of your characters might have been, in the novel you were writing, more important than a complex individual characterization.

PM: Are the symbolic qualities stereotypes?

Dr. H: Yes. We don't mean hackneyed . . .

PM: That's an odd . . .

Lee: I don't think we were talking about the main characters as much. I think we would agree that Merle is the strongest character and the least stereotyped. I just want to talk about her. I've rehearsed the question. I don't think we thought of them as stereotyped, although they were highly symbolic; she embodied so much of whatever message there was in her own personal history. I think we were talking more about Harriet in that particular case and Lyle, some of the more secondary characters.

Dr. H.: Well, then we're all talking about different things. May I put a parenthesis in here for a moment? Then I'm going to quit and let you talk it out. In this review, we read, ". . . As the characters acquire symbolic resonance, we see that Alan represents an effete civilization that pledged its soul to the gods of technology. Harriett embodies the suicidal impulse of the Western psyche. Saul represents the possibility of transformation and renewal." Now, this man has it all figured out on that symbolic basis, and putting these two things together, I thought this was the sense in which Eisenberg meant: if they had that symbolic value or types representing these qualities, then it was a good thing for them to be types rather than highly developed individuals. On the other hand, Alan is talking about something quite different, and I'm interested in your reaction to all of that. Now you all go ahead. I yield.

PM: I think why I'm a bit confused is because you're implying that the symbolic content that a character might embody also makes of him a kind of stereotype, and that to me is not really . . .

Dr. H: No, but it's bound to make him a more primary type.

PM: Perhaps so, but again you go back to complexity. A character can operate on that level of symbolism, but—this is what I was striving for—he can also be a person, a character, a complex creation. Yes, I wanted all of these people to stand for very definite points of view, but I also wanted them at the same time to be people, to matter to you, to interest you on the level simply as people. There are two things going on.

Dr. H: But you do see that sometimes they can be in conflict? If you want to have a major character represent this force or element in our world and you bring him to a scene where, for example, Harriet sees the children on the beach, overcomes her resentment, goes to the larder, cuts off the end of the loaf of bread that they never eat anyhow, chooses five eggs out of the two dozen to give the children, and the other parceling out in this rather . . .

PM: . . . sparing way.

Dr. H: . . . sparing way, she represents the colonial policy beautifully. But she contradicts herself as she has been through the book earlier, because she has never been mean like that. She's never had to be; she's a wealthy Main Line girl who parcels it out, I should say, without much thought for the individual human people involved in it, as a philanthropist. So that here—it's the only place I can cite to you where you didn't succeed in doing both for me—but here I felt you were unfair to the person and very fair to her as the colonial power. You see?

PM: That's an interesting reaction to that.

Dr. H: I never thought of that when I was working with you, reading the book as your editor.

PM: It's interesting because you see that as the first instance where Harriet betrays herself, but she does before, Hiram. That whole scene with the pullet eggs that she makes for the children who are hungry there at the house, just this minimal little thing that she knows cannot possibly . . .

Dr. H: That's all there is.

PM: I know, but if she were really a philanthropist, you know, there is the village shop . . .

Dr. H: All right, all right . . .

PM: . . . for one goes and puts the crumbs on the table, you see.

Dr. H: All right. I drop the philanthropy. I drop the philanthropy.

PM: It's always that Harriet stands for that little piecemeal giving that's so typified.

Susan: I thought of asking you about the whole scene where she talks about giving the toys to the maids' children. She doesn't want to part with the doll and she says, "No, I love my doll." She wouldn't give it up, and I was thinking that you had said she had never been mean before, and there were other instances . . .

Dr. H: All right, I guess I'm knocked down. It still serves the purpose, which is that it's terribly hard to leave an individual character the freedom to become himself if he's going to represent a consistent symbolic value at the same time.

PM: And it is hellishly hard to do the two.

Dr. H: But you didn't keep up.

Susan: But even if it's representative of something, the colonial powers haven't been consistent in their activities, either.

Dr. H: But we're abstracting them. We're not dealing with the literal colonial powers.

Susan: This is what it's representing, She's not being inconsistent in her symbolism either because if she's . . .

Dr. H: Well, look, Susan, you're starting from the point of view, as Mrs. Marshall herself said, of these people, and from their point of view, from Merle's, for example, and the other people behind her, there has been an overall large consistency in colonial powers of oppression.

PM: . . . exploitation . . .

Dr. H: . . . exploitation, and so on. Now, we're abstracting them, right, from this if they're representing something like that in an individual character in the book. Therefore, you do, I submit in those cases, impugn a kind of consistency. That's what it stands for.

Susan: I thought of that, but I was thinking more in terms of all this being given. There are a few crumbs dropped here and there and that's exactly what Harriet was doing. In that sense, it was consistent even though . . .

Dr. H: Okay. Well, I think you all have backed me down. I think that I lose that discussion, but I'm glad I raised it anyhow because it is a difficult thing. Now, just a last word. There was no question at all about Merle. Everybody felt that she was a wonderfully complex and realized character. As I said yesterday, that she was "quivering with life." So, when you thought we meant something different by stereotype, no. Now, I return the conversation . . .

Alan: I have a question about Merle. It seems to me that Merle dominates this book in so many different ways, and certainly when I think of this book in the future, I will think of her character. I think this is good because she did sum up so much of what was going on. But then I thought about it and, not until she really has her affair with Saul, does she really become a character in the plot actively. I mean, she's active in the plot, but the activities are just to map out what happens: some people come to Bournehills, they live in one house, they move into another house, they interact with other people, and she's constantly there guiding them and commenting. She's like a chorus; she's always summing up things, talking. Then, in the later chapters, she starts telling more of her past and becoming more like a plot character, and then she has an affair with Saul and eventually really takes over the plot at the end. She starts to take action instead of just standing on the sidelines to some extent. I wonder if you ever thought about writing this book with her as a more active character in the plot?

PM: More active in the first part of the book?

Alan: If you start to write this book about a woman who grew up under her circumstances, where she was the protagonist in a more conventional sense. The story could be called "Merle" or use her name as the title of the book.

PM: That would have been another book as you said. Yes. But in this book, technically I couldn't have done it because, you see, Merle is so strong. Even though she's not actually present in the first half or more of the book, one has a sense of her always, of her looking on, reacting, what have you. But, I could not have gone on with her and that kind of verbal outpouring that you have at the beginning when she's first being introduced at the party and at the reception at Lyle's house. She would have just been too much. She would have overwhelmed the whole thing. I had to let the other characters emerge, and I had to work very hard with Harriet because Harriet was an interior person, a person who really lived within herself; she kept people off from her. A lot was going on. With Merle it was just all coming out, you see.

Alan: I agree that it was a much more successful way to do it. If I had to think about myself writing a book with a character that was that strong, I would automatically take that more obvious road and, I think, suffer from it. So I wondered if you ever thought of that.

PM: Yes. I was very conscious of what would happen to the book if I really let Merle go on as she had started in the beginning, just talking and controlling everything. She would have just eclipsed the other characters. And even though she is not felt that much physically in the early part of the book, she's there; one senses her. She doesn't have that much to say after the scientists get started in their work and I describe what Alan does and describe Saul and Harriet setting up the house. One senses her always there in the background, but I couldn't tack her there as present, center stage, because the other characters wouldn't have a chance to live, to breathe.

Alan: Did you consciously think about portraying scenes through dialogue or through description, or did you just write it and see what happened?

PM: All of this has to do with the whole mysterious area of how the novelist chooses to handle his material. One of the criticisms that I've gotten from one or two people about the book was that so much of the book was narrative. They would have hoped for more dialogue, they would have hoped for more humor. Well, I dismiss that. I forget about the humor though I do think about having more dialogue. And that dialogue for me is hell. It's very difficult. I have to work over and over and over on dialogue, so that it's my particular bent as a novelist, it's my prejudice. I prefer narrative; it's easier. I mean, it's all hard, but narrative is less hard.

Alan: I think I liked Merle, or felt her presence all the time, because in the beginning when the car is on the road, she didn't have a chance to talk. It was description: "The woman came . . ." And so she stuck in your mind. I think if I had heard her blabbing on and on right away I would have been offended by her a little bit, I would not have been prepared for her. But by introducing her through description and then letting her betray herself with dialogue, I think she came across successfully and sympathetically instead of just as a strong character who sort of grated on you.

PM: Yes, well that was the fine point that I had to get to, where I wouldn't become too excessive because she was excessive. I mean, she talked too much; she was too dramatic. To get that across without myself as novelist becoming too excessive and overdramatic was quite a trick.

Alan: How much is she based on a person or people you know?

PM: She is based on a number of people. Something about the people I come in contact with stays with me. My characters are pretty much always composites . . .

Bob: I'm wondering if you believe that, in any case, reconciliation is possible.

PM: Well, I think you found one of the basic themes of the book. It is not as strongly stated as some of the others but you've caught it. And that is the conflict, as I see it in myself and as I try to express it in my work, between the longing for reconciliation—and that can take place between two people, between two nations . . .

Dr. H: . . . even with our lives.

PM: . . . yes, I'm talking about it in a very general sense—the conflict between the longing for reconciliation and the realization of how almost impossible that is. That was one of the definite themes of the book. It sounded like a leitmotif throughout—the moaning for reconciliation. I'd like to see people be decent to each other, I really would, you know, but from all that has gone on before, I see how really impossible that is.

Dr. H: But Paule . . .

PM: Just let me pursue that. One of the places where it's very clearly stated—my whole longing for reconciliation even though it's impossible—is on page 109 at the bottom where they meet for the first time. They've just come to the guest house and Merle is introducing all of them around.

> Motioning over Alan, who, his bulging briefcase in one hand and the jar of zinnias in the other, had paused shyly a little distance away, Merle made the introductions. And for the short time that they stood there with Vere's easy smile like a source of light and energy they could all draw upon, they appeared to comprise a warm, close-knit circle. Their small gathering almost suggested a reunion: the coming together of members of a family who had been scattered to the four corners of the earth and changed almost beyond recognition by their differing circumstances, but the same still. They might have been searching for each other for a long time, seeking completion. And they had met finally, (although it was

too late and could only last the moment), here on this desolate coast before this perpetually aggrieved sea which, even as they stood questioning Vere about the places he had worked in America, continued to grieve and rage over the ancient wrong it could neither forget nor forgive.

This sums up the conflict between the longing for reconciliation, the coming together of peoples and nations, and as I see it, the impossibility of that.
Dr. H: Well, "and now therefore to speak concerning hope." There are symbols in this book that represent the other thing. Do any of you recognize them as I say that? What of the symbols that suggest Ben Jonson's poem? "A lily of the day is fair a flower in May"? And now I skip a couple of lines. "And then short measures life may hurt me." I think you have some of those short measures.
Susan: Something struck me when Anne was talking about "the only possibility for change was in revolution." When we came to the part after the cane mill had broken down, after the press had broken down and the people of Bournehills did get together and cooperate and work together to get their cane across the hill to the island, I kept thinking that if it was possible in one instance, perhaps it was possible in another instance. Maybe it wasn't all as hopeless as everybody had assumed. That was the one that seemed the most blatant; I don't know if that was the kind of thing you were talking about.
Dr. H: Uh . . . well, that was the big thing I was thinking about which is just the tremendous quality of the people of Bournehills. I mean all of them from the old man to the ones who gather at the rum shop to the ones working in the fields to the ones standing by the roads. To me, this quality is the most exciting thing in the whole book. By their finding their place in the natural landscape, which is so bleak and so deprived a life to the Westernized eyes who look at it, they're the ones who have found the reconciliation in their linking of the past with the future and in their deep living with this magnificent natural scene which you've described so beautifully both in the ocean and the fields and the hills and all. They found some recognition, some reconciliation, I think.
Bob: Then why did they put on the carnival?
PM: Yes, but they have also refused to become reconciled too. They absolutely refuse to become reconciled to the kind of change that is offered to them—the piecemeal thing that Harriet symbolized.
Dr. H: They are reconciled to the eternal order and not at all to the social situation and the political situation. I was thinking more, when I spoke of hope, of things like flowers and trees, but I feel less about those people too.

We've lost such rhythms, such long, swinging cycles of life . . .
PM: Yes, yes, and that they do have the long view.
Susan: But the flower and tree is momentary just as the passage that was read telling how "they were there together . . ."
Dr. H: That's why I thought of the Ben Jonson poem.
Lee: Isn't it possible that the fact that Merle finally does tell Saul about her past and the fact that Saul tells Merle about his past isn't just another one of those things on an admittedly different level? It didn't really hit me as hope at that point, but looking back, if there's any ground for hope or reconciliation, the fact that these two people did get together and talk to each other this way seems to constitute some type of reconciliation.
PM: I would classify it as a small sign of hope, not really a reconciliation. I would see it more as one of the few hopeful signs that we can always pick out here and there. But in terms of the larger theme—is there really a possibility of reconciliation? I remain doubtful.
Lee: Are you saying you are doubtful on both the interpersonal and social levels?
PM: I would say that it's more likely that there's a possibility of reconciliation on the more personal level, but on the political, social level, given what has gone before, it's very unlikely.
Elliot: I can't define exactly what started me on this, but I kept running across instances that made me feel exactly as if I'd been there, but it was with different characters in a different situation. It seemed as if what Vere thought that the girl had done to him (aborting his child) was the same as what he thought Merle had done to him and the same thing that Sasha thought Saul did to her. In each case there involved a child.
Dr. H: With each of these three couples there's a big sense of wrong in one member of each couple, and it has to do with the child that came from the couple. That's another something that you may have done without realizing you were doing it, and I want to see whether you can accept it as making sense to you.
PM: Yes, in the relationship of Vere and the girl, there is the whole issue of the child who stands as a symbol of his manhood that this girl almost deliberately killed. And with Merle's marriage, even though the child there does not figure that strongly, she's declined her child.
Eliot: In which case the child is killed, the child is "stolen," and in the last case the child is "lost." It dies before it's born.
Dr. H: When I looked at that and I heard Bob, I thought that there was a mystical tie this way: that reconciliation was not effected in each of these

three cases, but the suggestion implied behind it was that if the child could have survived, the child could have brought a reconciliation. This sort of fit your Messianic concept to the book. It suggests that the child is simply hope or a final harmony that you said yourself was possible. Susan found it in the way the workers went to work when they were all deprived and collaborated with each other. This is the mysterious way that writers' minds work possibly, and that there is a link between those two—this single strand of two people and their child with the question of why we don't get reconciliations. Does that just about appraise it to you?

PM: No, not at all. I don't think that's what motivated me to have the child be so important in these relationships; I think something else was operating here. For the first time I'm really thinking about it clearly and I'm very preoccupied with children; they're not major, characters in the book, but children are always present. Children are the ones who are present at Harriet's death. They are present at her entry into Bournehills. I think they're so important to me because I'm very aware that children are the ones who suffer most in conflicts between adults and they are the ones who suffer most because of the sins nations commit against each other. So that when you have those children, when Harriet first comes to the guest house, standing there with their pot bellies and their spindly legs like a kind of statement that she has to engage, standing there like Pirandello figures, waiting for someone to give them life, to give them voice, this is to suggest the extent of the crime being committed against those children standing there. This is why they occur time and time again throughout the book—just little studies, still-life figures of them. Again, in the relationships between the people, how people abuse each other, it's not only nations that abuse each other but people, and the ones who really suffer are not only the two people involved but the child or the children. I think that's why it's kind of picked up.

Dr. H: That makes it far clearer than my groping attempt, and different from my groping attempt.

Bob: Your attempt, I think, gets at the paradox of reconciliation. While it's impossible through the perpetuation of the species, there's a hope coming up through the children.

PM: Yes. Again, that has to do with that whole longing for reconciliation, you know. If only somehow we could do right by the children. But again, you see, that's impossible. You say it's possible; I say it's impossible.

Dr. H: We have to believe it's possible, though everything that happens says it isn't possible.

PM: Yes, right.

Alan: Those are the two things that are somewhat contradictory until you bring in the aspect of the hope. I tried to think of it more than being dark but rather somewhat hopeful and optimistic because, if you take the individual thing of reconciliation that Bob traced as being a hopeless one, the social theme of revolution really is based completely on hope. The whole idea is by acting something good will happen. If you take the theme of reconciliation and its impossibility too strongly, then you take the wind out of the sails of revolution. If reconciliation is so hopeless, then why even bother getting ourselves excited so that we can become villains?

PM: Well, Bob takes it and gives it a much larger meaning. In terms of this book, both exist: the theme of the impossibility of reconciliation and the theme of hope. For this book, the two operate together because I'm really trying to do two things here, and if I might talk about this just a minute. The book is really trying to project a dual vision of what I see as what's going on in the world. On one hand—and this has to do with the impossibility of reconciliation—I see no hope of the West and the rest of the world, the darker peoples of the world, ever being reconciled. I mean, I'm really saying that in this book. I'm trying to trace the decline and fall of the order of the West. This might be a very unacceptable thing to the people in this room. Okay? But that is my theme. On the other hand—and just as important a theme—is the whole hope and looking toward that third world of darker peoples emerging. This is the dual vision that holds true for this book. Bob is taking that whole theme of reconciliation and trying to enlarge its meaning outside of the province of this book, you see; and I am talking to that point when I say, "Basically, personally, I see very little hope of reconciliation."

Dr. H: Listen, here's something that I think we ought to speak about. Paule, early on, when we weren't really getting each other very clearly and there was some confusion you said, "I'm sorry, but I just can't make it more explicit than that. That isn't the way I write at all." Now this interested me, because I think yesterday, out of the many, many affirmative things, the one strongest negative thing felt by the most people was your tendency to be, from their point of view, too explicit, to render a theme and have the reader feel that he really was with it and really dug you, and then you would go on and state it over again. So that here is your sense that you're not really explicit and their sense that you're over-explicit. Would you comment on that?

PM: Well, what I'd like, before I try to do that is for someone to give me an instance in the book where they felt that.

Dr. H: This is not really a negative judgment. You would have been even more effective if you hadn't commented upon what you had written.

Alan: Page 46 is the one we talked about yesterday, beginning with the parentheses. I'll read it. "(Which was also the case. Whenever he tried getting her to talk about her relatives, her childhood, her marriage to Andrew Westerman, wanting to have more of an idea of what her life had been before they had met, she would very skillfully, without appearing to, evade his questions; and he found that privacy of hers, which almost seemed to him at times a desire on her part to blot out her past, to treat it as though it had never happened, vaguely disturbing.)" I marked that when I read it, and somebody brought it up yesterday too, saying, "If we know Harriet, we know that already. And if we know Saul and Harriet, we see them acting, we see them together."

PM: But do you know it already, because it is so early in the book?

Alan: We don't, but I think that we felt that we would have gotten it sufficiently by seeing them live together and by seeing her actions rather than having to be told about it. When we see Harriet in her letters and in her treatment with Gwen's children and the way she takes over, all the things that she does—I suppose the best example of this is her carnival experience where she won't give it up and she won't include him in it—I think we felt that she was well-enough drawn and we didn't want to be told any more. I don't think we thought that the major things were explicit. We found them somewhat mysterious to some extent. We were still searching for the Messianic quality and what it was with Bournehills that we couldn't put our finger on, but some of the more superficial bits of characterization, some of the more day-to-day things that happened that you could draw significance from, we thought were sometimes unnecessary.

PM: It was done in too great a detail.

Alan: Unless you talk about keeping things inexact, I think that's very true that some things are inappropriately detailed. But the specifics are very, very, exact; and maybe that's why we were so surprised at the mystery of Bournehills. Because we had been told so much else.

Dr. H: Well, as far as the mystery of Bournehills goes, I have been more and more satisfied as the discussion went on that really perhaps all of us, me included, when I was reading back yonder, don't want to understand. Not consciously don't want to understand, but . . .

PM: There are those other levels.

Part II

Students Present: Pat McLaughlin, Sandy Schmuhl, Kathy Schultz, Marc Rosenberg, Craig Scott, Denis Mercier.
Assistant: Susan Fry

PM: Well, what does that parade say to you? What does the whole carnival ritual of Cuffee Ned say to you? Is it just a parade or do you see any other meaning in it? That's one thing I would like to explore very closely, if possible, with you and with the other people here. What does the carnival presentation, the whole masque of Cuffee Ned, get across to you?
Denis: I was just going to say their preoccupation with timelessness, with their sense of history, their reverence to the past.
Sandy: Also their honesty because they don't super-glorify it. You know, at the end, Cuffee Ned is killed; there is recognition of the whole reality of the thing, not just a part of it. And this is perhaps a strong feeling of the people.
PM: Yes, but in addition to the fact that he is killed, which is the end of the masque, what else is that saying to you?
Sandy: It's almost giving a rationale for living the kind of life that they do every day.
PM: What I'm trying to get at is what do some of the specific things that happen in the enactment of that rite say to you? When he goes up the hill and grapples and defeats the man at the top—it's not just a parade! What is that saying, you know, in terms of what the book is about? You didn't see any more than just a parade?
Marc: No, it's clear there are two kinds of time going on: historical time and mythical time. During the carnival, the people of Bournehills are living in mythical time. The Cuffee Ned episode of the past is in fact ritually created in the present. And for the time they are acting out this mythical event, they are reliving this time. Their sense of identity as a people, their sense of wholeness, is recreated for this period of time, which goes back to what the Times review was saying, which I disagree with. I don't think it's as optimistic a book as he would lead us to believe. That last sentence in the book is very pessimistic. The whole point of the carnival seems to be that if the people of Bournehills are going to get together again and be a people again, and rise out of their defeatism, they're going to need somebody like Cuffee Ned. They're going to need to surreally exist in the mythic depth that they experienced during the carnival.

Sandy: But unlike the other carnival groups, this group had not only a historical honesty, but an honesty to themselves. Their portrayal was very real to them in a way that a group of teenagers playing Castro-ites wasn't.
Dr. H: How did you happen to choose that?
Sandy: Well, because that speaks of July. That's what the other group was. That was the group that Harriet was caught up in.
Dr. H: I misunderstood, I'm sorry.
Sandy: Because that was the thing that was very real to them as a group, not something they had borrowed from another island, borrowed from somewhere else. Instead of borrowing it from the Colonials beforehand, the teenage group borrowed it from Cuba. But the Bournehills people took something that was their own and they were continuing to live their own way in a way that the rest of the island wasn't and people like Lyle and the others weren't. Maybe they were backward, but they were what they were, with no pretense about it. They didn't change their program from year to year because, so long as they were expressing themselves, that was better than to conjure up something else.
PM: Did anyone think that the reasons for the insistence of the people of Bournehills to reenact the Cuffee legend had first of all to do with the fact that they did consider themselves the timeless people, their place the chosen place because it would serve as a monument to the crime of Colonialism and slavery committed against them? The place stands as that, and they saw themselves as having as their mission in life to, year after year, remind the rest of the island, "This is what happened to us."
Sandy: And is happening.
PM: Yes. And is happening to us. Did anyone see something of this in the whole insistence upon reenacting the carnival myth?
Sandy: And the fact that for a short period of time the rest of the town was swept up with it. They didn't want to be, but they couldn't help being swept up with it. But then again, they were "townies" in a sense. The Lyle Hudsons and the others perhaps are imposing another kind of Colonialism on these people.
PM: And on themselves at the same time.
Sandy: This is the "now" significance, which I think is more important to what they were doing than to remind them of a period that was a hundred years ago.
PM: I'm also wondering if anyone, in reading that Cuffee episode, picked up on the fact that what they were saying, in reenacting the rite each year, was that Bournehills people are insisting upon revolution. That's what Cuffee

stands for, and it's not just the whole business of looking to some one person who's going to bring the light, who's going to be the Messiah, but the fact that Cuffee Ned, in his person and his life, epitomized revolution, complete overthrow, complete change in a sense, and the Bournehills people are insisting on that. The refusal to have television, all of the meaningless aspects of what are taken to be change, progressive change, they refuse wholesale to be reconciled to. They are insisting upon what Cuffee Ned insisted upon when he went up that hill, when he took power. Did anyone see this at all? What went on in that carnival scene?

Sandy: The difference—I couldn't help but contrast them with the Castro-ite teenagers—that it's the difference between revolution and rebellion, which is action just sort of for the hell of it. You know, let's do something different. Doing very specific things for very particular goals which are defined by the group is revolution as opposed to rebellion. Rebellion is sort of, you know, "Let's play around." The rest of the island had rebelled, but they were not revolting.

PM: Well, what's the difference between rebelling and revolting to you? One is just a kind of play?

Sandy: Rebellion is for the joy of doing something different, not knowing where you're going, but that you're somewhere other than where you are.

PM: Well, then I think you misread the whole carnival scene with the teenagers from Harlem Heights, because even though they appeared to Harriet not to be going anywhere but straight down to the river, to the bay rather, to be destroyed, still, with all of the firing of the guns and the noise and the brouhaha, there was a direction and there was some measure of control so they didn't all just fall right into the bay, you see. The same kind of discipline that was brought to bear with the successful revolt that took place in Bournehills was also what was operating in the whole Cuban thing. I was simply trying to link up the past with the present, to show that black people are simply trying to achieve what our forefathers started a few centuries ago. It was expressed in Cuba and what Cuffee Ned tried to do. I would like other people to react to how they saw that carnival scene because it is crucial. This is where the book reaches its high point. I mean, if you don't understand what that scene is saying then—perhaps as whites you can't understand it; it's too painful. Or on the other hand, maybe the writing wasn't all that clear.

Sandy: We almost came to blows yesterday talking about some of the characters—what they were like as real people, and whether they were more important to you, in writing them, as complex individuals or as symbols, as vehicles for saying something, broader, deeper.

PM: Both. As both. This is why it was such a struggle, as I said this morning, because being a storyteller and considering myself as one who's really committed to writing stories and novels, I'm interested in having my characters come across as people. Yet, because I'm also interested in the larger meaning, in getting across ideas and my point of view, in what I feel deeply and intensely about life, I have to also find a way of using those people so they say for me what I want to get across, so that they stand as symbols for ideas, for points of view. I'm trying always to juggle these two things and it's not easy. That's why the book took five years and more.

Sandy: When the character first comes to mind as a fairly complete entity, how predestined is he then? For example, I had a very strong feeling from the beginning that Vere was doomed to die in that automobile race.

PM: Yes, well maybe I did that a little too obviously . . . I'd like to pursue this thing about Saul's being Jewish and whether that was relevant to the book or whether that was just a kind of extreme thing on my part. I don't know. Maybe over there . . . do you have any thoughts about that?

Denis: I was just going to say that Saul was the only one who could empathize with these people. In the book, he was the one who had the most insight into the problems . . .

Dr. H: Well, you dismissed the tale of Christian symbolism in the review; you said you felt it must be much more than she intended. But, we discovered this morning that the reason Saul was named Saul was that Saul of Tarsus became St. Paul on the road, etc. I mention it now only because perhaps it will help a little bit to make a connection in terms of what you're talking about.

Craig: Well, I'm not saying I don't see why you did it; I'm just saying I don't think it was done as effectively as it might have been.

PM: Oh, I see. Well, what do you see as my reasons for having him a Jew?

Craig: I think it's basically the identification between peoples.

Dr. H: How does it fall short?

Kathy: It's perhaps a little too clear that this is the point that's being made.

Craig: Yeah. I think the symbolism is there, but there just isn't enough flesh to it underneath the story.

Dr. H: Let's take the likely contingencies that one of you two were working on this book. You would choose to replace Saul with what?

PM: He would give more flesh to the symbolism.

Craig: Yeah. I think Saul is symbolically Jewish, but he doesn't make sense existentially being Jewish . . . if that makes any sense at all.
PM: People have accused me of being too compassionate. The whole black community feels I've been too compassionate!
Pat: My point about Harriet is that her inability to deal with her family seems to be the basis of her neurosis and it's easy to feel sorry for her for that. But it seems that you start out with Harriet at seven years old, more or less already irreparably damaged.
PM: Not irreparably damaged. You see, again, you have to try to create character and also use that character to get across certain ideas. I wanted, on one hand, to show that Harriet, from the very beginning, was someone very strong-willed; that she was, from the very beginning, something of a rebel in her way. This is why she is the one who leads the revolt from the nursery window with her two brothers. She is a woman who has in her the need to act independently, not to go along with the prescribed order. And you see this from her childhood. Yet on the other hand, she is, because she bears the history, bears the weight of all that has gone into making her, she is still a representative of that white order that has to go. So I had to do two things with her. She was, on one hand, a person, but she was also a symbolic figure.
Pat: Maybe I'm going too closely, but it seems to me that on the personal level, just as a person, Harriet has found her tradition unworkable. Harriet has grown up in a terribly unhealthy family to grow up in, with a mother who always found her disappointing and a father who locked himself up in his study. No matter who she was, I don't think you could have had much hope for her.
PM: I'd like you to give me your reaction to this: even though she has rebelled and rejected all that has gone into making her—that whole WASP life, yet still and all, what does Harriet have? What is the overwhelming feeling on her part? She has to manipulate and control. So that even though she has rejected that whole background that has gone into her, yet still and all, she operates the duels with life on that level.
Pat: Is it because she's rejected it without looking at it?
PM: No. She does not examine her past. Yes. Because she's afraid that it'll be too horrifying. And that's why, when Lyle touches her and she senses that his touch has left a kind of blot upon her, it hasn't got to do with the fact that he's black so much, but with the fact that it has evoked in her things about herself that she cannot recognize and deal with. On the one hand, you have somebody who's rejecting a whole way of life, but on the other, she is caught up in it, she reacts out of it. She could not, say, get interested in a

man like Lyle Hudson because he was a man who was completed, finished; he had succeeded at his life. She could not be attracted to a man like that. It had to be to a man like Saul who had been damaged by life, that she could then reconstruct. I mean, it's power, and I'm talking about power, not only about individual level as we see it all the time, but power as the West utilizes it, uses it against other people. She just couldn't give up being a WASP. She couldn't, even though she would in her personal life reject the fashionable school and all of that business, she couldn't really give it up.

Pat: Don't you think in a way it was because she couldn't do without it? I mean, did she have brothers or sisters?

PM: Brothers. She had two brothers.

Pat: Well, her brothers who were comfortable in their tradition probably didn't need to manipulate people.

PM: Oh, but they did. They did it very clearly and probably very coldly. But her rejecting it all did it, but without her realizing that she was.

Dr. H: What did the brothers do?

PM: They were both . . . well, this is the part that the group this morning wanted me to cut out. I talked about them all living in the country, big families . . .

Sandy: They weren't criticizing themselves. This is the point that I wanted to make earlier; it was really critical at that point and now is less critical because I don't have your exact words in my head any more. But, if you really take what I thought you were saying about the Bournehills people and what they symbolized, and if you put it next to the idea of sticking with what is yours, not taking from the Colonials, not taking from anyone else, being what you are—if you take this beyond a level for the blacks and put this on a universally human level, then you're blaming Harriet for doing that thing which a moment ago you were holding up as an ideal—the fact that Harriet does not renounce what she unmistakably is.

PM: Oh I didn't hold it up as an ideal. Not at all.

Sandy: But there seemed to be a contradiction there. I'm sorry I don't have your words in my head right now because there seemed to be a contradiction in what you were saying about when one stands for what he is, when one says, "This is what I am." There's a line from Lorraine Hansberry. She says, "We are all shaped by the rim of that particular bowl in which we swim," and Harriet is what she is and she does not completely reject that.

Dr. H: What Sandy is asking, though I don't agree with her, is why isn't her loyalty to her tradition as appropriate and right as the Bournehills peoples' loyalty to their tradition?

PM: Yes, I know that's what she's saying. My reaction to that is that Harriet knows full and well that her tradition is wrong. That is why she has to shut out the past. That is why she refused to think about the widow, Susan, and all that has gone into making her. She knows it's wrong. She knows that it's a system based on the oppression of another people. She knows that. She is in flight from that, you see.

Dr. H: She knows it how, dear?

PM: She knows it to the extent that she refuses to engage it. She knows how terrible it is.

Dr. H: Except when she reproaches her husband.

PM: Right. Or, for instance, the scene on the verandah when Lyle talks to her about the products that were sent down to the West Indies and says that people made their fortunes off of selling rotten codfish and rice to us. And she thinks back to the widow Susan who dealt in slaves and in those various products. But she is reluctant . . . she refuses to try to change. She refuses to relinquish a necessary part of the power she has to change that. This is why that's not an ideal for me. This is why she has to be defeated in the end, because she refuses to give way. She recognizes that her position is wrong, that you cannot be an oppressor, you have no right to be. But she refuses to deal with it. Once that's brought home to her, then she just turns it all off, and I've seen this happen with whites. They just go blank. They refuse to listen any more.

Dr. H: I think the kind of thing that's stirring the pot down at this end of the table is that now you have begun to generalize about whites—and you mean to. See, there are two dialectics involved as I listen to you. On one level, you would acknowledge in terms of individual character, in terms of social, economic, political influence, quite evenly. But you are also an embattled and militant person in terms of the central cause which lies behind your book, and in the use of that dialectic to you, we all are just one thing. You speak of whites, you speak of WASPs; there are no real individuals because each of us is to you—in your militant incarnation—each of us is to you simply a part of that big white pot.

PM: I'm trying to deal, Hiram, with the symbolic content of the book. Don't get me started about what I feel personally; it's another whole thing. I'm really trying to deal with what the book is about symbolically and for me, Harriet is not only that little rebellious girl who all the time wanted to break out of what she saw as a narrow world, but she is also what, to my mind, stands for Western civilization. She was married first to a man who was very involved with manufacturing nuclear weapons, you see. When she dies at the end—and maybe that was a little too obvious now that I look back on it—

what she hears in the sea is detonation of bombs, and so all of this is going on. They are characters, but there are other things I'm trying to get across because I'm trying to say something very serious about what I see happening to Western civilization. Whether people want to listen to it or not, and whether they want to even see it in the reading, that's their problem. What I'm trying to say is that in my mind, this is a civilization committed to its own end. Harriet is committed to her own end, but she's also a character. That's what I was trying to do with all of them in the book.

Sandy: Then your final pages in the book are more hopeful than I thought they were . . . because Harriet is out.

Dr. H: This is what I was trying to get out. They're both. They're both. The book is deeply pessimistic in one sense; and in a different sense, it's very optimistic. We used different terms this morning, but I think that's a point I'd like the others to shoot at to see if we can see why, and then I'd like for you to speak to it.

Sandy: That's what I started to say.

Dr. H: Because you always get the better of it, because you get so condescending when you come back to me that you win. Now, go ahead. Say it.

Sandy: What I was in the middle of trying to think through was the ending of the book—and I liked the fact that it was unclear, that it was ambiguous. Was Merle going to come back? Was Saul going to succeed? The whole thing was left up in the air. And if Harriet does stand for all that you have said she does, and she leaves the book, she leaves the place, this would, on a very symbolic level, seem to imply that it is the Sauls and the Merles who will finally succeed, that your final vision is very hopeful. While in the reality of the book, it is left very unclear as to how these people as characters personally will succeed.

PM: You have no sense that Merle will really make it as a person, aside from what she means symbolically? You have no sense at the end that she really has begun, first of all, to come through, to overcome that long nightmare from recovery from her marriage and her breakdown and the whole thing? You have no sense that she's going to come through?

Sandy: I have a strong hope that she will and a feeling that she will, but not a sure knowledge, which is what I liked. I would much sooner be left with that than be left being told, "This is, period, what happens," and some kind of statement that *Merle Will Come Back*.

PM: An Epilogue. I don't go in for epilogues.

Sandy: And Saul, similarly, as a person, is ambiguous. But if you place him in context with the other characters—Vere is dead, Harriet is dead, the white

South if you want to really make a point out of that is dead—and your sympathetic characters are the ones that are left, this would seem to . . . is this what you're getting at?

PM: If you go back to those last few pages, I don't see how you can get the impression that Saul has been spared in any way because he's going back to defeat. "Saul left a few days later, feeling as he sat squeezed in among Delbert, Stinger, Ten-ton and one or two others from the shop in the Ford like someone being exiled permanently from all that he loved." Now that is not meant to convey a sense of this character being saved or too much hope for him, because he's going back to a place which he's been convinced all along is like being in a house where the owner is upstairs waiting to die. He's always felt that in a very intimate way about his own country. This is what has set him wondering, this is why he tried in his youth to bring about change but was defeated at every turn. He knew he could not sell out, and so he had to find some means by which he could live outside of the country. You don't get the impression of very much hope with Saul, but I certainly wanted to make the point of a kind of hopefulness in terms of Merle because she is, for me, symbolic of the third world that has to come into being . . . I don't know why you're insisting on outlooks. I mean, the book provides you with a number of outlooks. As I was saying this morning, I saw it, when the idea first occurred to me many, many years ago—a way of my projecting a particular vision of how I, in here, see the world. And it is a dual vision. I see, on one hand, the demise of the West, a demise brought about at their hand. When one considers all of the weaponry and the means for death that the West has created as its great contribution to man, then you almost see a civilization committed in some weird, irrational, way to its own end.

Dr. H: Very like the Roman Empire.

PM: Right. So on one hand that's how I was dealing with the book, and for me that's how I used Harriet symbolically. On the other, I saw, and I have to see, the possibility of a third world as a kind of phoenix that will emerge from ruins. For me, that is epitomized in the character of Merle, who does, despite the great abuse she's been subjected to, still have a great vitality. She still has a life-giving quality about her that will survive. And I'm saying that through her, the darker peoples of the world will have their chance to take center stage, their turn for power. Really. It's these two things constantly playing against one another in the book. I think that tension is why most people, most white people, resist the book.

Dr. H: When do you stress power there, Paule? That doesn't seem to me what Merle stresses. That seems to be simply the black counterpart to the

white part. It's their turn to take the power to do themselves in, in the same fashion that the white suppresses. That's the implication.
PM: Merle says it. Merle says it.
Dr. H: That's it. I mean, she foresees that and therefore . . .
PM: No, she does not.
Dr. H: Your third world, I think, is inchoate hope.
PM: Well, that's all we're left with, Hiram, in the final analysis.
Dr. H: You're not listening. Look, Malraux's *Man's Fate* sees the whole Communist drive in China in two visions: one is the Marxist vision of collective power, and one is the vision of brotherhood. And, it seems to me that the alternatives for the third world you're talking about are: one, yes indeed, we get done in, primarily by ourselves, and the darker peoples of the world take over; or two, brotherhood. This seemed to me clear as long as 25 or 30 years ago. Which of these two interpretations will it be? Will you—I don't mean you personally—will you take it for the power, or isn't it possible that it may be an ideal of brotherhood that will overcome it, as I see in individual statesmen such as the man whose brother was killed—the mayor of a Southern town.
Sandy: Medgar Evers. Medgar Evers's brother Charles.
Dr. H: . . . his vision of what it means to have that authority and that responsibility ought to make everybody who's lived around there fall on his face in both shame and respect. So that you say third world—what does it mean?
PM: Well, Hiram, let me put it this way, to see if I can get it across to you and to the other people in the room. When I talk about power, I don't talk about it in Western terms. I don't equate power with abuse, and that's what power has meant to the West. You've got to get out of a whole way of defining things, you know. Power has meant for the West a kind of subjugation.
Dr. H: All right. But then when you use it, you've got to redefine it.
PM: That's not my role, really. If you're going to take the meaning of power simply in Western terms as the way the West has used power, I'm not talking about that. I'm talking about coming into power where you begin, as a people, as a nation, to control your life. Okay? I'm not talking about abusing other people. If you get hung up in the way the West has operated . . .
Sandy: It's the same as genuine independence.
Dr. H: It works, then.
PM: Right. When I talk about taking center stage, that does not mean exterminating all others, because, as I pointed out, what's frightening to me is that the West, the white West, seems committed to its own end. You know, the darker peoples of the world, when one compares their whole history

to the West, almost appear as humanitarian. The kind of brutality that the West has perpetrated over centuries, I don't know if you can find examples of that, really, among the darker peoples. So power does not have to have the negative meaning. That's what I meant.

Dr. H: But you are, my dear. There are all sorts of ways of doing it. You don't have to be on barricades when you write a book like this.

PM: I know, but I feel that I should be, and that's where my conflict comes in. But, you know, I could not create a character that did not incorporate some aspect of me. I would suspect that with a character like Merle there is very little of me. She is, in many ways, the kind of fantastic and vital person that I would like to be but could never be. She's sort of an idealized image. Who could be a Merle and carry it off successfully? And Saul, that kind of wandering all over the place and seeking to have a sense of place certainly reflects much of my life because I've wandered all over South America and the West Indies, never feeling very much at home here. Harriet—that whole sense of being very inside oneself is certainly an aspect of me.

Dr. H: I'm glad you explained that because you said before this similar thing in different words, and then you said you picked different parts of them from different people. I've always felt that that is impossible. I've felt that it makes a sort of Picasso-fractured person instead of an individual. How can you put them together when every individual is the particular composite of things that he is? Now I understand that you mean that out of that sense of being trapped in oneself, which you say you share with Harriet, out of this sense I would guess the rest of her character begins to evolve. It isn't so much that you chop up pieces of yourself and insert them in different characters as it is that you have one thing in common with each: the wanderer with Saul, the shelled-up compartment with Harriet. And that's only a starting place with a character with you. Would you accept that?

PM: In part, but because I'm very involved with how people appear on a page, how they come across physically, I always have to look to people I know. The character is a composite in a physical sense. There are bits and pieces of people that I know or have met that has stayed with me, as well as of what they are like inside. I'm involved in that interior self also. I think any serious novelist has to be, in a way. There's got to be that kind of personal involvement.

Dr. H: Oh yes. Well, I think we could throw it wide open now for the last half hour. That was a very lively discussion and different approach to the book from this morning. It was totally opposite, and deeply interesting.

Susan Fry: Did you feel that Vere was sort of a lost person himself in the

sense of being lost to his tradition. He had sort of copped out of the materialism of the white society.
PM: Not that he had copped out, and I think I said this earlier on, but that he was desperately looking around for the means by which to prove . . .
Susan Fry: His manhood.
PM: Yes. And how difficult this was for him to do within the context of his own society.
Susan Fry: How difficult this was in terms of the actual tradition of Bournehills or the symbolic kind of tradition of Bournehills, or both?
PM: The actual situation of Bournehills, because Cuffee Ned certainly had no difficulty in proving his manhood. Vere came back, didn't work for a while, and so wanted to prove it in such a dramatic way because he had suffered such insult by the way the woman had treated him. He was almost desperately looking around. I mean, he dreams on the plane of how, when he gets this car and he puts it in the race, everyone is going to be standing on the sidelines sending up a hosanna. This is where I should hope that the book is universal—these are feelings we all have. It isn't only because he's black; it's because he's a man, and it's difficult in this world to have a sense that you are.
Marc: How do you feel about yourself as narrator and the narrator's relation to the action of the book?
PM: I try very hard to be detached. I don't know if I really succeed at that. Perhaps I've got the feeling recently that too much of the book is given over to narration, and maybe I should have had more dialogue, but the only way I could manage the material was to be the narrator, to do it in the third person, to look on and describe.
Marc: I was just wondering how much you let yourself know. It seems to vary from part to part. Sometimes you come on as if you don't know all there is to know, and others you come on and tell us things that you could only know if you were . . .
Dr. H: You mean it's a limiting point of view?
Marc: Sometimes the point of view is limiting, and other times it's not. There's a shift.
PM: I might have done that for effectiveness. For instance, in the very beginning when I don't really give her name but just talk about "the woman," that was only a device to capture interest.
Marc: But you also say on page 4: "Someone, perhaps the woman herself, may have taken a sledge hammer and batted it in," and the "perhaps the woman herself" suggests that you as narrator really don't know.

PM: Yes, those are tricks. You found me out.

Marc: I'm not concerned with their being tricks here, but what do they mean—to you, to writing that way?

PM: Well, part of it is the whole feeling that I've always had that I cannot be that intrusive in the story, that I cannot give that impression—because I'm so much in control as a writer. Maybe I do it somewhat awkwardly, but I'm trying to appear detached and sometimes as unknowing as the reader. This is why I'll say, "Perhaps the woman herself," knowing full well who has done it, but that's all my attempt not to appear as omniscient as I am.

Marc: So you don't feel obliged, then, to maintain any kind of consistency in your relation to the plot.

PM: As long as it works. If it works, I'll do it. And if it doesn't make me feel uncomfortable. If I feel it's right for that particular part of the story, then I'll do it. It's all about how effective it is to the reader. Some people may be put off by the fact that I'm too present in the book.

Marc: It wasn't a matter of your presence or your detachment; it was that you kept shifting.

PM: Yes. It does shift.

Sandy: When you began this novel, at which level did you begin it? As a symbolic concept, or with the characters themselves, or with the place, or something else?

PM: Well, in that long will and testament to you, Hiram, I tried to talk, but it's almost impossible to talk about how a novel begins. I suspect that for me, certainly with this novel, it began with a kind of confluence of a number of things. There was the very rare life situation many years ago: I was living for a while in the West Indies and a group of American social scientists came down, fussing about the place doing some kind of study. I got interested in what happens when people from one culture come into another place that is very alien to them, about what happens, not only in the situation itself, but with them inside and with the people with whom they are working. That just stayed with me, but I didn't think of doing anything with it. The idea to do a novel about the confrontation of haves and haves-not, black and white, was with me for quite some time. I've come across a fascinating character in my travels who, in a sense, serves as the base for Merle. Something about this dynamic and completely out-of-her-mind woman appealed to me. I didn't know what I would do with her either, but all of these things came together over a period of time and sat jelling until I sat down to write. This took place over a number of years, because after the bud of the idea was there I did a tremendous amount of research, visiting libraries and museums in the West Indies, gathering material about early slave revolts and the struggle for in-

dependence and freedom in the islands, and so on. It was good because I got a lot of material, but it was bad because a novelist should never go about a book that way. Research is the worst possible thing.
Dr. H: Well, you sort of disproved it.
PM: Well, Hiram, the book would have been done five years before and I wouldn't be an old woman now.
Dr. H: Five years ago, it wouldn't have had nearly its just due, if not in understanding at least in appreciation.
PM: Perhaps so.
Dr. H: And maybe perhaps not quite so much influence. It just suddenly fascinated me to realize, and I remember your mild explosion on the phone, that for the first two visiting novelists we have, each has written a novel about a slave revolt.
PM: Oh really?
Dr. H: You know who the next one is. You said, misunderstanding, "I don't want to be there when he's there."
PM: Oh.
Dr. H: It's William Styron, who wrote Nat Turner.
PM: Oh! Confrontations I can take, but not that. Uh-uh. But . . . so that's how it all sort of came together along with the research, along with ideas, along with feelings about people, along with ideas that have been with me a long time. How does one—and I'm talking very personally now—how does one, as a black person deal with one's rage? How do you use it in, to my mind, a very positive way? The book is also about that. So it carries quite a load. I think that's why people find it kind of hard going. It's an intense book, and it takes a close reading, and it's a quite traditional novel. I'd like to talk about that a bit. How did you see it in terms of style? Is this the kind of novel that most people can take nowadays? They've gotten used to the more introspective kind of psychological novel and very little patience with plot and story and development of character and that kind of thing. Did you find it a somewhat alien or different kind of book from what you're used to reading in terms of contemporary literature?
Denis: My first reaction to that was, "This looks like an old-fashioned novel." I mean, you describe yourself as an old-fashioned novelist, and you do round out everything. You take great pains to describe scenes, to describe people, to flesh out the characters and so on. I did have one reaction when I read your questionnaire last night. That is, that after reading the novel, I could anticipate many of your answers except one, and that was the one about writing dialogue and the ease with which dialogue came to you.
PM: Did I say that?

Denis: No. You said that it was very, very difficult. "It was difficult for me." I found that almost impossible to believe because I thought that it was in the dialogue where the characters really lived. Maybe I thought that because of my orientation to the modern novel, but this is where I really put the flesh on the characters. And oddly enough, despite the lengthy descriptions, I found it difficult to visualize some of these characters as black people. I had to be reminded that, for example, that Lyle was black.
PM: Well, what to you is black?
Denis: I mean, just as a physical description of the person.
Dr. H: Yes, but her question . . .
Denis: I know. I know. I'm not sure. I don't know what the problem is there, but Vere was another one. I kept visualizing him with his high cheekbones and hollowed-out face looking more like a Mexican person. I mean, I kept thinking West Indies . . .
PM: What you've got to deal with then—and I can't help you in this respect—is your conception of a black person. If you give what makes up the character and personality of a person, you know, and you cannot accept this person's being black, then that says a hell of a lot about your conception about who and what is a black person . . . I think perhaps that with this novel I felt kind of pressured to make things a bit more explicit than I should have so as not to fall into the trap that I did with the first one. This has to do, unfortunately, with reacting to criticism and stems from the first novel, which was read and criticized and reviewed totally on that first level. Nobody really saw other meanings to it. One should not react to criticism in that fashion.
Dr. H: That's interesting, because in between you produced *Soul Clap Hands and Sing*, four stories that are interrelated only because the theme of all of them, although utterly differently treated, is a man on the edge of old age and catching him at the moment when he, to all intents and purposes, will die and renew himself. With this group of short stories, it's very tight prose, very implicit prose, wouldn't you agree, Paule?
PM: Yes, it was fun doing it. But again there, the critics said it was too cold because it was too precise. "A cold note entered in."
Dr. H: You can't get away from it.
PM: So I'll just have to continue doing my thing, that's all.

Re-creating Ourselves All Over the World: A Conversation with Paule Marshall

'Molara Ogundipe-Leslie/1977

From *Moving Beyond Ourselves II: Black Women's Diasporas*, edited by Carol Boyce Davies (New York University Press, 1994). Reprinted by permission of New York University Press.

The following conversation with Paule Marshall was conducted on 28 January 1977 by 'Molara Ogundipe-Leslie in Ibadan, Nigeria. Paule Marshall was in Nigeria attending FESTAC (Festival of African Arts and Culture) and visited the University of Ibadan during her stay. The context of an African-American writer returning to Africa is important, as are the boundary-breaking implications of a black woman writer being interviewed by an African woman critic and writer, on home soil.

'Molara Ogundipe-Leslie (MOL): It has been said you've been influenced by Thomas Mann. Could you say how and why you find him artistically attractive to you?
Paule Marshall (PM): I consider Mann one of the influences. I don't consider him so much an influence now because I really think of him as a writer of my adolescence, in the sense that I read him when I was just beginning to contemplate the idea of becoming a writer. But he is of value to me on two counts, firstly because he handles so well the full-blown, the large-scale novel. *Buddenbrooks* and *The Magic Mountain* were instructive to me because I knew early on that that was the kind of novel—in a sense the traditional novel—that most interested one because of its form. And Mann was such an expert at handling this great mass of material that I learnt tremendously

from him. The other aspect of Thomas Mann that I found exceedingly rewarding was his handling of characters, which more or less coincided with the way I wanted to deal with people in literature. Because literature, or good fiction, is the ability to make your people come alive on the page and Mann was an expert at that for me. When you think of Hans Castorp, the protagonist of *The Magic Mountain*, you find in him a fully realized, a fully delineated human being on the page. He is there with all his foibles, shortcomings, his positive attributes as a human being but at the same time, and this is why Mann is also important to me as a literary artist. Hans Castorp in *The Magic Mountain* and the artist Gustav Aschenbach in the novelette *Death in Venice* are not only characters, not only people, but Mann invests them with symbolic meaning and this was important for me. I wanted my characters to exist on these two levels. To be people in their own right, to have them come across on the page, to help the reader identify with them; yet on the other hand for them to serve as symbols of principles. So Mann was extremely helpful in that regard.

MOL: Did you use this approach to characterization in *The Chosen Place*? Could you say you were somehow dramatizing some ideas?

PM: Yes, I would say so. I was largely dramatizing political ideas. I like to think of *The Chosen Place, the Timeless People* as a strongly political novel. I was trying to sort out what was happening to black and colored peoples throughout the world. I was trying to deal with what I see as the new colonialism. The white woman character in the novel, Harriet, is not only a woman who I hope comes across as a character, but she was also symbolic of the western principle in her need to control, to dominate, in her basic feelings of superiority. She embodies some of the unhappy aspects of the western personality. The main black woman in the novel, Merle Kinbona, meaning 'good kin,' for me is not only a black woman who is struggling for her identity, struggling to assert herself, to give meaning to her life, she is also reflective of the horrendous colonial experience we have all undergone, and her struggle to bring together all of these influences that have gone into making her so that she could fashion out of it a whole person. So she in a sense reflects the struggle of black people to come into her own.

MOL: Would you say, like Mann, you're concerned with the underworld of the bourgeois experience, that you're concerned with purpose and the disorderly aspects of western culture, such as his concern with the incest theme, for instance? Such themes indicate a concern with the decadence of western culture.

PM: Yes, I'm very concerned with that. I see decadence as one of the insidious exports of the western world to the Third World: a whole emphasis on a kind of cushioned and comfortable but essentially meaningless bourgeois life. And to make that so attractive that people become centered on self, which makes it almost impossible to think in terms of nation, to think in terms of the good of society. The emphasis resides mainly on how-am-I-going-to-make-it-for-myself? In *The Chosen Place, the Timeless People*, the character who epitomizes this dilemma is the lawyer, Lyle Hutson, who, as a young man in England going to the London School of Economics, is a devoted socialist. He sees the only solution to the problems in the West Indies is for the societies there to move towards socialism. Yet when he returns home he fits into and conforms to the bourgeois mold and he abandons all his idealism, the radical position of his youth. I see that happening time and again, not only in West Indian societies, but in African societies and in black American society. So that the book really should not be seen so much as a West Indian novel, it is simply that I was using the West Indies as a kind of place, I was selecting it as a sort of focal point because it is a small society and I was hoping to use it as a kind of microcosm which would have larger application and meaning.

MOL: I would want to call the novel a 'Third World novel'—would you agree to that description?

PM: Very definitely. I would like to see it described as a Third World novel, because it is set in a mythical island in the West Indies. Readers spend an awful lot of time trying to identify the place rather than seeing its larger meaning; the fact that it makes a statement about what is happening in the Third World in general.

MOL: Politically and psychologically?

PM: Yes.

MOL: What other writers would you say have influenced you?

PM: Well, any number, because I was a voracious reader from very early, as a little girl. I would say Ralph Ellison, the author of *Invisible Man*. Not so much that novel, but his collection of essays on literature and society called *Shadow and Act*. I find them seminal to my approach to writing. Because what he insists upon is that there is a whole culture, a whole field of manners about black American life that has to be first of all acknowledged and celebrated. That we are not, as so many of our detractors would like to insist, a people without a culture. That out of the painful experience of slavery and the aftermath we have been able to mold a culture which is unique to us. That culture has to be made available to black readers and it has to be celebrated. This makes for our strength and our validity as a people. And I think that that aspect of Ellison has been very helpful to me. I see it as one of the major influences on me as a writer. One of the things that really prompted me to write was the fact that I came out of a family of poets. My mother and her friends spent endless afternoons talking when they came home from work. They worked as domestics. And their whole ability to convey the character of the women they worked for taught me about characterization. Their ability to tell stories in a colorful, exciting way taught me about the narrative art. It was then in those early years just sitting and listening—and in those days children were seen and not heard—just sitting and listening and absorbing in the blood their African ability as story-tellers, folk-oral you see. Re-creating, they were highly political people. They would sit around and talk about Marcus Garvey, the New Deal, the Depression; talking about Roosevelt so that they gave me a sense that women could be involved politically. This is why *The Chosen Place* is essentially a political novel. They were the main influences in terms of technique, because those women had taken a language imposed upon them, English, and had brought a new dimension to it. They made it into a language which reflected them, with their use of imagery and metaphor, making their points through story. They taught me how one uses language in a creative and vital way.

MOL: That's very interesting. In that way the women are poets, poets of the human experience. Which writers do you admire?

PM: Well. I mentioned Ellison. I also admired Joseph Conrad during my adolescence. Again for this marvelous use of language. I found *Heart of Darkness* valuable because the theme is that man is complex, and until you begin to deal with all the dimensions of his personality, the sort of dark underbelly of the human personality, you are not dealing with him in his full dimension. I find that there is a reluctance, an inability on the part of white writers sometimes to acknowledge the multifaceted nature of the human personality. And one of the things that I am always trying to do as a writer is to suggest how complex and sometimes contradictory human nature is. So Conrad was also helpful. From the contemporary writers, I find Sartre exciting, John Updike because, again, of his use of language. I read a lot of Paul Laurence Dunbar because in his dialect poetry he shows what blacks have done with the language imposed on them. It is the kind of thing I am attempting to do in my work.

MOL: . . . trying to bring the language across, create a new language and literature to express the black consciousness. So what is your view of the current black aesthetic movement which is going on both in the States and Africa?

PM: I think it's all to the good. Because we are attempting to reconstruct our personality in our own terms. I see writers as image-makers, and one of the ways that we can begin offering images of ourself which truly reflect us, which begin to throw off the negative images the West has imposed on us, is to begin having our literature offer to the black reader the image of himself that is positive and creative. I don't think a people really progress until they think positively of themselves. Cultural revolution is about how you see yourself. What you think of yourself is part and parcel of other aspects of the revolution, the political revolution. You can't have the one without the other. And the black aesthetic, with its emphasis on the celebration of blackness, of seeing beauty in blackness, an emphasis on using some of the traditional forms, rhythms, and imagery in the work and dealing with themes that have to do with black life, is one of the ways of creating this positive image. We are in the process of re-creating ourselves all over the world and it's a fascinating task.

MOL: How would you say this is expressed in your work? How does black aesthetic appear in your writing?

PM: Interestingly enough, with *The Chosen Place* someone said to me, "Why is it that the way you describe things is not done in terms of western metaphor and imagery but largely African imagery and metaphor?" For example, there was a description of the man who owns the rum shop in the novel. When I describe him, I say he is almost like an African chief, presiding at the counter in the rum shop, with the rum bottle almost as if he is pouring libations, like a god who has had an injury. I was trying to show the way in which you can draw on the traditional material to make it a vital part of your fiction.

MOL: You tend to compare people to masks. I thought that was very effective, using African masks to describe the facial figuration of people.

PM: Yes, these are the ways I am attempting not only to make the connection between the black experience in the western hemisphere and in Africa, but also to infuse the work with a new kind of imagery, a new reference.

MOL: . . . and vision. Are there African renderings of form in your style?

PM: I think it's basically African. Also in a sense basically universal. Storytelling is an ancient art, it is not the exclusive domain of any people or civilization. The basic forms of story-telling are true in China, in Africa, wherever you find people telling stories. So I don't think of my work as reflecting the western tradition so much but rather as a part of a universal body of fiction. There are things that make a story work—characterization, the way you use language, how you orchestrate your plot so that you engage and hold the reader—and these are principles which operate in no matter what the society.

MOL: Don't you think there are certain combinations of these basic elements of fiction that are typical of people, that are determined by their culture? For instance, the attitude towards the work itself or the handling of time and plot structures? Don't you think that certain handlings would appeal to a people?

PM: That is probably true, for example with Amos Tutuola you get a different way of handling plot, you get a kind of stream and flow, the character moving constantly through a world that is both real and unreal. With myself there is a use of reality to suggest what is not real. In *The Chosen Place* the situation seems very real on the surface. There you have a small, somewhat underdeveloped village which has been pretty much isolated and forgotten. It seems real enough, the people working in the cane fields, going about their daily task, yet there is a dimension of unreality to those people. I tried to suggest it by the way they greet people by raising a hand as if they were witnesses on a stand. They are witness to their history and their suffering: the whole history of slavery and its aftermath. I begin at the level of reality but suggest there is another dimension, that I am after another statement which I am making through the use of reality.

MOL: And Carrington the maid is one such figure?

PM: Yes, when I describe her with her full breasts—the mother figure who suckles the world—I was trying by that to suggest that we as a people have been used to feed the world. Not only with our raw materials and resources, but our historical role has been the force that suckles the world. So this is why even though she is a very peripheral figure, I wanted to strike that note of how the black person has been used by western society.

MOL: How do you feel your work fits in with black American literature and Caribbean writing?

PM: I think that I am in a unique position. I know that people have trouble defining me as a black American or Caribbean writer. I fall between two stools, I'm neither West Indian nor black American. My parents were from the West Indies and they gave me a very strong sense of the culture out of which they came. That was one of the things that molded me as a person and a writer. Yet on the other hand I was born in Brooklyn, went to public schools and I'm very much a black American. I have got my feet in both camps, so that I am able to understand and respond to black American culture as well as West Indian writers who feel their situation is unique and apart from the black American experience. Similarly, I have no patience with black American writers who feel that the Caribbean is exotic and curious and different. To me it's all part of the same thing. There may be differences of expression, but at the base it's the same cultural expression.

MOL: Yes, the same historical experience of oppression and slavery.

PM: This is what my work is about: to bring about a synthesis of the two cultures and, in addition, to connect them up with the African experience.

MOL: I know writers don't like to talk about each other, but would you make a comment on Caribbean writers briefly—an appraisal or evaluation of them? Which ones do you like?

PM: The Caribbean writers I read—people like Eddie Brathwaite—are very interesting because they attempt to reach out to the African component in our experience and celebrate that. Given the fact that ours is basically an existential situation, we can create our history and personality. Writers like Brathwaite and Sam Selvon are saying, "This is the kind of personality I am going to create for myself as a black man, a fully faceted figure, by bringing into play the importance of the African aspect." So I like Eddie's poetry, also some of the things George Lamming does in his early novels where he exposes West Indian society, its hypocrisy and dependency on England and the need to break away from that and form a West Indian personality. In terms of writing, I find that the ability to describe the West Indian landscape by writers like John Hearne and Naipaul is just fantastic, they make that landscape live for you. These are some of the writers from the West Indies that I admire.

MOL: What do you mean by saying yours is an existential situation as black people . . . ?

PM: Here we are presented with this absolutely absurd history, certainly with blacks in the western hemisphere, and in Africa: the horrendous severing that took place, the separation from the motherland, the source. Then the traumatic business of slavery and colonialism, the insult of our color making us a lesser people, the notions of inferiority on us as a people—these are all things that have no sense. How can we, given these facts, create out of this horror a personality which would be positive and assist us to erect a new society, a new nation?

MOL: And, of course, there are the psychic effects of these experiences which you find even in Africa, even though the immediate, material severance is not that obvious.

PM: This is why the writer is so important. The writer feels the battle is the psyche; is that whole area of what people think of themselves, how they see themselves, what happens to them. It is the writer's great contribution to create new images that will overcome the negative psychological images we have because of our history. I don't think the political thrust can be really effective until there is a new thinking on the part of the black man. The cultural and the political revolution of China is so important. China closed its doors to the insidious influence of the West. They said: "Keep out your televisions, keep out your materialistic values, we are involved in the serious business of not only transforming our society materially but also making for a new man in China." What distresses me so about the developing nations as I see them is that all the emphasis is placed on the economic and the political advancement to the detriment and neglect of the real battle which, to my mind, is the way we see ourselves. If we take on western images, western values and attitudes, then all the work that is being done in the economic sphere is of no use.

MOL: And that would affect the way we proceed to galvanize the society; our mentalities are so important. So what are the trends in black fiction today in America? I am sure this kind of image-building and re-creation of self must be going on?

PM: Yes. In the serious fiction being written by black Americans today, I see two themes dominating. First of all, an examination of how black men and woman relate to each other, why we have had such a troubled history relating to each other. I think the fiction is concerned with this problem because there is recognition that we need all the forces within our community working together in order to make progress. If we spend our energies opposing each other in conflict, this takes away from the struggle. So there is an examination of this by some of the young writers. The other aspect which characterizes black fiction at this point is going back and dealing with some of the aspects of our culture which make for strength. Our legends and myths. We are saying essentially that man is not only defined by what he is materially. There is a whole aspect of the human personality which has to do with his spiritual quality, which we are examining. In the book that I am working on presently, I have gone back to some of the legends that are an important feature of early black American life and try to hook them up with the legends in the West Indies. One of the things that is striking about them is that those legends reflect a tremendous nostalgia for Africa. In black American folklore there's a notion about people flying. There are stories of how a man working out in the field, a slave, would suddenly throw down his hoe, abandon his plough, just spread his arms and take off to fly back to Africa. All these have to be made available for our young people to show that we had a culture, a tradition, and a history. And that this has to be used to form the new personality.

MOL: Is fiction exclusively your medium? Have you tried your hand at poetry or drama?

PM: I started off with poetry. I wrote poetry when I was twelve years old, very bad poetry. I haven't written any since then. But I like to think of myself as using poetry and prose so I use a lot of imagery in my writing, but I don't write poetry as such. I tried my hand only once at the dramatic form. I was asked to do a dramatic adaption of *Brown Girl, Brownstones* and I did that. It was a television play and came off very well, it won the award for that year. But I recognize that I only have a certain amount of energy and I have decided to devote that to perfecting myself as a novelist. I feel most comfortable with that form.

MOL: Do you feel that there are urgent themes that should be given priority over others in literature in general?

PM: Maybe! I can't speak for literature in general, but one of the things I'm preoccupied with is the need to celebrate black experience. History has been hidden from us, especially in the western hemisphere. I feel we have to go back and re-create that past so that we can use the lessons from that to aid us in the present struggle. I'm using the past as a way of "existing" us in the present and in the future. So there is a reappraisal of our past and a celebration of the positive aspects of our experience. Those are the two things which I feel have greatest priority in my work.

MOL: What do you think about the teaching and uses of literature in schools?

PM: I went to schools where I was never made aware that there was a body of black literature. I read people like Thomas Mann and Joseph Conrad, James Joyce and they are fine writers but I was never aware that there was a Richard Wright. I discovered black writers on my own. Even though I know there are any number of detractors now of the Black Studies programs and feel that blacks should be addressing themselves to technological knowledge, I still think it is important that this dimension of our experience be made available to our students. For a period of three years, I taught Black American Literature at Yale and what was so encouraging about it, was that I had black biology majors coming and taking a course on black autobiography. They did not know about people like Frederick Douglass or DuBois, the great leaders. It was a chance for them to fill in this tremendous gap in our education. So I think that the schools have an important task to fulfill in making available to young black students our history and our literature.

MOL: Thank you very much.

In Celebration of Our Triumph

Alexis De Veaux/1979

From *Essence* 10.1 (1979). Reprinted by permission of Alexis De Veaux.

I was in college when I was first introduced to Paule Marshall's highly acclaimed pioneering novel, *Brown Girl, Brownstones*. Of some thirty-odd books on the required reading list for English 295, hers was the only one written by a Black woman. A novel written by a Black woman? How many others had I read then. One? Two? Would it reflect me? I read it hungrily. I read it for breakfast on the bus, during lectures, in the tub for dinner, dissecting frogs in the bio lab with the book hidden on my lap; and at night between Richie Havens and Aretha Franklin, I'd let *Brown Girl, Brownstones* rock me to sleep. Years later I am sitting across the room from Paule Marshall in her Upper West Side apartment in New York City. She is a small woman. Her Black skin is island smooth, with Caribbean plum purple tints beneath her cheekbones. She is neat, meticulous, composed. Her hands are handsome and delicate. A scarf of African material is tied around her head in a turban style. The browns and beiges of her slacks and turtleneck sweater fall soft and mannered against her slender frame. Arranged on her sumptuous leather couch against the wall, Paule (pronounced Paul, she emphasizes) blends with the muted browns of the room overlooking Central Park. On the surface she does not look like a pioneer. She reveals none of the trappings: The boldness in her face is softly disguised; the charismatic flair is deliberately understated; the daring force and outspoken energy that mark every pioneer hide behind the few paintings and art objects placed in perfect order around the sparse but tasteful room.

So what's all this talk about a pioneer? Because like Gwendolyn Brooks, Ann Petry, and Rosa Guy, Paule Marshall is one of the few Black writers who came to be recognized in the fifties as an important and indefatigable talent.

A forerunner of the literary explosion of the sixties (the "New Renaissance"), she is as much responsible for opening the way to younger writers, particularly female writers (by the mere fact that she was seriously writing) as was James Baldwin, Richard Wright, John Killens and Ralph Ellison. These were writers who went the road alone with no vehicle to make comfortable their journey; no viable connection to an already well-established white literary movement; and yet they wrote and they told their stories, and they survived as artists, as individuals. They survived the best way they could. Each one, in his own way, was turning over new ground, helping to place the image of Black folk in literature in proper perspective.

And Paule Marshall took upon herself the pioneering task of creating an image of the Black woman in fiction, not simply as a product of America, but one whose story is as equally tied and bound to the West Indies as it is to its source—Africa. The Black woman in Paul Marshall's work is West Indian and, therefore, African by nature, a primary connection that has to be recognized and respected. Long before the women's movement, long before the current numbers of long overdue books by and about Black women, Paule Marshall was carving a respectful place for us in literature. "Women do figure prominently in my books," she says. "And I'm concerned about letting them speak their piece, letting them be central figures, actors, *activists* in fiction rather than just backdrops or background figures. I want them to be central characters. Women in fiction seldom are. Traditionally in most fiction men are the wheelers and dealers. They are the ones in whom power is invested. I wanted to turn that around. I wanted women to be the centers of power. My feminism takes its expression through my work. Women are central for me. They can as easily embody the power principles as a man."

This love and need to explore women in fiction, especially the Black woman, is a direct outgrowth of having grown up during the thirties in Brooklyn's Stuyvesant Heights (now Bedford-Stuyvesant), surrounded by hard-working people who set young Paule's imagination aflame with their story-telling. "Perhaps the most important influence in my becoming a writer is due to those fantastic women, my mother and her friends, who would gather every afternoon after work—they did day's work—and talk. We lived in an old brownstone house, which we leased. It had a huge, old-fashioned kitchen with a coal stove. An almost daily ritual for them was to gather there and talk. In that kitchen I was in the presence of art of a very high order because those women, in their talk, knew what literature was all about." Her voice is a steel-drum band. It hints of reggae, rhythm and blues and Bajan melodies blown off island waters. When she speaks about "those women," she is one of them, and she loves them, those talking-women she grew up with. "My mother and her friends would talk about their madames, as they were called then, and in describing them they taught me about characterization. How you pick up the detail that is striking about a person. I grew up among people to whom language was an art. Art which was present in the most ordinary things they said. They *created poetry* as they sat around a table talking. It wasn't that they read. There weren't books of poetry around the house as such, and no one read poetry. But their ability to recreate scene, to talk about people, to dissect character, that was the stuff of poetry and literature. It was just there, in the most natural kind of living way, as Africans see art, an integral part of life and not something set apart in a museum or theater or what have you. There was theater taking place in that kitchen each day. Theater of a very high order." Initiated into the art of oral rituals at a young age, she was in awe of the "actresses" who created them. "I was always so intimidated as a little girl by the awesome verbal powers of these women. That might be one of the reasons I started writing. To see if, on paper, I couldn't have some of that power."

The story-telling sessions she witnessed had an indelible effect on her, for not only were there discussions about woman's work but politics as well. Politics was important to these women, many of whom, like her parents, had immigrated to New York from Barbados during the post-World War I years of the Harlem Renaissance to fill the surplus of jobs created by the war effort, who sought the overrated promise of a better life in America. "Marcus Garvey was their great hero," she recalls. "When these women first came to the United States, they were his staunch supporters. They, out of their meager salaries as day workers, contributed to his movement; they were members of his Nurses Brigade. They marched down Seventh Avenue in the Garvey Day parades. These were women who were *involved* politically. Even though Marcus Garvey was no longer around, when I was a girl, their talk made him vivid for me. Those women in my mother's kitchen were the most striking influence of my early years. Though I was very close to my father, I never saw him, never heard him and his friends engage in the kinds of political and social questions my mother and her friends did. So my world was largely a world defined and formed by women." It was this strong image of the women in her mother's kitchen, an image of women concerned not only with household chores but with the politics of world affairs, that was later to be the impetus of Paule Marshall's life/work.

A bright and compulsive worker in school, surrounded at home by a cadre of women who transformed humiliating experiences into creative ones, Paule Marshall soon began to develop a keen sense of language as oral art. Books became the natural recipients of her love for words and the library a natural place to nourish that love. And so armed, she first tried her hand at writing as a teenager. "I went though the typical adolescent business of writing poetry. You know, the sensitive, misunderstood. alienated little girl, that whole bit, dreadful poetry," Paule cringes. "After I got over the spell, I didn't write for quite a while. When I started college I was fully committed, as were most young Black women at that time, to being a social worker. That was the thing. You were either a social worker or a teacher."

In 1950, two years after she entered Hunter College in New York City, she married her first husband. Then in her junior year illness forced Paule to leave school temporarily. Now with lots of time on her hands, she wrote letters to her friends. One suggested she consider writing as a career. "So I started writing short, little descriptive things. Vignettes. Then when I went back to finish school, I majored in English literature. I thought then of doing something having to do with writing, but I really didn't think of being a fiction writer. When I graduated, I tried finding work with a magazine or newspaper. But of course they were not hiring." They were not hiring women. But she'd made up her mind, so she kept looking. "And finally there on West 43rd Street between Sixth and Fifth avenues, on the second story, a little obscure, dirty window said *Our World Magazine*. I went trudging up this little narrow, dark flight of stairs. And there sat a man by the name of John P. Davis, the editor and publisher."

She is tickled as she remembers these days and working for *Our World Magazine*. Initially hired as a researcher for other writers, she soon began to write for the magazine's fashion and food section and then on to her own feature stories. The pressures of writing on the spot were complicated by the fact that she was the only woman on staff of the small Black publication. To her it seemed the men were waiting for her to fall. And why not? What woman then could be expected to survive the rigors of working in a tiny, noisy office of a struggling magazine, pouring out pages of copy on every current, often controversial, topic?

She could and she did, but magazine writing did not appeal to her, so, "In the evenings after an exhausting day at *Our World*, I started working on *Brown Girl, Brownstones*. I was living in St. Albans then. My first husband and I had just bought a house. And that stuff just started coming out of me. I have *never* had a more exhilarating writing experience. It took me a long time. It was a lot of pain because in writing that book I was actually learning how to write. With the publication of *Brown Girl* five years later in 1959, Paule Marshall, now 30 years old, added her name to the small but growing list of Black women writers, creators of an image of us in literature as intelligent, capable women. Images of women not only in touch with their sexuality but women who reveal their strength as well as their vulnerability: vulnerability to society, to themselves, to their men, to their history. Thus even as a young writer, Paule Marshall sought to instill in her female characters a sense of themselves as forceful people.

The powerfully lyric story of a young Bajan (Barbadian) girl, Selina, *Brown Girl, Brownstones* explores the world of her girlhood, her problems and pleasures. In language steeped in the tender unfolding of a teenage girl thrust into a half West Indian, half Black American mode of living, Paule Marshall's first novel paid homage to the women who first instilled in her the gift of oral art. These same women enliven the kitchen of Selina's house. We hear their stories, witness their rivalries.

That same cadre of women who had so captured Paule Marshall's attention now threaded their way through her first major literary effort. Was it autobiographical? "It was autobiographical in the sense that I was writing about the general world that I grew up in. Bajan Brooklyn. But the people are composites. They're made up of people I knew and people I imagined. There is no one you could point out in the book and say this person actually lived. Certainly not the girl, Selina. If anything, she's a kind of idealized image of myself. The kind of person I would have liked to have been: assertive, forthright, taking life in hand. Those marvelous qualities she has were not me at all. I was always so retiring, with my books all the time, and terrified of life. But that force Selina has is, I suppose, a kind of wishful thinking on my part." When she stops to reflect, I can see Selina's eyes opening behind Paule's and the eyes of Selina's family opening one behind the other: Ina, the older sister; Silla, the mother; Deighton Boyce, the trumpet-playing sweet father man. Opening. All the way back to Barbados and back again to the time way long before slave traders and tourists.

Brown Girl, Brownstones was well received by the reading public. It was a critical success. It got rave reviews in the *New York Times*; the *New Yorker* magazine and what was then the *Herald Tribune*. Not since Zora Neale Hurston's *Their Eyes Were Watching God* (1937) had a book written by a Black woman with such integrity, passion and anger done so much to dispel existing myths about the Black woman as a source of power in fiction. Yet despite all the reviews and attention, *Brown Girl* was not a commercial success, partly because a book about a Black girl's painful awakening wasn't a popular idea for a book. And partly because Paule is not "interested in selling the book." Television and radio appearances, book parties, public debates, cocktail parties and the like do not appeal to her. She simply refuses to cultivate a marketable image: Vehemently avoiding such occasions, she will, more often than not, opt for the comforts of her own private environment. Even personal interviews such as this one unnerve her initially, and it is only after several meetings and telephone calls that she allows herself to feel angry and, perhaps, hurt when this topic is brought up. Although she tries not to show it, she is hurt because her books have not received a larger following, and as an artist, she wants to be recognized, applauded and understood. Though not wanting attention focused on herself, she does want attention given to her work, and that is the paradox Paule Marshall finds herself constantly caught up in.

After *Brown Girl, Brownstones* Paule Marshall published a collection of short stories, *Soul Clap Hands and Sing* (1961). "It was an easy book to write. But it was also difficult in the sense that I'd just had a baby. And even though my first husband liked the fact that I was a writer, he couldn't quite reconcile himself to the hard work involved. He objected to the fact that I was away from the house working on the book. With the money I got from *Brown Girl*, I went and got help to stay here with my son. I went off to a friend's apartment and worked every day on *Soul Clap Hands*, and there was strong objection to that. Yet I went ahead and did it. There were, he sensed it, I knew it, my need and determination to be my own woman. To do my own thing. I think this is something women have to acknowledge about themselves—their right to fulfill themselves." Stubbornly determined, she kept going despite the strain on her relationships, the demands of motherhood. She grimaces remembering, "It has not been easy for my son, being the child of a mother who writes. It's not only my work." She's thinking about the years. All the years. Feedings. Short stories. Walks in the park. Ideas for books. Report cards. Bruised knees. Priorities. As we talk, her son is in the back cleaning his room. I can hear the vacuum cleaner coming and going. When he comes into the living room, there is a certain sense about him. It is practical, solid. He does not talk about literature but of other things like finishing high school, applying to college and becoming a naval architect.

Though a short book mainly concerned with the lives and activities of men, *Soul Clap Hands and Sing* did provide Paule with an opportunity to explore the West Indian motif weaving through her life and work. "In my writing I am always dealing from a base that happens to be me. It is, frankly, a means by which I can deal with aspects of my own personal history. I am both Black American and West Indian and, by ancestry, African. The West Indies is so very important to me because it is part of a history that as a girl I tried to deny. I went through torture as a girl growing up in Brooklyn, going to school with those heavy silver bangles on my wrists, and when we went to the West Indies and came back with heavy West Indian accents, the kids used to laugh at us. It was dreadful. So I went through a whole period of rejecting that part of myself. Now the West Indies represents an opportunity for me to fill in something I tried to deny, and it provides me with a manageable landscape for writing. I am overwhelmed by the complexity of America. People are annoyed with me because I don't deal with it directly, but I am just not going to take it on. I feel I can say something about Black people whether here, in the West Indies or Africa—wherever—by dealing with a more manageable environment, which to my mind has the same problems."

If *Soul Clap Hands and Sing* was her easiest book to write ("It only took two years"), then *The Chosen Place, the Timeless People* must have been the most ambitious and the most difficult of the three she's published so far. She was to spend the next six to seven years writing it. Published in 1969, *The Chosen Place, the Timeless People* is the dramatic twofold story of the "birth" of a woman, and the island people of Bournehills (an island in the Caribbean directly east of Africa) who fight desperately against the intrusions and corruption of their traditions, in the name of progress, by representatives of so-called liberal, humanitarian organizations from America. "As strange and as difficult as they are, as supposedly backwards as they are, they have an astonishing sense of history. They know that until a people, an oppressed people, have actually wrested power from their oppressors they cannot really come into their own. The Bournehills people refuse the many stopgap measures offered to them because, in their minds, the change necessary is a revolutionary change. They will not accept anything less than the complete independence their hero, Cuffee Ned, demanded in his time. Making it on their own. It's the kind of thing that the Cambodians are doing today." Leaning forward she says emphatically, "Move all the goddamn people out of the cities. Go back to the land. Learn to feed yourself. Be your own people. Own your soul. Close the door to the West, like China did for years. Close the West out until you're strong enough to deal with them on an equal level. That's why the Bournehills people are so stubborn and far seeing. They are absorbed and obsessed with the past. They *know* what history is about; they *know* what revolution is about."

She is speaking with a power now and a grace and a fervent commitment to what she is saying. Know your history. It can never be taken away from you. It can never be replaced with brass trinkets and glass pearls. That is what she is saying, and the multidimensional characters she has created for us echo these thoughts. They are heroic, unforgettable, timeless. "I tried to suggest their timeless quality in the ways I described them. For instance their eyes. They are a people who have the ability to not only see ahead in time but back in time. Or the way they said good-bye, as if they were witnesses. Witnesses to their own history but at the same time rooting them in the present. So there they are in those canefields, very involved in real, day-to-day living. I was trying to suggest links and connections and continuums."

And to epitomize those links and connections, she chooses to give us a pioneer/woman of tremendous and dynamic emotional complexities—Merle Kinbona. "Merle is the cultural broker. She negotiates between all the cultures and classes of Bournehills. She links it all together. She is as much one of the Bournehills people as the villagers. Her mother was a cane-cutter. She comes from that source, and yet she's been educated in England. She has her connections in town. She is able to wheel and deal in all these worlds. She is not only the link that connects, she is the history of the hemisphere. And one of the things Merle wrestles with is how to make sense of it all. And yet I see Merle as someone who is terribly uncertain and dependent, almost psychotic when we first meet her in the book. She lives alone in an isolated guest house by the sea; she talks endlessly. This is a woman who has been spurned by her father, whose mother died shortly after her birth, who has never been accepted by her society because she was illegitimate and dark-skinned. So her feelings about herself are fraught with insecurity and self-rejection. In that sense Merle is the historic Black person who has been almost brought to the edge, who has almost been done in psychologically, and so the book is concerned with pulling her back and the means by which she finds to *retrouvè*, to find herself again."

Symbols of chaos and uncertainty are brilliantly presented for our inspection by the writer throughout the novel. And yet it is a deep, intuitive sense of triumph over devastating obstacles that Paule Marshall instills in Merle. "I am very concerned with the environment of my characters. Take for instance the cassia tree that blooms in Merle's yard shortly after Carnival. I use it in a couple of ways. First, to highlight this marvelous flowering of Merle after she and Saul (the American social scientist) sleep together for the first time. Significantly it blooms for a few days and then things go back to normal. The tree suggests that although the affair was important to

Merle at the moment, she would soon be over it and back to her old self. Secondly I use it to suggest Merle is Everywoman, just as they have Everyman in eighteenth-century literature. She has these periods when things begin to happen to her, and she has a sense of coming into her own. Here is a Black woman who has been devastated by history. And the tree, which is mentioned earlier in the novel, standing barren almost as if it were dead, suggests symbolically that in the midst of death there is life. And Merle, even though she has been devastated both historically and personally, has within her the wherewithal to flower once again, because I am always speaking to this sense of triumph in Black people. W.E.B. Dubois talked about it also when he said that this tiny group of white people who are in a position of control at the moment are only en passant. There is nothing, as he says, that can deter the anointed people. And this is what I'm trying to suggest in the *Chosen Place*. It is there not only in the cassia tree, but in the emergence of Merle. In the end this woman, who is the illegitimate child of a plantation owner, emerges out of the psychological chaos of her history."

And so the community of women/folk heroes we became acquainted with in *Brown Girl, Brownstones* becomes singularly focused in Merle's character, and she inherits their collective American, West Indian and African strength. But as Paule Marshall's interests as a writer broadened, so too had the architectural imagery of women in her work. "I wanted the women in *Chosen Place* to embody the whole power struggle of the world," she says forcefully. "Merle embodies Black history and triumph. Harriet (Saul's wife) symbolizes the West: She cannot share power; she can go through certain meaningless motions, but to give, to really and truly give, she cannot do. Through Harriet I try to talk about that Western need to exercise control and power over others. For example her relationships to her first husband and to Saul, whom she tries to re-create with her money and influence. In this society women like Harriet are not allowed to realize themselves. They have to do it through their men. On the other hand there is Gwen (a local Bournehills woman). She is important because she symbolizes Black people's ability to endure, to survive and to continually astound and astonish white people."

Although, as a writer, she has been tackling the image and complexities of the Black woman long before it became fashionable, Paule Marshall does not consider herself a pioneer. She is somewhat embarrassed by the reference. To her pioneers are writers like Zora Neale Hurston and Dorothy West. Nevertheless she does hope her work has made some contribution, not only to the way we see ourselves as women but also to the questions we face as a people shaped by a profound, dramatic history. And that concern is the thematic motivation behind her work. "I'm trying to trace history. First of all to make some sense of my own history and also to make some sense of the history of Black people. To take, for example, the infamous triangular route of slavery and to reverse it so that we make the journey back from America to the West Indies, to Africa. Because I am convinced that, as a people, we have not as yet really engaged our past. Part of the reason for this, of course, is that we have been brainwashed into believing it's shameful—who wants to talk about slavery, for God's sake. But I think that until you do, you really can't begin creating your own proper image and proper self. Our history is not delimited by our presence in this part of the world. There are links and associations to a larger Black world. That's why it is so important at the end of *Chosen Place*, that Merle goes to Africa in search of her husband. And that's what I'm searching for in the work. To make that trip back. I'm not talking about a trip in actual terms. I'm talking about a psychological and spiritual journey back in order move forward. You have to psychologically go through the chaos to overcome it. One of the criticisms of my work has been that it dwells too much in the past. But the past is important to me because I'm really convinced one *has* to engage the past if you are to shape a future that reflects you. You have to deal with it rather than accept the kind of past that has been fostered upon us by white historians."

Paule Marshall is not a safe writer. She does not avoid the problems and conflicts of her people. She sees them and she attacks them as monumental themes in her books: sexuality, oppression, relationships, history, slavery, revolution, independence. Whether you agree or disagree with her perceptions is not the point. The point is that Paule Marshall is painfully aware of the importance and power of history creatively written. We are advised through the pages of her books to question the fabric and threads of this society and to make uneasy the one-eyed weavers until our image is sewn correctly with our own two eyes. And that is probably why her work has been "overlooked" by those who can (and do) make the difference as to whether or not a book will sell.

Still the lack of mass recognition and attention has created in Paule a strong sense of herself, and just as the women in her mother's brownstone kitchen were creatively able to rise above negative experiences, so is Paule Marshall able to transform and objectify personal experience, to have power over the circumstances of her own life story. To give it shape, meaning, form.

And there are several forms to choose from: poetry, essay, drama, fiction, journalism. Some writers explore several approaches during the lifetime of their writing careers. Not Paule. "My approach has been to concentrate on the novel and the short story and to try and perfect the form rather than to spread myself thin. There have been any number of inducements for me to go and do other things." One such inducement happened when she adapted *Brown Girl, Brownstones* for the CBS Television Workshop. Her award-winning adaptation was so successful there was a great deal of outside pressure put on her to write for the theater. She was even the recipient of a Ford Foundation grant in playwriting. "I was briefly tempted. And then I just recognized that wasn't what I really wanted to do. I just wanted to remain in the area of fiction. It's a stand that I've taken. Other people's approaches have been to try their hands at many things. That's not for me. One of the greatest battles has been for me to say, No, I'm really a novelist or trying to be a novelist, and this is what I do."

Her direction is clear. Her mind is firm. She will not waver. Do not ask her to write poetry. Nor articles for magazines. She will tell you quite frankly she is a novelist and a fiction writer and that's all. But like so many artists faced with the problems of how to support themselves, Paule Marshall turned to public-funding sources for financial assistance. Her books, though never commercial successes, had received rave reviews, and on the strength of them she was able to get writing grants from such notable organizations as the National Endowment for the Arts and the Ford Foundation. With the help of these and other grants over the years, she has been able to support herself. Crucial to the development of her craft, they allowed her to buy time to concentrate on writing with less anxiety about getting the bills paid and helping to feed her son. It has also meant some personal sacrifice, but it is her way. And she'd rather do her way.

A rigidly disciplined writer on her first three books who often put in six to eight hours at her desk writing and was known not to answer her telephone before four in the afternoon, Paule Marshall's writing habits have changed in recent years. At forty-nine she isn't so hard on herself anymore. She says she recognizes her limitations and her age now, and she doesn't try to fight it. Since the publication of *The Chosen Place, the Timeless People*, her writing habits have not been the only thing that's changed. After thirteen years her first marriage ended. In 1970 she remarried. She and her second husband, a Haitian businessman who lives in Haiti, have what she describes as "an open and innovative marriage" in which they visit back and forth during the year. They are both financially independent and are both dedicated to their own lifestyles and careers. It is an arrangement that allows her time and the maximum amount of freedom possible.

Another change in her life revolved around the matter of financial support. As monies from public funding sources became less available in the late sixties and seventies, she took up teaching at Yale and Columbia universities to support herself. But she was to discover that she was not comfortable teaching. "I'm a practitioner. It's hard for me to talk about writing in technical terms since I'm used to doing it in a very practical day-to-day way with my own work. Then too I have worked in private for so long, just me and the typewriter, that it was difficult to suddenly go from my study, a very private place, into a public place like a classroom. It was so painful a lot of the time." And yet her work has a tremendous following in academic circles all over the country. "I think it's because there's enough about the work that is challenging to a reader, to young critics, that they find something there to work with. I think it's unlikely that I will ever make it commercially with best sellers and that kind of thing, but what has been very heartening and reassuring is that the people who read well like the work. And that, I tell you, is just so gratifying."

She rests her teacup on the small, wooden table between us. She jokes about her homemade cookies. It has been a long interview. The silhouettes of Central Park trees peek in the windows. We take our second wind. The conversation changes to politics, writers and the future. Is she a political person? Yes, though she is not actively involved in any organization at the present. She was, for years, a member of the Association of Artists for Freedom, an organization created shortly after the infamous church bombing in Birmingham, Alabama, in which four little Black girls were killed in 1963. Instrumental in the association's formation were a group of Black artists, including Ruby Dee, Ossie Davis, John O. Killens, Paule Marshall and others. Their concern was to impress upon other Blacks the necessity to be actively involved in the independence of their own people. To demonstrate the acute level of their concern, they proposed a national economic boycott the following Christmas. However, without the aid of the NAACP (who flatly refused their request for help), they were not able to pull such a boycott off.

These days find Paule Marshall meditating before work, riding her bike through the streets, exploring the nooks and crannies of the Upper West Side and Central Park, eating natural foods, taking care of her body, enjoying the company of good friends or an evening at the theater, maintaining a low public profile and working on a new book. Recently she was awarded a grant from the National Endowment for the Arts in fiction. She will use it to live off while she finishes the new work. What's it all about? "It is about a theme which has always concerned me: namely the materialism of this country and how it often spells the death of love and feeling, and how do we, as Black people, fend it off. The book is about this terribly uptight, middle-class, middle-aged Black woman who undergoes a profound change on a cruise to the West Indies and Central America. She suddenly begins to question her life and the kind of grasping for things that has characterized her marriage."

Paule admits this book is not an easy one to write because her writing habits have changed and because of her desire to have a more integrated life: to live as much as she writes each day, to participate more in her own relationships. And so the work comes slowly. She often puts in a seven- or eight-hour day at her desk only to find herself with a headache, in need of rest and with not many pages written. She reminds herself to relax. To let it flow in its own time. So we talk about writers who have influenced her. "When I was a teenager, I was influenced by all kinds of writers, from Emile Zola to Zane Gray. Then I went through a very heavy Thomas Mann and Joseph Conrad period. Thomas Mann's *Death in Venice* was a seminal book for me in my early twenties. I was also influenced by Richard Wright, to a lesser degree. Of course there was Paul Laurence Dunbar. Women writers like Zora Neale Hurston and Dorothy West I didn't discover until later on. I was very taken by the heroine in Dorothy West's *The Living Is Easy*. I loved Lucille Clifton's poetry. That's my kind of poetry. Also early Baraka. One of the people who is absolutely crucial to me is Ralph Ellison. Even more so than his *Invisible Man*, my literary bible is his collection of essays, *Shadow and Act*. He is so committed to the notion of the worth and validity of our experience and the responsibility of the writer to celebrate that experience and not fall into the trap white sociologists have set for us in viewing our lives as totally negative. It is not one bleak history of degradation and despair. Ellison states it for me so well. Whenever I get a little shaky, and unclear, I go back to him. Jimmy Baldwin has been equally as important to me. His essays have been crucial in my formation as a writer and a thinker."

Sitting here in a room of an apartment she has lived in for several years, Paule Marshall is comfortable with herself and her life's work. It is true that it is changing, but there are always new plateaus to climb, things and people to weed out and replace. Nonetheless she has always had her work to measure the ups and downs by. It has often been a slow and painful process. Often lonesome. Often questioning. But she has done it. Without the glitter and glamour supplied by public relations folk. Or the mass recognition. Or the National Book Awards. There has been no overwhelming controversy over her books, but there has been the lyrical, image-laden, complex volumes of her work. Her work. It has grown with her. It has worked at the technical kinks. There is a brevity in the lengthy sentences. An architectural order to measure the paragraphs by. To measure and unmask the raging conflicts of pioneering Black women on paper. "Our survival, Ellison says, has been one of the great triumphs of the human spirit. And that's what the writer has to speak to. And that's what I'm committed to as a writer."

A Talk with Mary Helen Washington

Mary Helen Washington/1981

"A Talk with Mary Helen Washington," from *Writing Lives: Conversations Between Women Writers*, ed. Mary Chamberlain (Virago, 1988), 161–67. Reprinted by permission of Mary Helen Washington.

Paule Marshall, whose parents emigrated from Barbados during the First World War, was born in Brooklyn, New York, in 1929. After graduating Phi Beta Kappa from Brooklyn College, she worked as a magazine researcher, a librarian and eventually as a writer. She has published three novels, *Brown Girl, Brownstones* (1959), *The Chosen Place, the Timeless People* (1971), and *Praisesong for the Widow* (1982), and a book of short stories, *Soul Clap Hands and Sing* (1961). During the 1950s and 1960s, Marshall was associated with American Youth for Democracy and also with Artists for Freedom, a militant Black movement formed after the bombing of a Birmingham church that killed four little Black girls. Although she was a successful writer in the 1960s, Marshall came into her own in the 1970s, the decade of feminism.

From her mother and the Barbadian-American community in Brooklyn, Paule Marshall inherited an entire cultural and linguistic vocabulary, one that combines idioms and myths from Afro-American, Afro-Caribbean, and African cultures. Marshall's very special relationship with her mother who embodied those cultures has resulted in a unique example of "mothering the mind" of a creative artist. Marshall says that her strongest and most truthful writing is a celebration of the art she learned from her mother: "She laid the foundations of my aesthetic, that is the themes and techniques which characterize my work.

"The dynamic of that early struggle had a profound impact on what interests me as a writer. It also influenced me in terms of style. The imaginative and poetic approach to language was as natural as breathing, and I sensed that her power came from her manipulation of language. I couldn't hold forth on my feet but because I had absorbed their [those Bajan women's] ability to work magic with language, I was trying to duplicate it in standard English, in being as careful and precise as possible and trying to imitate their tough, lyric way of dealing with language. This artistry with language—the marvelous phrases, the strong, artistic quality of Black language, that core of expressiveness which is developed when we Black folk are not allowed other outlets—is expressed in those areas where we're not censored or oppressed, where we can fully express ourselves. It's a solidly African-derived kind of thing."

In a 1973 essay "Shaping the World of My Art" and in a recent article ("From the Poets in the Kitchen," *New York Times Book Review*, 9 January 1983), Marshall has explained the ways her creativity was nurtured by her mother and the other women in the Barbadian-American community. These story-telling women, themselves artists, provided a model of woman as artist, thereby giving Marshall the freedom to become one. They left the houses where they worked as servants and gathered in her mother's kitchen after work to talk—about "this white-man country," about economics, psychology, sociology. These poor peasant women, recent immigrants from Barbados in the 1920s, recounted many of the tales found in her first novel *Brown Girl, Brownstones*. Their angry recollections of poverty and colonial exploitation in Barbados, as well as the racism they encountered in the United States, were the content of their "exhaustive and vivid discussions." Paule sat unnoticed in a corner, listening, absorbing the insight and irony they brought to words, and above all, "their poet's skills": "All that free-wheeling talk together with the sometimes bawdy jokes and the laughter which often swept the kitchen, was, at its deepest level, an affirmation of their own worth; it said that they could not be either demeaned or defeated by the daily trip out to Flatbush. It declared that they had retained and always would a strong sense of their special and unique Black Identity.

"There was this very real situation: my mother and her group of women sitting there in the kitchen after work. These women were extensions of my mother—impressive, powerful—they were the only adults in my world. Men were very scarce and I never got a sense of them sitting around talking with each other. The forces in my world were these women. For them it was a struggle just to be women—they had to 'tie up their bellies' and keep going. They saw those duties as having to work and to take care of a family. They looked to each other for their social lives, not to men. Men and women seldom went out together. Their social lives were among their own sex—an African-based pattern."

Language for these women of Marshall's youth became both refuge and weapon, a form of self-expression as well as a means to interpret and control their lives: "In this white-man world you got to take yuh mouth and make a gun" (*Brown Girl, Brownstones*). As these women sat in her mother's kitchen each afternoon, narrating their lives and memories, they not only showed women in the powerful act of story-telling, they formed a peculiar female kind of folklore. They had words for pregnancy: the expectant mother was "in the way," or "tumbling big." A woman who was too free with her sexual favors was known as a "thoroughfare," or she might be called "a free-bee," which was Marshall's favorite of the two: "I like the magic it conjured up of a woman scandalous perhaps but independent, who flitted from one flower to another in a garden of male beauties, sampling their nectar, taking her pleasure at will, the roles reversed.

"What I did with my mother's voice was to transform it. I was using her approach—her care with telling a story well, finding the telling phrase—I retrieved these things. I am using the voice of the community."

The dynamic of that early relationship with her mother has profoundly affected the style and themes of Marshall's work. Her own struggle to be in her mother's presence her own person, to break away from her domination, to match her mother's power with words is recreated in *Brown Girl, Brownstones* in Selina's seven-year battle with Silla. As important as this relationship was to Marshall's development as a writer it was, in many ways, problematic and negative:

"The influence was absolutely fundamental and crucial but it came in a negative way. My mother never directly encouraged me to write. What I absorbed from her was more a reaction to her negativity. It was her saying to me when I was in Junior High School after I'd won all the medals, saying to me out of her own defeat and failure, that I was a failure. No, the influence was not positive, it was full of problems, stress, antagonisms.

"My mother was well aware that it was a power struggle, that I was seeking to replace her. She called me a 'force-ripe woman'; 'two head bulls,' she would say, 'can't reign in a flock'; or, 'Here you've come to read the burial service over me'; 'Look how I done brought something in the world to whip me' . . . Because of all my grand ambitions she used to call me 'poor great'. She wanted me to get a job as a secretary, not to go to college. She wanted to get along in a kind of minimal way and she disapproved of my ambitions. She was always telling me that I looked as if I were living my old days first."

Writing became for Marshall a way of imitating her mother and of throwing off her domination. She hoped her success as a writer would please her mother so that she would have to retract her verdict of failure.

"My mother's powerful ability to handle language was something I wanted to emulate and to do one better—with the hope that this would please her and she would take back that awful thing about my being a failure."

Success with words would also signal that eventually she would reign as "head bull" in the flock.

Marshall insists that the mother-daughter bond, important as it is for revealing character, for allowing women to be the central characters in their lives, the activists, the centres of power, has a significance for Black women far greater than their individual lives. She repeats the theme that recurs throughout Black literature: "selfhood must be conceived in political terms.

"The element of struggle has deeply affected my writing because it reflects my own struggle to be in her presence my own person, and that struggle—that need to break away, to move away from domination, to prove your own worth—is connected to the larger struggle of the Black people. The woman in the story 'Brooklyn' throwing off domination to become a political person is an example of how the struggle with my mother influenced the themes in my work."

In the quest for traditions to illuminate the meanings of the mother-daughter bond, white feminist writers often turn to Western myths—the myth of Demeter and Persephone as an example of generational continuity between women, variations of the Medusa myth as the terrible but powerful mother, mothers and stepmothers in fairy tales who predict an archetypal mother-daughter hostility. That bias towards Western white models ignores African mythology as a source of Black maternal imagery. Without sufficient knowledge of African myths, I cannot trace Marshall's symbols back to their ultimate African sources, but there is enough evidence to suggest that the image of the Afro-American slave mother is one of the sources for the characterization of Silla Boyce. Everything about Silla's portrait suggests the slave mother—her standing on the corner waiting for suburban housewives to offer a day's work; the emphasis on her body as an instrument she uses to protect her children; her working out all day and then returning home to make Barbadian delicacies for her family; her manlike strength. In the one well-known narrative by a slave woman, Linda Brent's *Incidents in the Life of a Slave Girl*, the mother-child bond is central to the entire text. Unlike the male slave narrators, who were often willing to cut familial bonds to escape slavery, Brent will not take an opportunity to escape to the North because she refuses to leave her children in bondage. Like that slave woman, Silla remains behind with the children while Deighton devises a number of escapes from the bondage of his life.

The historical mythology of the slave mother as a way of envisioning and defining motherhood maintains the importance of understanding motherhood in its political context. It challenges the fiction of mother-daughter hostility and the traditional ways of seeing mothers as powerless in the world of men. Clearly, Paule Marshall's mother nurtured her creativity in this tradition. In Marshall's later novels, *The Chosen Place, the Timeless People* and *Praisesong for the Widow*, the mother-daughter relationship is not treated directly; she writes about two women—Merle Kinbona and Avey Johnson—in larger social and political contexts:

"In *Praisesong* the widow moves back into the past because that past provides her with the power to live in the present. In the legend of Ibo landing she sees a possible way of dealing with America, with establishing a psychological and spiritual distance from its ethos, its values. But her composure and peace are false. She has to move back to a centre she once had."

However, the themes generated by that early relationship are still present: the concern with oppressed people engaging their history, facing up to colonial oppression, moving to control their own lives and refusing to be dominated by the materialism of the Western world:

"That whole concern with dealing with history and with third world peoples facing up to colonial oppression—that power dynamic—people moving to control their own lives—the basic pattern is still there but translated into a larger kind of concern."

Talk as a Form of Action: An Interview with Paule Marshall

Sabine Bröck/1982

From *History and Tradition in Afro-American Culture*, edited by Günter H. Lenz (Campus Verlag, 1982). Reprinted by permission of Sabine Bröck.

Q: I've read that you got a lot of impulse for your writing as well as literary material out of remembering the kitchen talk of your mother and her friends . . . took that out of *Brown Girl, Brownstones*. Can you recall other sources for your creativity, e.g. did you read any novels by black women writers of that time?

A: Well, the period that I was talking about when I referred to the kitchen talk were the thirties, when I was a little girl growing up in Brooklyn, and the forties, and at that period women writers who were around or who had been published by then were just unheard of, were just unknown on my community. They weren't taught in the schools that I attended, people like Jessie Fauset, people like Zora Neale Hurston, they just were not taught. And that's one of the great deprivations of education in this country and more specifically the black community in this country. We were just not exposed to, were just not given the privilege to read Black literature. The books that made up the curriculum in the English department were drawn from so-called Western and American literature, American meaning excluding Blacks, even though they might occasionally teach a Black male writer. Back in those days almost never would they teach a Black woman writer. So certainly there was not any opportunity for me in school to be put in touch with Black women writers in the thirties and in the forties. The things that I read as a little girl growing up were the standard kinds of Nancy Drew books about becoming a nurse and the Little House on the Prairie books. The better kinds of literature that I got to later on in High School are Jane Austen, later on in college Joseph Conrad and Thomas Mann. And I began after a time to be somewhat influenced by these writers. I still had not made the acquaintance of Black American writers. When finally I got to read people like Wright, I found that although I was pleased in the sense that I was reading about Black life, I was yet having the sense that my particular experience as a young urban Black American woman was not really being dealt with in that literature.

And very slowly the idea of trying to do *Brown Girl, Brownstones* came about, came out of that sense that there was nowhere in the literature where I could turn where I saw not myself so much reflected but young women like myself reflected. Gradually, I mean these things are not conscious, some deep inner place I began wanting to attempt that story, to attempt to get something of the reality and texture and meaning of their life down on paper. Then something marvelous happened. It must have been in the fifties that I came across *Maud Martha* by Gwendolyn Brooks. I read it and found it a remarkable book. Not only from the point of view of style—that kind of spare poetic, very delicate but very sturdy kind of style—a way I couldn't write and don't—mine is much fuller. But I like that kind of poetic approach to prose. And I also was very much taken with *Maud Martha* because I think she in a sense was a truly vanguardal breakthrough character in American literature in the sense that Brooks took the life of a terribly ordinary young woman and made of it something of art. And in a sense even though I hadn't started writing at that point, I sensed that this was the kind of thing I would attempt when I started writing: to say that there was something of worth, something to celebrate, that there was something to acknowledge about the life of women who had been simply dismissed by society. That in the small number of Black books that I've read mainly by men I haven't seen the life, the ordinary community life in any way dealt with in its fullness.

And I think I wanted to do it for a couple of reasons: first of all, as I might have said before, I wanted to tell the story of the young urban Black woman—that's a very narrow sphere. On the other hand I wanted to in a sense tell the story of a young woman in relation to her community. What I sensed in so much of the literature, Black literature that I began reading at that point, this is in the mid-fifties, when I started thinking about writing—what I sensed in so much of the literature was that the reference was constantly the larger oppressive racist society, and that that defined almost totally the hero or the heroine. I had a sense that even though that was valid, yes, that a whole dimension was missing, that in the face of racism, in the face of oppression, there was a Black community, that Blacks had been able to elaborate, to make, to fashion a life in a community that was a means of sustaining them. And that our lives were not solely defined by racism, that we did most of the time love our children, our husbands and our wives and we had a family life and these were things that have to be celebrated because by celebrating we said that in the face of an oppressive society we were still able to maintain a sense of humanity.

And this was the thing that I think I was after in the work, and this is why women, the kitchen talk, the women at the kitchen table, my mother and her friends were so important. Even though I couldn't have spelled it out, even though I wasn't conscious of what was happening at that table I sensed that they were artists. They were not permitted—given the nature of their lives—the means to develop as artists and so they had to find a medium through which they could give voice to this tremendous reservoir of expressive quality that they had. And so it was done through talk, and it was talk that even though it was spontaneous on one hand was on the other very finely tuned. So it was an artistic expression. I mean they just didn't sit around the kitchen table and tell a story "in any ole kind way"; a story was told with an eye to its structure, with an eye to the people they were talking about in the story—characterization, it was told with a sense of drama in mind. And so it was there in those early years that I really had sense of what went into making stories. And so this is why they were so important. And I wanted to write about them when I came to *Brown Girl, Brownstones*, because there was something of their lives that needed to be recorded, because it said something about the way Black women were able to make of their lives a kind of artistic expression through their talk. They were able not only to make an artistic expression, but for the hours that they would spend sitting around their kitchen table talking they were in a sense controlling their lives, and that's central. They spent most of their day working as domestics in the homes of white people being exploited, being disregarded, being considered the pariah of a society, but when they were able to gather together in a kind of a community of friendship and support which those sessions at the kitchen table represented, they were able to give vent to their artistic impulses and at the same time to, in a sense, control their lives, so the two things were at play and I wanted to capture something of that quality in the novel.

Q: I like this idea about taking control, something like the moment you're able to speak about hurt it's like you are not this helpless victim any longer.
A: Yes, so that my women, the women in my novels really represent a depar-

ture from the kind of women that you see so much of contemporary Black women writing. They are not victims. On one hand they are oppressed women, they have to go out and do the menial work and they are insulted and humiliated and so forth, but their whole way of reacting to that, their whole ability to find means of giving vent to their anger and frustration, their ability to exercise a kind of control of their lives, even if it's through talk, suggests that they're not victims. I think that's very important because there is in the dominant culture here a whole desire to see Black life as totally in disarray, as being truly shattered by the experience of racism. And I think this is one of the things that my work represents, it really is a departure from that prevailing notion that the women do find means by which they can escape being just simply victims.

Q: I think Robert B. Stepto wrote in an essay about Richard Wright when he talks about the women's writing after Wright that the difference between the women's writing and the characters in most of Wright's writing is that the women are oppressed and they are in a way poor creatures but they dream just the same. Do you think this is about the same as what you are saying: that there is this vision of being able to create or being able to love and not resigning to circumstances?

A: Yes, yes. With them, with the women, especially in *Brown Girl, Brownstones*, it was not only dreaming. They did dream, I mean they had very practical dreams, they dreamed about property, they dreamed about making it in terms of the American materialistic ethic, they dreamed alright, but they also acted. I saw their talk as a form of action, because both the women in the novel and the women I knew as a girl growing up—their talk was not confined to the usual things that women are supposed to talk about, gossip, their husbands, how much food is in the stores and so on. These were women who talked about the economy, this was during the period of the post-depression and Roosevelt had just come along. They talked about Roosevelt who they considered their great savior, they were politically aware women, they talked about Marcus Garvey who was their great hero. When they came here as immigrant women in the early twenties and got their first jobs as domestics and so on, as sleep-in maids or just as day-workers, they contributed out of their small salaries to the UNIA movement which was Garvey's movement. They were members of his nurses' brigade and marched in the Garvey Day parades of 7th Avenue in their white nurses uniforms. And they contributed to the buying of the ships, the Black Star Line. I don't know how many of those women would actually have gone to Africa, if Garvey had achieved his dreams, you know, the whole repatriation. I don't think one of them would have gone, but their embracing of the movement, their support of Garvey suggested something to me when I thought about it years later, which has been very important to my writing. Not only did it say that they had a political perspective, but they also saw themselves in terms of the larger world of darker people. And even though they might have had some of the same unhappy stereotype opinions and attitudes towards Africa, at that point their allegiance, their dedication to Garvey said that they saw themselves not just as Black Afro-Americans or Afro-Caribbeans living in this hemisphere, but they saw themselves as part of that larger world. And this has become, of course, one of the themes of my own work.

Q: I want to ask you about these very practical dreams you were hinting at. The criticism I read about was almost always in that vein, saying that this is a woman who is totally caught up in the typical American dream and she is all after power, and that was negative for these critics. They saw it as something which was not bearable or not right. I didn't understand it that way, I always thought it was a very avant-garde way in the fifties to portray a woman seeking after power and admitting it freely, that would have been avant-garde even for white women, let alone for Black women who just came here I don't know how many years before. I mean she wasn't even a "true American."

A: I think a couple of things enter into it. The criticism of her that you've come across comes out of the stereotype of the Black woman, of this all-powerful matriarch figure. She has been seen in the literature and apart from literature as a kind of castrating figure, and I think that the criticism comes out of that. And it's unfortunate, because the critics who condemn a character like Silla are doing so because they have accepted the dominant society's view of Black women, which, of course, is to discredit her. If you say a woman is castrating, that's a total condemnation of her. What they fail to see is that Black women historically have been strong, have had to be strong, and that strength is a positive feature and that strength does not take away from their "womanly qualities," their ability to be tender, to be emotional, giving creatures. What has happened is that "strong, matriarchal" has taken on a whole unhappy meaning which casts these women as unfeeling, as castrating, as larger than life. What I tried to do in *Brown Girl, Brownstones* was to suggest that, yes, the mother is almost fierce in her desire to establish herself in this country, but that she does have needs. I'm trying to evoke memories of her as a young woman. There is the time when she is at the dance, there is the scene where she allows the father to take the money because they've had a night together, so she is not this iron clad, the iron maiden, so to speak.

Q: A lot of people saw her that way. I always felt just the opposite. The more detailed you described how fierce she was, the more I sensed her fighting against something in her own self so that this whole contradiction in herself was revealed without somebody being there to tell you, yes, sometimes she is needy or sometimes she is sweet, but you sensed it out of the writing.
A: Yes, that's what I was trying to convey. There are some negative features to her and I try to suggest those in the novel—these are the things that the young girl, Selina, questions about the kinds of values that her mother embraces. I think the mother's failing, the thing that makes for her emptiness in the end of the novel is that she has embraced the American materialistic ethic unquestioningly. In her whole ambitious drive to obtain the house, to see to it that Selina goes to college and becomes the doctor or whatever, she does it in such a way that she alienates the very people that she needs in her life, her husband, her children.

And I was trying to say something large, I mean my characters are on one level, yes, people in a novel but they are so on another level saying something about the larger society. So Silla is symbolic of the kind of thing that makes me so unhappy about American society: this kind of almost blind absorption in the material which makes for a kind of diminishing of life, of feeling. Because the book is really about the loss of love. In the face of her getting and spending this is what is forsaken, what is given up, this is what she loses. The book is also—as I see it—a kind of commentary on American society. So it's on one level about Black women who refuse to be victims, about a Black woman who is defined not by racism solely but by her community and by the people who made her up, the old woman who represents love to her, the old hairdresser, Suggie, the neighbor, who represents sexual love . . . so that you get in Selina the creation of a complex and intelligent protagonist who is seen in terms of her community. This might be some of the reasons that the book somehow has become a kind of classic, you know the fact that it has been brought out again and it's been selling fairly well, because not only do Black young women see themselves to a great extent in Selina, but she has a kind of larger application, because it's a story of the rites de passage and those stories were only told about young boys.
Q: What did you consider your audience to be like in the fifties, and has it changed since, and how would you explain the fact that your novels were lost to a wider audience after they received critical acclaim on their appearance? Barbara Christian told me that she remembers *Brown Girl, Brownstones* being taught in school, so that young girls read it at a certain time, but

she couldn't tell whether there was a larger audience to it, and she suspected that there was not.

A: When it first came out in 1959 it was very well received critically and there was hope that it would be a commercial success. There was Hansberry's play *A Raisin in the Sun* at the time and they had hoped that because that had received great acceptance that maybe there was room for an acceptance of a novel by and about a Black woman. That didn't prove to be the case. The book at that period was read mainly by people who were interested in a well-written book, who had some interest in Black literature. There was certainly Ellison very much on the scene and Baldwin, but because there wasn't that much interest in women's writing it did not have as large an audience as it does now enjoy. And even now it's being mainly read in colleges, new women's studies programs, Black studies and working class women novel courses—that kind of thing. It's having a much larger audience now than it did when it first came out.

I think there are some other reasons for the small audience when it came out. In this country it's not enough to write fine literature or to attempt to—because it's a country too committed to public figures, the writer has to do something else, the writer has to find ways of becoming a public personality, and I'm not very good at that. I have such a hell of a time to get the words on paper, that is such a struggle for me, that then to take on this other thing which is also a major undertaking is something that I've not been terribly good at. One has to find ways of promoting oneself in the hopes of promoting the work and my attitude was, look, I've written the book, I've got an agent and the publicity persons in the publishing house, let them go out and sell it . . . but it doesn't happen that way. So one of the reasons for *Brown Girl, Brownstones* not doing very well that first time around was in part that I didn't understand what the whole literary establishment was all about what it's like in this country. I'm beginning to learn now and even though it doesn't sit very well with me, I do try to attend a conference here or make a talk there, because that's all part of it.

Q: Did you feel you would have had a harder time trying to promote your work as a woman, especially because that scene was very "hero oriented" with Baldwin and Ellison being around?

A: Well, I think that even though there were Baldwin and Ellison there was also Hansbury who was very well known a that period, so that there was room for the Black woman writer, although not as much room as there is now. When Petry's *The Street* came out it was fairly well received and fairly well read, I think. Gwendolyn Brooks was a Pulitzer Prize poet, you see, so that there were a few Black women writers on the scene who had some popularity, some public acclaim and recognition. It just didn't happen, only with the mid-seventies and eighties, that Black women have come on the scene. They had been there, certainly in the Renaissance, e.g. Hurston and Nella Larsen, these were writers who were being published and who were fairly well known certainly in the reading portion of the Black community and to a limited degree in the white community.

Q: But both died in rather obscure circumstances?

A: That's true.

Q: And they had to be dug out again by women writers like Walker in the eighties?

A: Yes, America is such a crazy scene artistically—there is this whole kind of periods of soaring popularity and then one can easily disappear off the scene.

Q: So you don't think it's a special problem for women writers, this disappearing without anybody taking notice and being forgotten?

A: I think it's both. It's in part the way American society treats its artists, then as a further extension of it is what being Black means in this country. I think there is still a kind of amazement of a part of the larger society that Blacks and especially Black women maybe can write, that they can actually sit down and write a book. This is a definite problem. E.g. when I teach, I'll have my male colleagues say to me that their wives have read my book and they loved it. But they themselves, only very few of them will say that they have read it, because they see it in the domain of women and part of it is their sexist attitude, but part of it also is a sense that a book by a Black woman writer can't be alright serious . . . so let the wife read it.

These kinds of attitudes make it a real uphill battle for the Black woman writer. So that when you see the kind of extraordinary success of say a Toni Morrison, you have to look at that very closely, very carefully, because there is another thing that operates in the literary establishment. She has even talked about it: there is only room for one at a time. She laments the fact, e.g., that as an editor at Random House she has writers like Toni Cade Bambara whom she has not been able to really kind of push. (Bambara is the author of *The Salt Eaters*.) They have all these kinds of tacit agreements in the literary establishment that there is only space for one, maybe with a second edging off. So there is that to contend with, this principle of tokenism.

In the face of all of these impediments what does a writer like myself do, someone who has been writing since the mid-fifties, who has published three books. I should have published many more, but that's my own problem, I mean I'm a very slow, fussy, meticulous kind of writer . . . you have to understand the society, understand America's attitude towards her artists, her writers, and very quietly but very consistently continue with your work, and try not to take on all of that other stuff, because that can be the suicide. Or you start doing things that will get you the public recognition, you start making compromises. And one of the most rewarding and gratifying things that have been said about me and my work is that there is a kind of basic integrity there. I'm not going to use the kind of themes that are fashionable because they would sell, I'm not going to suggest that Black life is in such disarray, that our unity is so disintegrated that we don't constitute any kind of force in this country, I'm not going to portray Black women as the eternal victims, I'm not going to give the impression that the whole thing that one reads in so much of the literature of rape, of incest, and so on is a pattern in the Black community. Selina, I think, has become a kind of durable and enduring character because she is both ordinary and extraordinary. She is an ordinary young girl finding her way to womanhood, she is extraordinary for me at least because she doesn't go through all of those terrible things that are supposed to happen to Black people, to young Black women. She is not raped by her father, or her stepfather, or her mother's boyfriend, she does not witness physical brutality between her mother and father, she is not, in other words, a social statistic, she is rather my attempt to create life, the life of a young woman on paper. That's one of the ways in which she is kind of special, and it is one of the reasons why succeeding generations of young women Black and White, come to her and find something that says something to them, which is really most gratifying for a writer.

Q: When you talk about your description of the Black community, you certainly are not suggesting that things like rape or incest don't exist?

A: I'm saying that they do exist but that it's not the total story of our community, and I'm saying another thing: it's important to write about that but what happens (because the larger society is always trying to discredit the Black community) is that that view of the community tends to become the only view and my attempt in my work is to present other aspects of our community.

Q: In almost all Black women's novels the female blues singer plays a prominent role or you find the text of blues songs or hints at blues songs. Would you say blues singers or the songs were an inspiration to you?

A: No, I wouldn't say that they were or are. What I would say—the blues songs that I use in *Brown Girl, Brownstones*, the little "Romance in the Dark" e.g., that I use as an epigram. They are important to me, even though they were not a great influence on me, because they are about the texture of the Black community, they are about some of the things that give our community its unique and special quality. James Baldwin said in his early collection of essays: "It is perhaps only in his music that the Black man in this country has been able to tell his story." So that music is a very important artistic expression for Black people in this country, it has been the way we have been able to funnel a lot of our feelings and angers and hopes and dreams, and because that is such an important aspect of our artistic life, songs, blues songs and music figure in my literature, even more so in the book that's coming out in January.

Q: I was talking with Mary Helen Washington about this blues singer phenomenon, because I had the impression that there was a certain difference between the female blues singer and the novelist, the difference being that the singer could be more outspoken about certain internal aspects of the Black community, e.g. sexuality, or male-female relationships in general. Would you agree with that?

A: I think both the blues singer and the writer are dealing with those subjects in their own way. The very art-form of the blues is distillation, is finding a kind of metaphor, the song, to express some of the difficulties, some of the longings, some of the positive things about relations between black men and women—the novelist or the writer in her work is dealing with this in her own way. The blues is a tightness, a distilling. With the novelist you have a chance to expand it, to do it in greater detail, e.g. the whole trouble of relations between mother and father in *Brown Girl, Brownstones* comes out of some of the pressures that impinge upon them from the society, the mother's overwhelming ambition and the whole adjusting to a new society. A song would do it in a line or two, whereas I devoted a whole novel to it.

Q: Do you think the difference might also be in a different land of relation between artist and audience which is much more direct for a singer who sings in clubs?

A: I don't know if that's effective. I think that the demands of the form, of the particular artistic expression as such has these requirements and that in essence they are both addressing the same thing, coming up with the same reactions and feelings, but doing it in a different kind of artistic expression. I like to use lines from songs because they reinforce the material, they give it a kind of cultural authenticity.

Q: Did you know any other Black women writers at the time you wrote your novel?

A: No, not really. Even though at that time, when I started writing *Brown Girl, Brownstones* I had this terrible job working for a magazine, and just out of desperation I started writing this novel, and as I got into it I realized what an awesome undertaking it is to create life on paper, which is what artists like myself are all about. I just had the need to be with other people who were doing some things so awesome and so terrifying. And so I looked around for the longest time for a group and finally came across an organization called the Harlem Writers' Guild, a group of Black writers who met and read their work and discussed matters of craft. I don't know how much I got out of it in terms of real solid help for my own work, but just the kind of support from being with people who were attempting the same thing was at that point in my development very important.

Q: That would have been my next question. I wanted to know about this specifically in the sense of: do you feel you got support as a woman writing about another woman, because you said you felt like doing something that had not been done before. Did they realize it and how did they react?

A: No, I don't think they saw it so much as a woman writing about women, but rather they saw it as Black writers trying to get a hearing, they saw it as Black writers, male and female, supporting each other so that within the Harlem Writers' Guild there wasn't, at least I didn't sense it then, this whole kind of stated or unstated war between the sexes, but rather we were all so eager just as Black writers to get a hearing.

Q: What did this group do? I read you got politically involved during the Civil Rights Movement.

A: Yes, we were involved, not only this group, but I was member of a group called The Association of Artists for Freedom with people like Ruby Dee and Ossie Davis and Lorraine Hansberry and James Baldwin. I was part of the whole ferment of that period. And for me it was something that I came to in a very natural way, because, as I said, there was always this talk of politics when I was growing up so that I had the sense when I started writing that it wasn't enough to try to get the story of my community told but that it also had to have this larger meaning. And that's why when you read *The Chosen Place*, you'll see a very sharp political direction which that book takes.

Q: How do you recall the fifties in terms of possibilities for Black women? The reason I'm asking this question is, I went through the Afro-American Women's Journal at Howard, which came out from 1940 to 1946 (nobody knows what happened to it, unfortunately). The main goal of this magazine was to promote consciousness among Black women to find jobs in the defense plants and to become professional, and then suddenly you get this rupture in 1945, after the war. You sense this big disappointment because the jobs were given back to men and there was a backfall for black women. How do you remember this time?

A: Let's see if I can. As I recall that time, and I'm really seeing it in terms of the reality I knew growing up in Brooklyn, there was an expectation on the part of young women like myself who were from lower middle class families which might even be from poverty line families, but families with upward mobile aspirations—there was the feeling (and I think this has to do with the fact that it was an African West Indian community largely) that you went on to college and that even though your choices weren't very great, that you became a social worker or an English teacher—that was all that was for you, but you did try to go on to one of the free city colleges. There was an expectation that young women would do something with themselves, but, of course, there was the expectation that one married, no matter what you did, you married. So that personally I have the sense that it was a period when young Black women were encouraged to do something more with their lives, while at the same time the old demands were being made upon them, demands of marriage and so on, very strongly in the fifties.

Q: Do you think it affected Black women as strongly as it did white women, I mean all these things Friedan is talking about in her book? Black women had to work all the time so they just couldn't stay at home and be nice, like white suburban women could.

A: Well, you have to understand one thing about American society: that it really is comprised of several cultures and that even though there are points of convergence sometimes, Black people in this country really do constitute a nation apart. So that what goes on in the larger culture sometimes really doesn't apply. I think that the whole business of the feminist movement in many instances doesn't apply to Black women, to the Black community, because Black women have always had another kind of experience, and another kind of life. First of all they always worked, there was none of this business of sitting around and being taken care of by some man. So the whole question on the part of the feminist movement to get the women out of the home is not true for the Black women except when it has to do with the fact that the Black women has been out there working, but in the most menial jobs. And, let's face it, the white woman has been the oppressor, because she has been the one that Black women had to go to work in their kitchens. There are divergencies, what Friedan is saying in large measure doesn't apply to Black women.

Q: Would you say that the new Black feminism which has emerged in the last years among the mostly intellectual Black women is due to the fact that it deals more with themes like pornography or sexual violence or sexism on a more psychological level than on topics like equal work and topics Freidan dealt with in the fifties?

A: No, I wouldn't say that. I think that the Black feminists are concerned about adequate salary, better working conditions for women, and that their concern about that is to my mind as strong as their concern about the kinds of abuses women had to very quietly accept for so long. I would suspect that what has been given more play in the press (which is not controlled by us) are the more sensational aspects of the movement, whereas the concern inside the movement for issues which have to do with the economy is just as great.

Q: Can you recall having had discussions with other women about things like the blatant sexism of, say, *JET* magazine, e.g. pictures of naked women on its cover or—seldom enough—of babies. And they had always light-skinned, very soft-haired women, pale beauties.

A: Yes, I recall anger and frustration, because I was very intimately caught up in all of this because, I told you, that I worked for a magazine, a counterpart of *Ebony*. I served as food and fashion editor, and the kind of outrage that I would experience each time I got around to my fashion stories and the models came in to be interviewed and my editor, who had the final saying, when I would present him with the photographs of the women that I wanted to use as models—he would make sure that he picked out those that were what you would call the Lena Horne type, and that's why I didn't last very long on the magazine.

There was this kind of ugliness within the Black community, this non-acceptance of ourselves, this looking towards those within our community who were closest to white in appearance. And, of course, this is one of the reasons the sixties were so important, that some of the psychological damage was confronted and an effort made to redress it.

One of the reasons I wanted to write the story of a Selina Boyce was to give an answer to the prevailing image, to say that she was not a topsy, she was not any of the characters which you found in *Gone with the Wind*, or any of the other stereotypes. These had all to do with white America's hang-ups. I wanted Selina to be a departure from all of that, this is why *Maud Martha* is important, because she is a dark woman as is Selina—you get away from this whole Nella Larsen theme, you get to a type of Black woman who truthfully reflects the reality of most Black women.

PW Interviews Paule Marshall

Sally Lodge/1984

From *Publishers Weekly* 225 (January 20, 1984): 90–91. Reprinted by permission.

On a chilly, wet, winter day a visitor to Paule Marshall's New York City apartment finds welcome warmth in the rich browns and beiges that dominate the decor. And Marshall herself, dressed in a long caftan of these same colors splashed with orange, radiates a great deal of warmth as she hangs up her caller's dripping raincoat and leads the way into a living room featuring plants large enough to qualify as trees. From the window one looks out over the bare treetops of Central Park, which even in November looks inviting from this vantage point.

Marshall is a beautiful woman. Most striking are her bright eyes and long, lovely hands, which she uses at just the right moments to accent her words. The reason for our visit is the publication of Marshall's *Reena and Other Stories* (*PW* Forecasts, Dec. 2, 1983), a collection of her early short fiction written between 1954 and 1969, out from the Feminist Press this month.

We wonder if Marshall finds it at all unnerving to be relaunching her early work after so many years, and the author responds with her light, ever ready laugh. "Yes, it is a little odd. On the one hand it is very gratifying that the work has a relevance today, that it is still up to date. On the other hand I tend, as I write over the years, to put things behind me. But what was enjoyable about putting this book together was going back and looking at those early stories, seeing their strengths and of course their flaws, since with the very early stories I was just starting out."

Marshall's very first published story, "The Valley Between," is included in the collection, and in her introductory comments to the story, the author notes that it was written "when I could barely crawl, never mind stand up and walk as a writer. I was a mere babe in terms of craft and technique."

Yet the author finds comfort in the fact that, as she puts it, "Even then I was on the right track in terms of what I was trying to say, even if technical things were a little off and my theme was a bit overstated. Still and all, it was firmly grounded in what are some of my main preoccupations as a writer: a woman's need for self-fulfillment, her reaching out for another self and the kinds of opposition and resistance that she runs into. These are themes that really only came into their own in the early 1970s, when there was a flowering of writing by women. But way back then in the '50s I was aware of all the constraints placed upon women, and in particular upon women writers, and I felt so strongly about this that I began writing about it then."

Marshall discusses several other influences that led her to become a writer. She was born in Brooklyn, of parents who had come to New York from Barbados in the 1920s, and some of her strongest early memories are of her mother and her West Indian friends, sitting around a kitchen table after a long day's work. Marshall speaks of the "insight, irony, wit and humor" that emerged from the conversations among these women, and of their "poet's inventiveness and daring with language."

The author sits forward as she recalls these very influential memories; her voice becomes almost a whisper as she slips back in time: "I was that little girl, sitting in the corner of the kitchen, in the company of poets. I was there, seen but not heard, while these marvelous poets carried on. And from way back I always wanted to see if I might not be able to have some of the same power they had with words—their wonderful oral art. I wondered if I could capture some of that same power on paper."

She made her first attempt at writing at the age of twelve, when she tried her hand at poetry: "Oh, it was very bad poetry, mainly because I was writing about things that I knew nothing about—apple trees, which I'd never seen growing in Brooklyn, kings and queens. I was trying to get out of myself and out of my world; not knowing then of course that writers should stick with their own worlds."

It was soon after her frustrated attempts at writing poetry that Marshall had a revelation that also fed her urge to write. She made an important discovery in the library, where she spent much time during her adolescence: "The library was a retreat, a wonderful way to discover new worlds," she recalls. "But I remember feeling that there was something missing, and then I came across Paul Laurence Dunbar, and learned that there was a black poet who had produced a thick volume of poems. Although I couldn't have said it consciously back then, he in a sense validated black experience for me. I went to school in Brooklyn during the '40s and '50s, and the black poets and writers—even the great writers of the Harlem Renaissance of the '20s—just weren't taught in the schools. Ironically, they were taught in the segregated schools in the South at that time.

"And so Dunbar made me aware that there was a mass body of material by black writers, and that if I ever hoped to write I should start writing about what I knew best, which was what growing up in that tight little island of a world of West Indian Brooklyn was all about. And that maybe there was something important and valid and sacred about that experience of being both Afro-American and West Indian."

Marshall admits that she then spent years thinking about writing, but was terrified to put pen to paper,—"because then you commit yourself—you find out if you are good or not." With a laugh she explains that she had "all kinds of delaying tactics. And then I reached a desperate place: I was working for a second-rate magazine, and I became frightened that I was going to spend my whole life writing mediocre material for this magazine. So I came home one evening and began writing *Brown Girl, Brownstones*; even though I had written stories, it took me a long time to get to the place where I felt strong enough and at the same time desperate enough to start writing a novel."

Brown Girl, Brownstones was first published in 1959 by Random House, where Hiram Hayden was Marshall's editor. In a quiet voice, she recounts an incident that she says made a very strong impression on her: "The day I received my contract from Random House in the mail, I had an appointment with Hiram, and I went off to the lovely neo-Renaissance Villard buildings where the publisher's offices were. There was a magnificent, sweeping marble staircase I had to climb to get to Hiram's office, and I remember running up those stairs with my contract in hand, and I can't tell you the feeling of exhilaration I had, thinking that the world had said 'yes,' and that maybe I did have something going for me.

"And there, coming down the stairs was one Bennett Cerf, and he recognized me as a new addition to Random House, and stopped to say a few words. He ended our polite exchange with words that were just devastating to me. He said: 'Well, you know, nothing usually happens with this kind of book,' and made a kind of dismissing sweeping motion with his hand. I can't tell you how this affected me; I'm sure he didn't intend to be mean, but for a minute or two that contract in my hand felt like a rejection slip. I thought about the incident a lot, and behind his words I think I found what it meant to be a woman in that society, and also of course what it means to be black; that even though my book was going to be published and the publisher found some literary merit in it, I was not really a part of the literary community."

Since her first novel, Marshall has published a book of novellas, *Soul Clap Hands and Sing* (1961), as well as two other novels, *The Chosen Place, the Timeless People* (1969) and *Praisesong for the Widow* (1983). The latter will be released in paperback this spring under Dutton's Obelisk imprint.

Marshall was very pleased that the Feminist Press reissued *Brown Girl, Brownstones* in 1981, and that it has been adapted for numerous courses—Afro-American literature courses, women's studies courses and ("Bennett Cerf should know this," says Marshall with a good-natured laugh) even in straight American literature courses. "I find it most gratifying," says the author, "that this novel is finding a new audience; a whole new generation is coming to *Brown Girl*, and these readers have found some of their own concerns and ambitions mirrored in the novel."

Between books, Marshall spends much of her time teaching. She has taught creative writing at such schools as Yale, Columbia, and the University of Iowa Writer's Workshop, and will soon leave to spend the spring semester at the University of California at Berkley. Marshall finds that teaching does feed her writing, even though she does not write while she teaches: "Teaching takes over my life, and I can't write at the same time, even though I take notes and think about what I want to write; I become too involved with my students' work and lives. Students give me a great deal, because they are experimenters, which I find exciting and instructive."

Experimenting is not new to Marshall the writer. Indeed, she has spent her entire writing life "trying to reconcile the different strains that have gone into making me. What took place in my mother's kitchen as she talked with her friends is my fundamental base, but what that also gave me was a curiosity about other voices. My writing is very concerned with voice in the sense of language. And though I wanted to capture that whole West Indian dialect, I also wanted to capture the black American English that is part of my heritage too. As a child I moved with the utmost ease between these cultures; it was the way the world was for me. With this double exposure, there was the desire in me from early on to play with a variety of voices, to always be stretching and exploring the English language. It has to do with the fact that I come from people for whom language is an art form."

Years later, the inspiration Marshall found in the conversations of her mother and her friends is still with her. Although her mother died before Marshall's first novel was published and never really knew the influence she'd had on her daughter, Marshall observes that the members of the West Indian community in which she grew up voiced what her mother would have said: "When *Brown Girl, Brownstones* was published, they were on the one hand very proud that a daughter of the sod had written what they called 'the big book.' On the other hand, they were a little annoyed that, as they put it, I had told the truth." One feels that Paule Marshall couldn't ask for higher praise.

Interview with Paule Marshall

Sandi Russell/1988

From *Wasafiri*, no. 8 (Spring 1988): 14–16. Reprinted by permission.

Paule Marshall, born in the United States of Barbadian parents, brings to the language and themes of her fiction the double inheritance of Afro-American and Afro-Caribbean culture. In her essay, "Poets of the Kitchen Table," she expresses a special debt to the women of Barbados living as immigrants in New York, whose forceful and inventive talk continues the oral tradition of their homeland. "They taught me my first lessons in narrative art," she writes. "They trained my ear. They set a standard of excellence. This is why the best of my work must be attributed to them."

Her first novel, *Brown Girl, Brownstones*, published in 1959, stands beside Zora Neale Hurston's *Their Eyes Were Watching God* (1937) and Gwendolyn Brooks's *Maud Martha* (1953) in its defiance of the conventional stereotypes of black women in both black and white literature. Out of sync with its time, Marshall's novel anticipates the complex treatment of black female characters in the work of Toni Morrison.

Paule Marshall's works include *Reena and Other Stories*, and *Praisesong for the Widow* (which, like *Brown Girl, Brownstones*, are both available from Virago). Two novels, *The Chosen Place, the Timeless People* (1969) and *Soul Clap Hands and Sing* (1983) are published by Harcourt, Brace and The Feminist Press, respectively. She is now at work on a new novel that explores, through a father/daughter relationship, the cultural politics of dominance and subordination.

I met Paule Marshall in November 1986 at her apartment in Richmond, Virginia, where she is Commonwealth Professor of Creative Writing at Virginia Commonwealth University. She has held similar posts at a number of American universities, including Berkeley, Iowa, Columbia and Yale.

The Richmond area is fraught with history. Richmond is the capital of the state of Virginia, where my father's people were held as slaves. It was the native ground of my mother's tribe, the Chickahominy, when the British colonized Virginia in the Seventeenth Century. So we met, Paule Marshall and I, as two black women with a long history of dispossession behind us, yet we came together in that place drawn by the need to re-possess ourselves.

SR: I'm interested in your Afro-Caribbean background. Can you give me a sense of that experience?
PM: Yes, my experience has been somewhat unique. I do have this dual heritage, but I shy away from saying "dual" because that seems to suggest a divide, and I really don't see it as a divide. There is the Afro-Caribbean aspect and there's the Afro-American. I was born and raised in Brooklyn, and was the child of West Indian immigrants who had come to America. There was a great flood of them in the 1920's and they were sort of the West Indian counterpart of the great migration of Afro-Americans from the South to the North. Blacks were just moving into the Northern cities and these West Indians came for the very same reasons as the Afro-Americans. So there I was, the child of these people from Barbados, and as soon I stepped into the house, I would go into a totally West Indian world.
SR: What characterized this West Indian world for you?
PM: The smells of food, the accents, my mother's voice, the ambience; all of it was solidly West Indian. And then when I stepped outside and I was on the sidewalk, I was this little Afro-American girl playing "double-dutch" and running up and down the street. So it seemed to me the most natural thing in the world, this moving between these two worlds. I never saw the division and I never saw the duality. I never sensed it until I was nine years old and my mother took my sister and myself to visit our grandmother in Barbados. We stayed there for a year. And because it was such a long stay, my mother put us in school there, which was the worst thing she could have done, when you know the British system in the colonies. They used to beat the children in school. You got caned when you didn't learn. So there I was in this totally strange and ominous setting and I didn't stay very long in school there. I just told my mother that I couldn't take it. First of all, I was not going to be beaten and I couldn't bear to see others being beaten, so I didn't last very long in school. But when I came back to the States, I had absorbed an accent, the West Indian accent. I also had both my wrists laden down with what are called bangles. These are heavy silver bracelets which are fashionable now, but in my day, and I'm talking about the late 1930s and early 1940s, to wear

them was a sure sign that you were West Indian. So when I went back to school in Brooklyn, and my friends heard me talk with this strange sounding accent and saw and heard me rattling around with these bangles, I started being teased. And that was the first time that I could sense that there was something different about me, different than the kids I went to school with, who were mainly Afro-American.

SR: How did you handle this problem?

PM: Right away I got rid of the bangles and I worked assiduously, by myself, at home, to rid myself of this dirty mark, this Barbadian accent. But it was only then, for the first time, that I sensed that there were these two things operating for me. And for a period I went through quite a rejection of the Afro-West Indian part of myself, because I so desperately wanted to be like my peers, which is, of course, so standard. And it wasn't until I was grown that I began to see the marvelous gift and the great benefit of that experience. I act as a kind of bridge. I do bring together in my person, and hopefully in my work, these two cultures. Because to my mind, aside from certain small differences and variations on themes, I see them as one. I see them as the African-American response—and when I say African-American, I'm talking about blacks from Brazil to Brooklyn.

SR: Yes, a response to our history in this hemisphere. There have been some differences in culture, but to my mind, not that great. Barbara Christian states in her book, *Black Women Novelists* that: "Black immigrants cannot easily merge into the Afro-American social fabric, for they themselves are not sure they can or want to be a part of that tradition." Do you agree with this?

PM: Yes, that's very true and she's talking there mainly about those who have just come over, like my parents. I don't think my mother ever really became a part of "this man country," as she referred to the United States, nor did she ever really have American friends aside from one close Afro-American woman, whom I deal with in part in *Brown Girl, Brownstones*: the hairdresser, Miss Thompson. But I remember that was her only real Afro American friend. Now there's a reason for that. The West Indian immigrants behaved pretty much like all immigrants, so that they came here very ambitious, very go-getting, and that has to do with the whole immigrant mentality, the whole immigrant personality. It's a kind of selective migration; those who come out are the ones with drive and push. You know this does not make them special people, it's just the power of selection.

Also, they weren't here for very long before they understood what America was all about, vis-à-vis black people. They saw, they recognized immediately that blacks were at the bottom of the heap, that they were the pariahs of the society. And instinctively, they wanted to put some distance between them and Afro-Americans, feeling that somehow, if they could establish themselves as different and other, they would be treated in another, more positive way. It's nonsense. I mean whites see only a black face until perhaps you open your mouth, and my mother would lament from time to time, "Oh my God, if we only had our own language." So that when she opened her mouth they would recognize immediately that she was not one of those. You see, this kind of thing is so, that without perhaps the dominant society working very hard at it, our house was divided. The Afro-Americans for their part, felt that the Afro-Caribbeans came here and set themselves up as superior and were overly ambitious. They also had their criticisms and so there was this dreadful kind of internecine warfare going on. It was very bad in the late 1930's and early '40's. I understand there's still some of it, but it is not as marked as it used to be in the earlier decades. It has been a factor, but it's one of the things that I don't really like discussing too much because I don't want to make too large an issue of it. Because my whole thrust and what my work certainly tries to do, is to touch upon what the similarities and commonalities are. One of the things that impelled me, for example, to write *Praisesong for the Widow*, was to deal with those linkages, those connections.

SR: Yes. You do that beautifully. The book is so vivid in your depiction of our need to understand those connections.

PM: So that's my response to the conflict. It is to say, I am Afro-Caribbean and Afro-American. I am embracing both these cultures and I hope that my work reflects what I see as a common bond.

SR: Suggie, one of the characters in *Brown Girl, Brownstones*, says when she speaks of what is expected of Barbadian women in America: "Be-Jees, I ain't gon be like them, all cut out of the same piece of cloth." Now, do you feel that West Indians, here and in Britain, have been able to retain their cultural identity? Are they still able to keep that wholeness?

PM: I think in part they manage to hold on to it, at least this was my experience. Suggie's statement has to do with what is true of many immigrant groups, because the pressure to succeed, to do well in the new society is so great. The pressure within their communities is equally great, so that everyone conforms, because that is the only way that one is going to establish a kind of beachhead, a toehold. This was certainly true in the world of West Indian Brooklyn, and I suspect that in part, it's probably true for the West Indian immigrant in England and in Canada, that you have to apply yourself in a kind of fierce, totally devoted way to making it; to making it in a material sense. Because this, in a sense, justifies your having made this long voyage up there. This will make it possible for you to help through remissions, through money and so on, sent home to help your family in the Islands. I mean there's tremendous pressure on conformity.

What Suggie is saying is that yes, she's come here, she works, but the need on her part to still be a person in her own right is very strong, which is also true of Deighton in the novel. He is also resisting that whole West Indian demand that he be like everyone else. And of course, the cost, the price he's made to pay for that, results in his death. But there is, and this is one of the things that I found so difficult to take as I became a teenager, there is that awful business of conforming to the code and the code has to do with success in very visible terms. In West Indian Brooklyn, it was in buying a brownstone house. That was the most visible icon of one's success. As I said, you become tolerant after a while, you understand why they have to do it. So I think that Selina, by the end of the novel, comes to a certain kind of understanding and tolerance even though she knows that is not her way.

SR: In your novel, *A Chosen Place, A Timeless People,* there's a scene where Merle is dressing and she has difficulty merging the different traditions she has "inherited," as exemplified in her various articles of clothing, into a true expression of herself. Do you see a sense of wholeness being possible for westernized black women today?

PM: Let me say a few things about the books, the books really express my search, and it is very gratifying that readers come to it and can identify with that search. But it really is a quest on my part to reconcile the many strains that have gone into making me the Afro-American, the Afro-Caribbean and a person in the larger American society. How does one, out of this kind of mixed bag, come up with a self? This has been my fundamental question, the thing that impels me to write, and I think I've come to some answers about that and one of them is rather exciting because it's about the creation of a self. I mean we are, as black people, in a kind of existential situation where we, in a sense, can create ourselves. Look, this is all that's been given. Some of it has been terribly negative, and we're going to try because it has been so negative, to throw that off. But we're going to look at the whole thing and take from it what is useful, what we can use to create a self, and we're going to try to bring together some of those forces into a kind of harmonious whole. This is really what I've been trying to do in terms of my life and in terms of the work. To say, "This is good from my Afro-American experience; ok, let's take that. This is positive from my Afro-Caribbean experience, I'm going to take that. This is good from America or Western civilization, and try to bring them together." One of the ways I try to do this is in the way I use language. I'm fascinated by language, because black people both here and in the West Indies have used language as a way of retaining their humanity. That's why it holds such meaning for me. They've also made such great poetry out of it. They've taken the English language which has been imposed upon them and recreated it in their own image. When I hear people from Barbados speak, I know that they have taken that English language, the "King's English" and have made it into an instrument which expresses them. So I think that is what I'm trying to do, to take what is useful and to weld them, to bond them, to bring them together into a whole. And you can use standard English: I've been taken to task for that, but that's ok, because it's part of my heritage. What language does for me is to say, there are all of these strains, let's bring them together. Let's see what we really can create out of them. And by extension, that's also true of what you can do with yourself in terms of bringing together all that's gone into making you.

SR: In reference to the larger scope that you feel encompasses black lives, you said that one of your characters, Merle, was a "third world revolutionary." Would you care to elaborate?

PM: What I'm trying to do in the work, is to take the black woman as character to another level, to give her an added dimension. Basically, there is the quest for self, the classic theme of identity, but at the same time, because ours is a very special experience, that's not enough for me, that really isn't. I'm always trying to link it up with what is the larger and broader struggle of us as a people. So it's not enough for my women characters to be caught up in a search for self. What I try to do at the same time is to *suggest* that their search is linked to this larger quest which has to do with the liberation of us as a people. And so Merle operates more successfully than some of my other characters. She operates on a couple of levels. She is the woman who has undergone all of these things in her life: her experience in the West Indies, her experience in England, a disruptive marriage, the loss of her child, her unhappy lesbian affair and so on, and she's trying to make sense of it all. She's trying to overcome the paralysis of her fractured life. And, because of her concern with what's happening politically, Merle then takes on a larger and broader political meaning. She has been shaped by forces in the West Indies and by England and so she, in effect, *embodies* the history of this hemisphere.

SR: Could you tell us about any new projects or books you are working on?

PM: My new book is underway, but one discovers what one wants to say in the process of writing. I mean, you can start out with an outline and some idea of where to take the book, but it's in the actual writing, as you develop scenes and characters, that you begin to discover what it is you want to say. I think that one of the things I'm reaching for is: what is the next step for this black woman who is trying to realize self? And for me, it is not only releasing self in personal terms but in larger political and historical terms. I think what I'm getting at, groping for, is the need to bring some kind of rapprochement, some kind of working relationship with black men. The way I'm going about it is trying to deal with a father/daughter relationship. Now that was partly true of *Brown Girl, Brownstones*, but of course you know that writers pretty much have their themes.

SR: How does this translate into larger, political themes?

PM: The father/daughter relationship is on one level, but at another level, dominant/subordinate relationships are being examined, because so often, that's the way the father/daughter relationship is spelt out. This is because of my need to work out my own relationship with my father. One has to, and sometimes it's very painful to have to throw off and cut away that kind of bond. You have to say that it's necessary and do it at a personal level, because that's the only way you then can take control of your life and shape it as you want to shape it. And this doesn't say that you don't have respect and regard for that person who was so dominant in your life, but that the dynamic of the relationship is no longer possible, that particular relationship can no longer work. Hopefully, there can be another kind of relationship, but *that* is no longer possible.

At the other level, this larger thing I'm reaching for is to suggest that in political terms it doesn't work either. Where there is this dominant figure and there are those who are subordinate, we have to come to some kind of relationship—black people, men and women—in a more egalitarian fashion. Now there are some historical models for that, and I'm very indebted to a seminal essay by Angela Davis, when she was in prison.

SR: How does Angela Davis' essay relate to a better working relationship between black men and woman?

PM: Angela Davis talks about the kind of equality black men and women under slavery had. She calls it the equality of oppression. The fact that blacks of both sexes were working side by side in the fields, made for a kind of equality. It made for a kind of black woman who was quite different from the way women are looked at today. If we could go back to that and tap those old relationships, that equality, that working together, then we might have a model that could serve us today.

A *MELUS* Interview: Paule Marshall

Joyce Pettis/1990

From *MELUS* 17, no. 4 (1991–92): 117–29. Reprinted by permission.

Interviewer: There are very clear pictures of the Caribbean in your fiction. Would you talk about its importance to you and to your work?
Marshall: Well I think the importance of the West Indies in the work started even before my first visit which took place when I was nine years old. It predates that because as I quoted in that essay of mine, "The Poets in the Kitchen," one of the things that was talked a lot about among the women was the whole nostalgic memory of home as they called it, home. It was very early on that I had a sense of a very distinct difference between *home*, which had to do with the West Indies, and *this country* which had to do with the United States. For a while it was a little confusing because to me home was Brooklyn and by extension America, and yet there always was this very strong sense in the household of this other place that was also home. I think that it began then, an interest in this place that was so important to these women and that I began to sense it was important in whomever I was going to discover myself to be. So when I started thinking about such weighty topics, not until much, much later in my life, twenties or so, the other home seemed important to me in order to answer certain questions about myself. Really in a sense that's what the work is primarily about; it's my trying to find answers I'm always putting to myself.
Interviewer: Were you aware of intraracial conflict growing up in Brooklyn? That theme is minimally present in *Brown Girl, Brownstones*.
Marshall: I was made aware of the fact that I certainly was Afro-American growing up on the mean streets of Brooklyn, and at the same time there was this other component, this other very strong dimension which was Afro-West Indian didn't see any contradiction or difference or problem with the

two until I was made aware of some of the conflicts between the two groups. This was very painful for me because I saw myself belonging to both. A conflict would almost suggest that there were parts of myself that were in conflict with each other. Then to reinforce the whole West Indian aspect there was the trip that my mother took us on when I was nine and my sister was thirteen to visit our Grandmother in Barbados. My mother had come into some money from a brother of hers who worked at the Panama Canal; and he had died there, as so many of those men from the West Indies working in the swamps and jungles of Panama didn't make it out. He died there but left some money. My Grandmother distributed the money among the children, sent my mother her portion. My father was trying to convince my mother that it made much more sense to take the money and invest it in a brownstone. My mother had this—to his mind—hare-brained idea of taking us home to visit, to see, to meet, her mother and so this is what she did. She lost the first money for the trip because she very unwisely trusted a fellow Barbadian who was a travel agent, and he absconded with the money. That was the delay and my father said, "See I told you, you shouldn't have bothered with this scheme at all. You should have spent this money in a wise way." That whole thing of money works into *Brown Girl*, although it is developed very differently.

Interviewer: Is the presence of the elderly female ancestor in your book connected to your Afro-Caribbean heritage and to your visit to Barbados?

Marshall: I don't remember that much from that first trip, but some things stand out in memory. There is the image of this old woman who came to meet us at the disembarkation shed where we landed and the image of her walking through it to meet us—a very small, dry, wiry, quick stepping, very black old woman, the grandmother. There was something so purposeful and so straightback about her walk that she became a very important figure to me. There was a lot of mythology about her in the family, as a woman who had had fourteen children, (including two sets of twins), worked her land after her husband died, and toiled to send her children away to America. This was an overpowering figure of the matriarch in the most positive sense of powerful. I remember too the sense of a place that was completely, it seemed to me, covered in sugar cane. I didn't know anything about sugar cane, but there were all of these tall canes all over this place and it looked to me like overgrown grass and I feared that I could get lost in all of that grass. That I remember. There was always the sense that the West Indies was in some way important to my understanding my self. So when I started to write, there was always that presence of the islands, that sense that that was part of the South. Then, too, there was the practical, technical aspect to it. I found that because the islands were small, they permitted me to deal with a manageable landscape. I could use that to say what I wanted to about the larger landscapes, the metropoles, but it would be more manageable by using the West Indies, and so I found them technically to my advantage.

Interviewer: Barbara Christian has written that *Brownstones* was a literary anomaly, not at all in tune with the published works of its period, and she means that positively. When you wrote the first novel, were you thinking of a literary community or aware of issues in the work of other Black writers? Did you feel the need to write that particular novel without regard to what else was being published?

Marshall: Well, there's a bit of a story connected with the beginning of that novel, the actual writing of that novel. I was working after I graduated from college as a writer for a magazine that was about to fold at any moment. It was called *Our World*. It was in serious competition with *Ebony* at the time. *Our World* was always in financial difficulties, and when I joined the staff even more so. But it was a great experience for me because it did teach me discipline. I couldn't sit there agonizing over the words at the typewriter; I had to knock out the copy. That came to my aid when I started serious writing. I became very distressed at the sort of thing that I was doing at *Our World* because the stories were very much early *Ebony* format, lots of stories about black entertainers. One evening in sheer desperation I came home and started writing *Brownstones*. I worked on it for five years in the evenings after spending my day knocking out that stuff at *Our World*. I was able to do it not only because I was young and had this marvelous energy, but also because the book in a sense had been there waiting for me to write it. Like many fledging writers I was afraid for a long time to actually be serious about writing because I would then have to discover whether I was a writer or not. I went through a period of talking a lot about wanting to write, belonging to various writers groups, finding excuses not to get around to the work, but never actually sitting down and doing it until I was compelled by experience at *Our World* magazine. When I say that it was there waiting to be written, I mean all that I had experienced all along, especially that seminal experience in the kitchen as a little girl, listening to my mother and her friends tell stories and talk about the world, and political issues and so on. There was all of that waiting for me to do something with it. Also, I wanted to see if I had the same power with language that I sensed the mothers possessed. None of this was very conscious, but there nonetheless. Then, too, I was a great reader in addition to the kind of exposure to great oral literature that I was exposed to from the mothers. In fact, I got through the trials and tribulations of adolescence in the Macon Street Branch of the Brooklyn Public Library. I would spend hours there reading, browsing, sometimes nodding at the desk. I remember being very disappointed because Black writers weren't that well-known, and you were not encouraged to read them. I wasn't aware that there were people like Zora Neale Hurston writing at the time; Nella Larson had books out. Once in a while you'd get a poem by Langston Hughes but other than that, no sense that there had been the Harlem Renaissance or that Richard Wright at that point was extremely popular. So, my exposure was to the so-called establishment writers, both American and European. I remember being very taken with Thomas Mann's *Buddenbrooks*, which is kind of *bildungsroman*. When I began writing *Brown Girl, Brownstones*, it wasn't in the sense of my doing something that was different from the writing going on at the moment, but rather taking as my model what Mann did in *Buddenbrooks*—the sense of a large canvas that would take a family and trace its experience over a long period of time through a couple of generations. That was the model that I used for the structure of *Brown Girl, Brownstones* and of course my instincts as a writer were fairly well in place at the time. I felt that if I was going to venture out, that it would be best for me to write about what I knew, at least in the beginning, something I knew in a direct way. Not that the events, and the characters, and the situations in *Brown Girl, Brownstones* actually took place, but they certainly are based on the life and experience of that community in which I grew up.

Interviewer: Did you have a friend like Beryl or is she completely fictional?
Marshall: She's based on a number of friends over the years with a large dose of imagination. She was interesting to me because Beryl represented something I had to work out for myself and using her as a character helped me to deal with this, to deal with the fact that my family did not follow the pattern of the typical Barbadian West Indian immigrant family. They never succeeded in purchasing the brownstone house, you see. We were never an entire family. My father, after I was about age thirteen, became so involved with Father Divine that he was no longer part of our household. In a sense he had sort of abdicated his responsibilities as father. So the set pattern for families that was so true for most of the West Indians that I knew in Brooklyn was disrupted for me. Beryl represents the child of those families who went the so-called established route. The Beryls have always been fascinating for me because, on one hand, they are the first generation children (I

think it may be second generation, I've never been clear about that) whose families have been successful, have realized the immigrant dream. A part of me always longed for that. At the same time a part questioned it and in a sense even rejected it because it seemed so narrow to my mind. And so using her as a character was a way for me to deal with some of those feelings.

Interviewer: When you wrote *Soul Clap Hands and Sing* did you envision it as a continuation of what you had achieved in *Brown Girl* or were you striking out in a different direction?

Marshall: Well, I wrote *Soul Clap Hands and Sing* mainly because after I finished *Brown Girl*, I sensed that the second novel would take me a long time, because while I was in Barbados working, rewriting, revising, overhauling *Brown Girl, Brownstones* I encountered the seed that was to be *The Chosen Place, the Timeless People*, and I knew it would take me a long time to do the research and the thinking and the actual creation of the novel—a long, long time. I didn't want to be known as a one-book writer from the publication of *Brown Girl, Brownstones*. So I decided that I would knock out the second book because the stories were just there waiting for me to put them down on paper. There were some questions after *Brown Girl* came out about whether I could write as effectively about men as I had written about women in *Brown Girl*. That was another type of challenge I thought I should take on by writing those four novellas, that made me put to rest the whole notion, that I could not write about men. Another factor that was very important about that book was that again I tried to answer questions I had been putting to myself. The question that really prompted that collection was how does one use well this gift of life. How do you really find a way to live fully? I suppose I was debating with myself whether I really wanted a total commitment to writing, and that was one of the ways for me to answer that question and to come to a decisions because the men that I deal with in the novellas fail to use their life fully and discover near the end that they have dishonored the gift. It was one of my ways, through these characters, to ease some of the tension of what I was feeling—how was I really going to order my life; how was I really going to commit myself to being a writer and all that that entails. How am I really going to use this time well? Those men provided me with a vehicle by which I could answer it, and I could also use women. This all goes back to Thomas Mann. The women would act as catalysts for these men. Through the women they finally come to look at their lives in a very clear way and to see how they had not used them well. There is a scene in *The Magic Mountain*, Thomas Mann's monumental novel, where Hans recognizes that being with a woman, and being able to perform well sexually with a woman, is a metaphor for being able to do well by life. That idea intrigued me when I read that novel in college; it stayed with me and I could see it working itself in the character of these old men.

Interviewer: Do you view women as catalysts because you consider them more capable of living fuller lives?

Marshall: I think women in my fiction have to do with the fact that women were essential to my world very early on. (It has to do with those poets in the kitchen.) They held up the world. They were simply housewives and domestic workers and women who wore these old dowdy coats and dresses from the bargain basement. Yet I saw them as powerful people, and what I discovered when I came into literature is that women were not ever central to the story. So when I started writing, it was with a sense of wanting to move women to center stage. They certainly were center stage in my life. They seem to have marvelous resonance, and that was the place for them. And so I saw them as agents of change, as embodying a certain power principle. So when I thought about these old men, who was I going to introduce as the one who would permit them to see their lives? It came very naturally to me that it would be women. I had a deep sense of a certain kind of power residing in women, and I didn't see the power of women as threatening to men, but just simply as power.

Interviewer: I know the origin of the title *Soul Clap Hands and Sing*. When you titled each novella with a place name, were you thinking about psychological bonds among people of color?

Marshall: Not consciously. All four places began with "B," which meant that I would be working with a wide canvass that would stretch from Brooklyn to Brazil. I would be able to say something about the human condition unconfined to one place, and examine what was going on in these very different parts of the world and with these very different people. All the men from different backgrounds—Max, for example, the Jew; Gerald Lockleak, who was mixed blood; the Brazilian and the West Indian—and yet they are caught up in the same fundamental, universal kinds of questions and problems. That I found exciting.

Interviewer. I think that Gerald Motley in "British Guiana" is the most complex of those four men, but "Brooklyn" and "Barbados" are the two novellas that have been reproduced most often in anthologies.

Marshall: I think it has to do with the rather striking role that the women play in those two stories, especially the Brooklyn story, a story of sexual harassment, which, of course, was a theme that came to be variously talked about in the feminist movement. Certainly, I was dealing with it before that period. I think that's one of the things that has made "Brooklyn" one of the more anthologized of the stories. "Barbados," the dramatic way that a young unlettered servant girl was able to look into Mr. Watford's life, has made that a story that has remained popular.

Interviewer: There is so much diversity among the characters in *The Chosen Place, The Timeless People*. Will you talk about how you conceived that work and what your goals were?

Marshall: I'm still recovering from that work. As I said, I knew that it was going to take me a very long time to do research for that novel; it was very extensive. I had to do all the research on Cuffee Ned and the uprising, the whole manufacture of sugar from the time it comes up in the fields until the time it's taken to the mill; to go Sunday mornings to the slaughtering of the pigs and be there and observe every little detail. It was a long haul of a research project for that novel, long and intense. I had a terrible time for a number of years trying actually to make the transition from research to fiction, just to put aside all those facts that I had accumulated and move into writing the novel. My sense of what I wanted to do, of course, was to have a kind vehicle that looked at the relationship of the West to the rest of us. That whole scene as DuBois stated it: "The problem of the twentieth century is the problem of the color line." In all its ramifications, to look at it, to examine it, to see how it has played itself out in this hemisphere. So, I hoped that the novel would not solely be seen as a novel about the West Indies, even though it's seen there, but a novel that reflects what is happening to all of us in the metropolitan powers, the power of Europe and the power of America. That's one of the reasons, for example, just a small note, that the car in *Chosen Place* that kills is made by General Motors in Germany. This brings together what I saw as two major powers that reap such havoc on the world. That was the large schema. I didn't set out with that absolutely, clearly, fixedly in my mind, but rather some people, some characters. I encountered models for them while I was there in Barbados working on revising *Brown Girl, Brownstones*. A group of social scientists from the States came down for summer field work and their reaction to and relations with local people struck me as something that warranted further thought, that might provide me with the makings of a novel. I didn't use those people exactly, but they provided me with the seed, and it began slowly growing, and all other kinds of themes and possibilities became evident as I started working, very slowly, trying to get some of the characters and some sense of a plot line and story.

Interviewer: Merle is obviously a riveting character in that book. Her "talk," for example, seems a deliberate artifice that she uses as a way to protect herself. It shields her psychologically and allows her to hide behind it too. Merle's talk is connected to the power of language expressed through the poets in the kitchen and linked to the power of language in the African American community. Did you envision Merle's facility for "talk" in this way?

Marshall: Talk has always been essential to the way I see the world, and I saw Merle as being very much like the mother poets in that one of the mothers was really a superlative talker. She was known as a "mouth king." I saw Merle as a kind of "mouth king," and I saw I could use that as a device, a technical device to first of all suggest her disjointed and fractured life, that she was a woman in serious psychological trouble. The talk was sort of expressive or indicative of the state of her consciousness of mind. Also, I could use the talk as a means of saying what is not to be said, so that she says things that one is not supposed to say. She says things about the political situation; she says things about the relationships of people on the island, those with power, those without. She can say all that because she is this woman who has had this breakdown, and the talk is the manifestation of this breakdown, the psychological and mental. It was also a way for me to have her state some of the concerns and themes of the novel, and it would be perfectly understandable because she is a woman who has suffered a psychological breakdown. But she is going to be dismissed as untrustworthy, a crackpot.

Interviewer: She is a passionate character, isn't she?

Marshall: She is, yes. One of the really fitting descriptions for her, I think, came from the person who did the review of it for the *New York Times*. He called her part saint, part obeah woman, part revolutionary. That really sums her up. What she is symbolically is the black man/woman of the Diaspora. There she is, a person who has come about in the classic way that so many of us have. Her mother, a woman who worked on the estate there and was used and then discarded by the planter who was himself of mixed blood. So this whole thing that is so much our history, Merle embodies. In her relationships abroad, there's a continuation of those fundamental relationships. I mean, I've been criticized for being homophobic, which is just a misreading of the relationship Merle has with the English woman. Because any examination of that relationship, any close reading, would clearly show that it's about the relationship of the English when they were the nation on which the sun never set, the British Empire.

Interviewer: Harriet continues that idea except that she is American. She is a woman who has inherited a sense of power and a sense of dominance because of her ancestry.

Marshall: Very much so, because one of the areas in which I did extensive research was the early years of the slave trade, how that whole triangular slave trade operated. An in-depth study of just how these American families were very directly involved—not only the men, the captains, brokers, and slave owners—but also how the women from respectable families of the North, not only the mistresses of the plantations who hated the black women that the practice used and abused. These women in the North had their side trade in slaves. I found it a fascinating thing, and so I wanted to use that in some way to show how deep-seated the ramifications of that whole trade were. Also, Harriet permits me to find a means by which Merle will finally be able to overcome that relationship with the English woman. So technically it was important that she reflect in an American way the same pattern of dominance and exploitation that the English woman represents in the novel. It was important that her background be such, but I also wanted to make the point of complicity that American women had in the slave trade. In the last scene between Merle and Harriet, when Merle is finally able to stand up to her and reject out-of-hand Harriet's offer to pay her way anywhere on the face of the earth, it is very much that same pattern that she is so familiar with during those years in England, that whole kind of control. Of course, it has to do with the fact that Harriet, although she is well-meaning, is very much an expression of the West in that her behavior doesn't go beyond a certain kind of well-being and tokenism. She will have the jar with the candies for the children who come, but the kind of real sharing of wealth which will in some way diminish her, she's not going to do that. Again too, Harriet's role allows me to look at women, to use them rather than the configuration of men as the brokers of power. Those two women in the novel are the ones who represent the two soothsayers of power.

Interviewer: Saul's involvement with both Merle and Harriet makes him seemingly understand both of them, although towards the end, I think he doesn't understand his wife. His understanding the West Indians and empathizing with them and trying so sincerely to help them makes his relationship with Merle acceptable. What was your response to the criticism of Saul's relationship with Merle?

Marshall: The book first came out in '69 during the height of the Civil Rights Movement, black consciousness, and the rejection of all things white. The affair was seem by some people, like Larry Neal, as a betrayal. That novel had a terrible time among black intellectuals when it came out.

Interviewer: I don't think it would have that same time now. Saul's identification with the oppressed seems clearly established.

Marshall: Yes, well I felt that if I used a Jew who had developed because of his own history and the history of his people, who knew about suffering (and I'm talking about the historical suffering of Jews) it would permit him then to be able to enter in. Also, these facts would permit Merle to accept him, although she never does even though, yes, they do have the affair. She always has to recreate him in another image so that he is palatable and acceptable. She makes him into one of the red people from Canterbury. I had to find a way that moves their relationship away from the whole standard thing of white man exploiting black woman. That was a real struggle for me; I thought I might be able to solve that problem by first making him symbolic of a larger suffering and perhaps a greater understanding, and secondly I had Merle transform him into someone that she could find acceptable.

Interviewer: Was *Praisesong* your most commercially successful book?

Marshall: I think *Brown Girl* has been. That book has almost become a modern-day classic. It has an interesting history because when it first came out in 1959, it got excellent reviews so that it was known as a critical success, but it was not a commercial success. As you might know, it was published by Random House, and at that time the publisher of Random House was Bennett Cerf. I remember meeting him once, and he made some remark about this kind of book really doesn't do that well, but he was really saying that even though his company was publishing it, he really didn't consider it part of American letters or me as part of the literary establishment. There was that kind disregard, certainly for black women writers. Even when you consider just a few years before *Brown Girl* came out, *Maud Martha* by Gwendolyn Brooks had come out the year before *Invisible Man* and got absolutely no attention whatsoever. Zora Neale Hurston's work was out of print. It was a very inhospitable climate in which I started writing. I had no mentors, no one that I could turn to. By that time I had started educating myself by reading black writers, and I did find that Gwendolyn Brooks's *Maud Martha* was extremely helpful to me, when I started thinking about *Brown Girl*, especially with its characters because in *Maud Martha* for the first time, you had the interior life of a black women dealt with in great depth. It was really helpful to me in designing and creating the character Selina.

Interviewer: What motivated Feminist Press to reissue *Brown Girl*?

Marshall: It went out of print until 1983. Florence Howe of Feminist Press called and said the one book she got a lot of requests for was *Brown Girl, Brownstones*; she'd like to bring it out. I thought about it for awhile, concerned that Feminist Press was an operation without financial wherewithal. Then I said fine because I knew there was an audience out there for it. I had enough interest expressed in the novel. So, they brought it out and what has happened in that whole relationship between *Brown Girl* and the Feminist press is that the press resurrected the novel, and it has done exceedingly well. On the other hand, *Brown Girl* has kept the doors of the Feminist Press open, so it has been a beautiful trade-off.

Interviewer: Is your new novel a significant departure from what you've done in the other novels, particularly in *Praisesong for the Widow*?

Marshall: Yes, I think so; it is a kind of departure. In many ways it's a kind of unapologetic, unabashed story. It's really not a story so much as a kind of *roman à clef* that has to do with my relationship with my father. At last, I'm dealing with that. That's what it is about on one level, and a kind of playing out of certain themes that I sensed in that relationship, which I suspect might be true for other young women in their relationships with fathers—themes of seduction, of dependency, and of dominance. When I say seduction, I certainly do not mean to suggest that as the kind of thing that is so current and popular and gets the headlines of the best sellers and so on, not the physical incestuousness, but the more subtle kinds of seduction that take place within families. For instance in my case, my father was a charming, poetic kind of person. Because for me the kind of ideal model; dependency, a kind of domination, took place there in that relationship because of his qualities, and it took me a long time to come out from under the shadow of that red rock, to quote T. S. Eliot. So much of my life was spent searching for someone who would come close to that sort of idealized image that he represented for me. My new novel is about that, but certainly the woman in the novel is not myself, but a woman who has the same kind of situation with her father. It also examines the themes of seduction, dependency and domination in terms of their cultural and political aspects. This is where it begins to come close to some of the things in the other works, how other cultures, especially the dominant culture of the United States, seduce the more fragile ones of the third world, and how hard it is to come out from under that. I think that is kind of what I'm reaching for in the novel, and that whole theme is played out with a number of women in the novel. Women from various backgrounds and so on, all in terms of one man. Um, well we'll see if it works!

Interviewer: Do you have a working title?

Marshall: Yes, it's called "Daughters."

Interviewer: I know you're very busy teaching and writing, but do you have the opportunity to read contemporary black women writers?

Marshall: I try to keep up, but one of the things—and this is a real plus—is there's quite a bit coming out, but I try to read some.

Interviewer. Do you feel part of a literary community, a member of a black women's network of writers?

Marshall: I don't think it's any formal or official kind of body or organization or what have you, but most of us know each other and there's a sense that we're all in our distinctive, individual ways, fine-tuned on one level to address the wrongs that have been done to us in the literature, the kinds of images that have been perpetuated over the centuries of literature in this country. To really depict ourselves, portray ourselves as we really are. To offer not so much the world, but ourselves (and by that I mean the black community) a more truthful and in-depth and complex sense of who we are in all our diversity. I think that is one of the most wonderful things that has emerged out of this small proliferation of black women writers. I would not go to the length of saying it's a huge thing, no, and it might be all very temporary, but I think that what has emerged is a more complex and truthful image of who we are and that is such a boon. This is something that motivates and guides my work, the sense that you can portray black women in a black community as it truly is, that you can do a great service to that community, because once you see yourself as you really are, and that doesn't mean a glorification, but with our failings and our strength, that you begin to have a sense of your right to be in the world; and that sense, when you see yourself reflected in literature as who you really are, has by extension the possibility of bringing about a greater strength in community. You can take hold; that you can do, you can unite. I find that the work can be very exciting because it goes back to that early experience of mine in the Brooklyn Public Library. In all of those books, as much as I loved them, I never saw me. It's very important to get a sense of self. If the work does nothing else but that, it will have been one of the most worthwhile things I could have done with my life.

An Interview with Paule Marshall

Daryl Cumber Dance/1991

From *Southern Review* 28, no. 1 (1992): 1–20. Reprinted by permission of Daryl Cumber Dance.

This interview was conducted at the home of Paule Marshall in Richmond, Virginia, on June 14, 1991.* Much of our discussion focused on Ms. Marshall's recently completed novel, *Daughters*, published this fall by Atheneum, which she characterizes here as "perhaps my most personal novel." There are, of course, frequent references to her earlier works, which include *Brown Girl, Brownstones* (1959), *Soul Clap Hands and Sing* (1961), *The Chosen Place, the Timeless People* (1969), *Praisesong for the Widow* (1983), and *Reena and Other Stories* (1983).

DD: When you spoke at the Humanities and Sciences Lecturer Award program at Virginia Commonwealth University, you talked a little bit about the seeds of your new novel, *Daughters*. Can you tell us a little bit about it? How did it come about?

PM: I like to think that the seed for the novel was a quote I came across about eight years ago in, of all places, a dance program. I was sitting in City Center Theater on West 55th Street in New York waiting for the lights to dim and the curtain to go up on a performance of the Alvin Ailey Dance Company. While waiting, I was leafing through the program and I came across an epigraph to one of the dances. I don't remember the name of the dance, but the epigraph struck me. It read, "Little girl of all the daughters,/You ain't no more slave,/You's a woman now." That line struck me, stayed with me. I don't remember anything else about that evening. I don't know if it was really that good a performance. I couldn't tell you the name of the dance, but I remembered that epigraph because suddenly there it was, a kind of James Joyce moment of epiphany when a meaning or a theme that has been eluding you suddenly comes clear. It had that kind of impact. "Little girl of all the daughters,/You ain't no more slave,/You's a woman now." The quote gave: the idea for a story about a group of four or five women—black woman—wandering around backstage in my mind like the lost souls in Luigi Pirandello's play *Six Characters in Search of an Author*. The characters in my head were waiting for me, the author, to come up the right story for them. And suddenly there it was that night in City Center Theater: the sense of the story I wanted to write about them. I could finally get these women out from backstage, out from the shadows, and onto center stage. *Daughters* was born that night.

DD: For the benefit of those who haven't had an opportunity to read novel, can you tell us a little something about the story that you wrote about these women.

PM: I'll try. Like most of my novels, *Daughters* is about people, politics, culture, history, race, racism, morality, marriage, children, friendship, love, sex, the triumph and sometimes defeat of the human spirit, as well as a few other things I threw in for good measure. Seriously, it's the story of a family, a marriage, and of the young woman, Ursa Beatrice Mackenzie, who is the sole issue of this marriage. Ursa is of dual heritage, American through her mother, a schoolteacher from Connecticut, and West Indian through her father, a leading politician on one of the islands, a man known all his life as "the PM," the Prime Minister. *Daughters* is, in part, the story of Ursa's struggle to come to terms not only with her family, especially her father, but with the two worlds she inhabits—America, where she lives, and the island where she spent her childhood. The novel is about the long hard battle we sometimes have to wage to achieve true autonomy. *Daughters* is also about the array of women who have an impact on Ursa's life in one way or another. These women are the "daughters" of the title. Ursa, in turn, is the little girl of all these "daughters." They're an odd lot, these women. They're from different backgrounds, two different parts of the world, even different periods of time. They range from a long-ago slave woman by the name Congo Jane, who became a warrior, to Ursa's mother, Estelle, a modern-day Delta *soror*, who falls in love with this man everyone calls "the PM," marries him, and goes to live on the island I call Triunion. It's the story of their marriage and the problems of a personal, political, and moral nature Estelle wrestles with over the years. Estelle's story is an equally significant part of the narrative.

DD: Can you speak about Estelle and her relationship with her husband, this marriage between the American and the West Indian? And is that marriage reflective of your *own* experience? Can you say if any events or conflicts or issues in the relationship of Estelle and the PM were inspired by any situation that you experienced or knew?

PM: Well, it's a mixed bag when it comes to the sources. Yes, I drew in part on my own experiences as someone who was once married to a West Indian with political ambitions, but I also made use of what I *perceived* to be the experiences of other people I came to know during the periods I spent in the Caribbean. But *not* in any direct way. It's always in bits and pieces. As with everyone, everything that has happened to me, that I have experienced firsthand or heard about or read about—however it's come to me—it's all stored in the data bank of the mind, this repository, this hopper. And in creating a story, in creating *Daughters*, I simply go to the data bank and *select*—and that word is crucial—*select* what I need, those elements that will help me tell this particular story. What I don't find I invent. I'm always inventing. I find that the most exciting, challenging, and fulfilling aspect of writing fiction. My imagination is always working overtime. And it's true, you know, that certain aspects of my life or the lives of friends or something I have read, et cetera, will trigger the idea for a story because it speaks to something deep within me. Yet the material drawn from reality, that I take from my life and other lives and what I've seen and experienced, is always altered, is always transformed; it's always reordered to fit the fictional reality that I'm creating.

DD: But are there no individuals whom you might be able to cite as direct influences on characters in *Daughters*?

PM: As direct influences or direct sources? Not really, because my characters for the most part are always composites. I'm always creating my people out of fragments of any number of people I've known. Sometimes they are just outright inventions: for example, the PM's keep-miss, or mistress, in *Daughters*, the woman Astral Forde is a total invention.

DD: Yes, but I'm sure you've known a lot of keep-misses.

PM: That's right, and I used them as a base for my invention.

DD: You commented in an interview in *Wasafiri* that "the books express my search." To what degree does this novel reflect your personal search?

PM: The writer Ralph Ellison has an interesting theory that might help me answer your question. In an essay of his on the relationship of the writer to his/her work he uses the phrase "completion of personality." By this he means that the writer, without being conscious of it, often injects into the work deep-seated and oftentimes troubling aspects of the self, and in thus externalizing them achieves a kind of completion of personality, a filling in of the gaps that can bring the writer closer to wholeness and healing.

Something like this happens with me vis-à-vis the work, I suspect. All of my novels and stories come out of questions I'm always putting to myself, sometimes without being fully conscious that this is what I'm doing. Writing novels and stories is my way of seeking answers. For example, one of the questions I'm always putting to myself is, how do I as a woman—a black woman—and a writer continue to function and to grow in a society that almost daily assaults my sense of self? That question in part prompted my writing the novel *Praisesong for the Widow*. Also, how does one grow old in youth-struck America? Another question which that novel sought to answer.

In the case of *Daughters*, writing it permitted me to deal number of concerns that have preoccupied me for years. The relationship of black men and women, for one. Through Congo Jane and Will Cudjoe, the long-ago slave heroes; through Estelle and the PM in the early years of their marriage; through even the little boy, Robeson his friend Dee Dee I could express my hope for reconciliation, cooperation, love, and unity between black women and men. It's a plea for dialogue, for a willingness to reach out and support and save each other.

How do individuals, how do countries and cultures achieve independence? Another question that I'm seeking to answer in *Daughters*.

At the individual level, it's Ursa's search in the novel. In the larger context of culture and society we see the irony of her father's nickname, the PM: that it is an empty symbol of power and authority in a country that still takes its orders from America and the West. The battleship, the *Woody Wilson*, comes to supervise each election. "How do you come out from under the shadow of that red rock?" to quote T. S. Eliot. Out from under the seduction of another's values and the domination of the Herrenvolk? Congo Jane and Will Cudjoe suggested "the way" long ago, as do other, more contemporary characters in the novel. It's about the coming together, the working together not only of black men and women, but of the entire black community throughout the world. Idealistic, I know, romantic even—I've been accused of both—yet the possibility, the necessity of that union sustains me.

DD: Let me ask you about the setting of a large part of the novel—the West Indian island of Triunion. Was the name Triunion designed specifically to indicate that idea of bringing together?

PM: Oh yes. Very much so. Triunion. Pure invention again, albeit bits and pieces of a topographical and cultural nature were borrowed from a number of islands to fashion it. They include Haiti and its next-door neighbor, the Dominican Republic, as well as several of the English-speaking islands. I wanted to create a place that would represent the three major colonial powers in this part of the world: the English, French, and Spanish. Again, my obsession with history. My Triunion was once under all three flags and although "independent" (in quotes), it continues to suffer from those divisions. The place is meant to suggest the weakness that comes from disunity. It's meant to suggest all the poor countries and communities, including the African-American community here, that fall prey to the seduction and domination of their former colonial masters because of disunity. Perhaps it's an impossible dream, but I long for the day when the islands of the Caribbean—English, French, Spanish, Dutch—will come together in some kind of federation or European-style political and economic entity. It's the only way I believe they will be able to come out from under the shadow of Big Brother to the north, be able to achieve real strength and thus be taken seriously in the councils of the world.

DD: You've mentioned Congo Jane and Will Cudjoe, and I notice in this novel as well as in *The Chosen Place* that you deal with slave rebel heroes. I suppose these are combinations also of the actual historical figures. I know there is a Cudjoe. To what degree were this hero and this heroine based upon actual slave figures?

PM: Before I answer the question directly let me say something about my interest in history, especially the history of black people in this hemisphere. By the time I got to high school I realized that the history taught me, the *little bit* of history taught me about black people, was far from the truth. I sensed that early on. Somebody was lying through their teeth to me, trying to undermine my spirit and my sense of self. Really out to defeat me and those like me. Then there was the happy darky, the faithful Dilsey, the tragic mulatto, the nigger wench. Stepin Fetchit was a favorite in the movies of my day, as was the bug-eyed Mantan Moreland; images that peopled my childhood in books and the movies, especially the movies.

History was an Africa without civilization and art, was West Indians as monkey chasers and African-Americans as mammies and Amos and Andies, black people denigrated at every turn. And so part of my preoccupation with history in the work is my need to set the record straight, if only for myself; to get at the whole story. History to me is an antidote to the lies, and I'm interested in discovering and in unearthing what was positive and inspiring about our experience in the hemisphere—our will to survive and to overcome. We have the unique opportunity to create, to reinvent ourselves. Since so much that's been said about us—all those negative and unflattering portrayals—was designed to serve the fantasies and motives of the larger society and had little to do with us, we can declare it all null and void, all that stuff, and fashion a self for ourselves that's more truthful and more complex. And I think that knowing and understanding history is an essential part of that endeavor. And that's why there's always the emphasis or the concern with the past in my work

But to answer your question about the slave heroes, Congo Jane and Will Cudjoe, in *Daughters*, I portray them as co-conspirators, co-leaders, consorts, lovers, friends. They are inventions essentially, but inventions based on a number of black heroic figures both here in the States and in the West Indies that I have come across in my reading. For Congo Jane I drew on the famous Jamaican heroine, Nanny of Nanny Town, who founded the self-sustaining Maroon colony in the Blue Mountains of Jamaica back in the early eighteenth century. Lucille Mair has written extensively about Nanny and other rebel women of the period. The crucial role that they played in the resistance has received, of course, little attention in the literature. It was important to emphasize in *Daughters* that it was Congo Jane *and* Will Cudjoe, the main point being that slavery, as painful and traumatic as it was, nevertheless was a time when black women and men worked and struggled together in a greater spirit of unity, mutual support, and equality. It's been referred to as equality under the lash. Lucille Mair examines her work, as does Angela Davis in a seminal essay that appeared in the *Black Scholar* some years ago. So it's all about that. It's about the direction and lessons that history has to offer us. That's what really fascinates me.

DD: When in college, Ursa wants to write her senior thesis on the relationship of Congo Jane and Will Cudjoe, and her professor refuses to approve her topic. Was that your personal experience?

PM: No, although I've heard any number of similar stories from black students. I simply wanted to make the point that there is a good deal of resistance on the part of even the most liberal whites to admit to some of the positive and even triumphant aspects of the African-American experience in this part of the world.

DD: Indeed to deny them.

PM: Yes. To deny them. That's what Ursa experiences at the hands of her white "liberal" professor. And it becomes a kind of mission to write about Congo Jane.

DD: Speaking of powerful black women, let's talk about Celestine, the old family retainer in the novel and another one of the daughters of the title. She's a very interesting figure, and I thought about Jean Rhys's similar character, Christophine, when I was reading your novel. Is Celestine to any degree influenced by her?

PM: No, not at all. Christophine . . . Celestine—the names are close, but that's about all. I read *Wide Sargasso Sea* many years ago and remember little of it. My Celestine, the young nursemaid who initiated the PM sexually when he was a boy and then the older woman who helps raise Ursa, is, along with Congo Jane, an ancestral figure in the novel. Celestine is based largely on my maternal grandmother. Although my grandmother has been dead for many years now, she remains an important presence in my life and in my work. She appears in one guise or another in most of my short stories and in *all* of the novels. She embodies for me that long line of unknown black men and women who are my forebears. It's about creating a history for myself. I once wrote a story about her called "To Da-duh, in Memoriam." Da-duh was her nickname. Most of the story was straight out of my imagination since I only knew her briefly and I was a little girl at the time. But even so I sensed her special force and her resiliency, her spirit—this woman who had fourteen children, including two sets of twins, and who managed, through acquiring land in Barbados, to send most of her children abroad; and who worked her land up until the day of her death. She was this stalwart black woman. I've always identified with her. In fact I've always felt that I was more *her* child than my mother's. And her heir as well, in the sense that I have the feeling I was perhaps put here on this earth to preserve and continue her essence. And so Celestine in *Daughters* is yet another incarnation of Da-duh. But then so is Great-Aunt Cuney in *Praisesong*, as is the old woman Leesy Walkes in *Chosen Place*, as is Mrs. Thompson, the hairdresser from down South, in *Brown Girl, Brownstones* . . .

DD: So she can be an American?

PM: Oh, yes. I don't make any distinction between African-American and West Indian. All o' we is one as far as I'm concerned. And I, myself, am both. Anyway, I'm sure that Da-duh will make her appearance in the next novel down the pike. I am in many ways an unabashed ancestor worshipper. I need the sense of being *connected* to the women and men, real and imaginary, who make up my being. Connection and reconciliation are major themes in my work.

DD: You have spoken often as well of your mother, but you dedicate *Daughters* to your father, about whom you've made only occasional comments. One can't miss, of course, the females in your novels who wrestle with romantic, charismatic, somewhat mysterious father figures. Are you working through your relationship with your father?

PM: [Pause] Yes, the dedication suggests that. I've finally overcome, as much as it's possible for me to overcome, some really deep-seated feelings of anger and hurt caused by that relationship. The greatest grief of my childhood was that my father deserted us to become a member of Father Divine's quasi-religious cult, a sect that was popular back in the thirties and forties. My handsome, charismatic father, who was given to wearing silk underwear and spats, who played the trumpet—or tried to for years—and who, like my mother, was a natural-born poet, would say to us in the morning, "Rise and shine and give God the glory!" This father whom I adored became a devotee of someone who decreed there were no mothers and fathers, parents and children, rather that *he*, Father Divine was father and mother to *all*. So that Samuel Burke, my father, forbade my sister and myself to call him Daddy. Finally, he disappeared out of our lives altogether to go and live in Father Divine's "kingdom" in Harlem, abandoning us to a cycle of poverty and my mother's decline into bitterness, cancer, and an early death ... It's taken me a long time and much interior work to get over my anger at him. And also to overcome the fear that I had been *contaminated* with what I sensed and saw as his failure. Failure it seemed he almost actively sought out. For years I was afraid that no matter how hard I tried, I'd never escape his bad luck and his failed efforts to be an artist. And then there was the pain and outrage at having been rejected by the one person you loved most ... That's, of course, how I interpreted it as a little girl, and that outrage and sense of inevitable rejection were, I think, to undermine the important relationships with men later on in my life. I've had to *really* struggle to undo that damaging pattern ... It's a very painful subject for me to deal with.

But through *Daughters* and the story of Ursa, my main character, and *her* relationship with *her* father, the tensions and conflicts there, and her ability finally to cut away that emotional dependency, I think I've also achieved a final purging. I've been able at last to forgive, bless, and to release Samuel Burke from my life while retaining and honoring the love I still feel for him. So *Daughters* in many ways is perhaps my most personal novel in that regard. Although I hasten to add that the personal and the autobiographical have been transformed, disguised, reinvented.

DD: And of course a similar situation is treated in *Brown Girl*.

PM: In *Brown Girl* not as fully. The greater emphasis in that novel was the relationship between the mother and daughter.

DD: But I was thinking about the father who actually does join a comparable

religious sect in that novel, provoking a similar response from his daughter.
PM: Very much so, very much so. From the very outset I guess I've been trying to get to the point where I could deal with it more fully. It's *always* been there, though, in the work.
DD: Let's turn again to the women in the novels, and to those in *Daughters* in particular. Even more so than in the earlier novels the women in *Daughters* are silent, it seems to me, or if they do talk they yell, but there's little real communication. Can you talk a little bit about the silence of these women?
PM: What you see as silence, or the refusal or inability of the key women in *Daughters* to express themselves verbally, is a technique I deliberately chose to employ. First of all, I felt that it was in keeping with the characters, their personalities. It also provided me with a chance to deal with the silence that so often characterized my own relationships. I used to find it exceedingly difficult to express what I truly felt with my partners. Perhaps the silence in *Daughters* comes out of that in part. I'm not sure. On the other hand, Merle in *Chosen Place*, who talked nonstop, and Silla Boyce, the mother in *Brown Girl*, who loved to boast that she had no cover for her mouth and proved it on every page of the novel, were idealized images for me, the kind of outspoken, assertive women I would've *loved* to have been. Also the talk was in keeping with the kind of personalities I created for them. Avey Johnson in *Praisesong* and Ursa and Estelle in *Daughters* are perhaps closer to me in what you view as their silence. And I know it's a kind of outmoded response these days. People are not only supposed to talk endlessly, but to divulge their most intimate feelings. I suspect, though, that silence is still true for a lot of women.
DD: Yes.
PM: I have my doubts as to how many of us are actually able to talk about our real feelings with the men in our lives. Many of us still sit out our grievances in silence until we explode and start to yell or take some form of action. Silent sometimes till the point when we finally pick up the gun and just blow him away.
DD: Deadly silence!
PM: I might be wrong and I hope I am. At any rate, let me emphasize that the silence of the women in *Daughters* does not preclude action. Although much of the talk in the novel takes place offstage, the women express their feelings in action. Estelle drives out to that airport in the dead of night in her anger over the PM's infidelity. And we learn in the scene with her friend Roy that she has really let the PM know what she feels about the situation any number of times before actually taking action. It is established also that Ursa

has told her lover many times in the past that his job is ruining both him and their relationship, and that serves as the background for the final blowup between them. As I see it, the book is filled with a good deal of talk—but also with large, enraged silences.

DD: It's interesting that some of these women who obviously are together so much, especially Estelle and Celestine, and who never are able to establish any line of communication and never understand each other, might *really* have been supportive to each other. But I suppose that's so often the case.

PM: That's true. Yet what I wanted to establish through Celestine's monologues was that even though she resents Estelle, the American wife, there is still much about Estelle she genuinely likes and admires. Estelle, after all, was the one who taught her how to read. Estelle insisted that she, Celestine, have her own bedroom with her own furniture. Celestine refers to all this even when she's in the midst of finding fault with Estelle. I wanted to suggest the complex feelings my characters hold for other.

DD: It's also interesting that Ursa, the daughter, and Astral, the PM's keep-miss, are brought together in the same kind of pairing, one transcends economic standing, and where they live, and whether the Americans or West Indians. There is always something that reminds us of how much the women share.

PM: Yes.

DD: With Ursa and Astral there is first of all the matter of the abortion. You begin the introductions to both of these women with an abortion and, in effect, the novel may be primarily about giving birth or the failure to give birth.

PM: Let's start with the two abortions detailed in the story. Ursa's, which opens the novel, is largely symbolic. It's meant to suggest her attempt to cut away the subtle seduction and domination that has long characterized her relationship with her father. She doesn't succeed in that first, which is why she continues to feel that "this thing, whatever it is," as she says, is still there. It's only at the end of the novel, when she brings about the PM's political defeat, that she's finally free of this incubus. That last day at the beach when she falls down on the rock pile and injures her hip, the pain cuts across her belly in waves. I wanted to suggest they were labor pains finally freeing her from the emotional dependency of years. So that opening abortion is designed to work double-time, as Flannery O'Connor would say (that is, to have several meanings). With Astral Forde, it's another matter. Her abortion is the real thing. Yet it was also personally therapeutic. Writing about it permitted me to deal for the first time with a similar trauma in my own life when I was a young woman. A date rape, an unwanted pregnancy, a back-alley abortion, which was the only kind available in my day. In Astral Forde's case, Ursa becomes the child she aborted—although, of course, she would never admit it. But it was important for me to establish this in order to underscore the point that Ursa is the little girl of all of these daughters, all these women.

DD: What about the fact that Astral, like Ursa, has this feeling that there's something left in there?

PM: Yes, but what is left in there is, as she refers to it, a wire thing. "It's like the man left the wire thing up inside me." This sensation of the wire still inside her is, she believes, the thing that has made her sterile. She intimates as much in one of her soliloquies. She was maimed, she was made barren by that procedure: "Who says I can have any blasted children!"

DD: Children are very important in this novel.

PM: Yes. A good deal of space is given to children in the book. I use them to suggest the future. This is especially true of the boy Robeson and his little friend Dee Dee. They are, for me, the modern-day counterparts of Congo Jane and Will Cudjoe—inseparable, supportive of each other, united in times of trouble. Dee Dee with those ever vigilant eyes of hers and her beaded hair in the Black Liberation colors of black, red, and green. Robeson, who stands up to the policeman and is "injured," as so many black men have been injured in one way or another in this society. There's Lowell, Ursa's lover, with his permanent frown of worry that is like the keloid of a wound that refuses to heal.

Robeson's mother in the novel, as well as Ursa's best friend, represents the consummate mother. Her goal is to raise a child who will be useful in the struggle, someone who can be depended upon to bring a bucket of water to the woods that are on fire—meaning our communities both here and in the West Indies. Viney tries to ensure Robeson's safety by surrounding him with an array of material things, only to be reminded when he is arrested that perhaps there's no real safety for a black child in America.

DD: Estelle is a major figure in this novel. Of course, there are many important women in this novel. But with the other women we generally learn about them in very direct ways through their conversations with good friends to whom they speak honestly and directly or through entering their minds. But with Estelle there's usually some distance. Perhaps the closest revelation of what we might see as coming directly from her is those letters, but of course, with letters we don't express everything, especially not to the people back home. And clearly the things that bother her most are never discussed in those letters, and the things that bother her most are told to us through Celestine or others, who are often *un*sympathetic toward her. Why do we learn about the traumatic events in her life through a second voice?

PM: Well, that speaks to some very fundamental issues about craft: how to reveal character, how to make your people come alive on the page and matter to the reader. As a fiction writer, you have at your disposal a number of ways to accomplish this—dialogue, description, action, thoughts, behavior, an array of techniques. With Estelle I decided try some of the less conventional means, in part to get away from the fairly standard methods used in portraying the other women in, novel, and also to challenge myself. I would tell Estelle's story largely through letters and a secondary voice, that of Celestine. One reason for the decision had to do with language. It struck me that there might too great a similarity in the voices of Ursa, her close friend Viney, and Estelle. A mainly urban, North American speech. What would be more interesting linguistically, I thought, would be to tell the Estelle part of the narrative in the different and more colorful voice of Celestine. I wanted to balance the voices in the novel. It was something of a risk, I knew, but I decided to try it. And I really don't think that Estelle is any less vivid or any less affecting as a character because of it. I may wrong, but it seems to me that she does reveal her feelings about problems she's wrestling with in her letters. Her miscarriages, her work, her difficulties adjusting to life in Triunion, the depth of her love for the PM. Later, she refers obliquely to her acceptance of his infidelity. "I don't even understand me anymore," she says in one of the letters, "the things I've accepted living here." And so I've tried to present Estelle at something of an angle instead of head-on.

DD: Is she also a character who is closer to your heart and therefore perhaps protected a little bit, kept a little distant?

PM: That's an interesting question. She is a composite of many people whom I've known, including myself, as well as people I've just imagined. I don't know that I have revealed less about her by the method I've used.

DD: Why hasn't Estelle developed any close friendships with women, as is the case with the other important women in the novel?

PM: She does have a friendship, although it is not as fully developed as the others. There is this strong relationship between Estelle and Roy, doctor-friend, as she calls him. So I do provide her with a key friendship, but it's a male, again trying to do something slightly different with Estelle.

DD: There are, in *Daughters*, very *vivid* pictures. The action is arrested and there is this *image* that remains: Ursa, the little girl, reaching up to touch the toe of Congo Jane's statue; the PM's mother, Miss Mack, hooking her cane around the neck of her helper in the shop; and Astral at the swimming pool holding the towel and the soursop juice for Ursa, reduced to a maid. What are the sources of such pictures?

PM: Again, as with my characters, images and scenes are sometimes drawn from life but transformed to suit my fictional purposes; usually, though, they're pure inventions. For example, Astral Forde, and the towel, and the soursop juice, came solely from my imagination. So, too, Ursa being raised on Estelle's shoulders to reach the statue in the first chapter. On the other hand, I used my Haitian mother-in-law for the woman with the cane. My mother-in-law was a shopkeeper who was known to hook her little helpers around the neck with her cane handle when they committed some infraction. And that image stayed with me. I knew I would use it in a story or a novel some day. And I really love doing that. I love working long and hard to make a scene come alive. I've been called a "picture writer" and I like to think that's true. I'm always trying to use language and imagery and description in such a way that the reader sees as I see in my mind's eye, with that same clarity, vividness, and depth of feeling. I work very hard at that.

DD: You weave many plots with many characters—what of little Robeson? Is he likely to show up in a future novel?

PM: It's uncanny that you should ask that, because in the novel that's slowly beginning to take shape in my head now there's a little boy who will figure as a central character.

DD: Are any of the situations similar to this one?

PM: Not really. Only the fact that there is this little boy. In fact the entire novel, as I'm thinking, might be told in his voice. He's not Robeson, though. All I know about him at this point is that he's the child of some jazz musicians who went to live in Paris, and when they die there, the boy is brought back to the States to be raised by his two rivalrous grandmothers. These two live across the street from each other in Brooklyn and have been at odds for years because of the marriage of their children. It will be a kind of Romeo and Juliet theme, with the old women—one from the South, the other from the Islands-suggesting the warring Montagues and Capulets, with the child, this little boy, caught in the middle of the fray. That's as far as I've gotten. But I am struck by the fact that you felt something more should be done with Robeson.

DD: You mentioned that the women in *Daughters* were there, in your head, before you even had a story for them. But were there any women who were not a part of your original scheme, who sort of *came* into it? Astral, for example, was she there from the beginning?

PM: Astral? Let's see. The women wandering around backstage in my mind were very shadowy. Estelle was there. And Ursa, certainly, because I was interested, I knew, in creating a story about a young woman would represent the coming together of two cultures—African-American, West Indian—someone expressive of my own background. There was, of course, the ancestral figure, who was Celestine. She was there. And, yes Astral Forde must have been present also, given the fact that the "outside" woman, the keep-miss, is such an institution in the West Indies. They have all kinds of interesting names for her.

DD: Keep-miss is most appropriate. And was Viney, Ursa's best friend in the novel, also a part of the original group?

PM: I'm not sure. Viney might have been a later addition. I needed to represent the world of the young professional African-American woman making her way through the mine field of men, work, children, racism and sexism of the society, and so on. Also Viney serves as a foil and alter ego for Ursa—she is the sister/friend, as Ursa calls her.

DD: Speaking of bringing the Afro-American and West Indian cultures together, Eddie Brathwaite, the West Indian poet and historian, has said that you probably would not have written your second novel, *Chosen Place, Timeless People*, had you not been a West Indian, and could not have written it had you not been an Afro-American of West Indian parentage. Do you see yourself as an American writer, a Caribbean writer, or is it impossible to make that kind of classification?

PM: Well, I was once accused by, I think it was Harold Cruse, in *The Crisis of the Negro Intellectual*, of being neither fish nor fowl, of fallen between two stools as a writer because of my background. And I've been at times loudly claimed by the African-American literary community as well as the West Indian, and occasionally as loudly *disclaimed* by both. It used to hurt and exasperate me years ago—the disclaiming part of it—and still does to some degree. But I simply go on being who I perceive my life and my work to be. And I like to think of myself and my work—especially the work—as a kind of bridge that joins the two great wings of the black diaspora in this part of the world. I really see it in that way. And agreeing in part with Edward Brathwaite, perhaps there *is* a certain advantage in being neither fish nor fowl; perhaps it gives me a unique angle from which to view the two communities: involvement on one hand, yet a certain objectivity and beneficial distancing on other. I don't know. What I do know is that there is this tendency to categorize the writers, to put us in pigeonholes. People want to be able to get a *handle* on you—and my reaction is to try *not* to take it on, but to go ahead with the work and to honor my imperatives as a writer. And my principal imperative is to give expression to the two cultures that created me, and which I really see as one culture. All o' we is one.

DD: Even before you moved to Richmond, Virginia, there seemed to be some fascination with the South in some important characters you created: Mrs. Thompson in *Brown Girl* and Aunt Cuney in *Praisesong*. In *Daughters*, Viney is from the South—Petersburg, Virginia, in fact. How did Petersburg win out over Richmond?

PM: Well, for one thing, Petersburg has bigger and more spectacular Civil War battlefields. I'm thinking of the famous Crater. In creating a personal history for Viney, I decided to put one such battlefield across the road from her family's house in Petersburg. The house is also put a few doors down from their church, The Triumphant Baptist (and there is a Triumphant Baptist Church in Richmond—that's where I got the name). Viney's Triumphant Baptist Church also faces the battlefield. And I just let that configuration of battlefield, church, and her family's house make their statement about an entire history.

DD: A lot of writers from the Caribbean suggest that on one level they *do* seem to relate to the South. Some of them have said there are things about the South that remind them more of the Caribbean than the North does.

PM: Well, it's odd. I find myself living here in Richmond, yet most of the time I'm not really that conscious of being in the South as such. That is, until I hear someone speaking with a pronounced southern accent or a clerk in a store "yes and no ma'ms" me to death or I happen upon a Civil War reenactment, which is what happened to me the very first week I came to live in Richmond. I was walking downtown and suddenly I saw a group of men in gray Confederate uniforms coming toward me . . . along with some women dressed in Scarlett O'Hara hoop skirts and bonnets and so on. And for a moment, before I understood what was going on, I could have sworn I was in a kind of time warp. I felt like a character in an Octavia Butler novel who has been suddenly catapulted back to the antebellum South. And I was really all ready to take the plane out of Richmond. It also took me some time to adjust to all of the statues of Confederate heroes lining Monument Avenue, *reminding* me practically every other block that these men on their noble steeds were fighting to preserve my enslavement. So it's taken a while to adjust to some of those things. Generally, though, living in Richmond these seven years has been a positive experience. It's slowed me down some, and after having lived in New York City all my life, I needed to decelerate. It's also provided me with the opportunity—because I find life here less pressured—to work on my inner being, so to speak, and to unburden myself of a lot of past negative programming. So I've become a sort of happier, more relaxed, and younger person even as I become a Gray Panther.

And Richmond has also proven to be a good place for me to get the writing done. But I'm the kind of person who can pretty much live and work anywhere. Essentially I am someone who has always lived on the periphery. I'm basically a loner by choice, someone whose day is pretty much given over to her work. I mainly need a congenial setting, that's what, really, Richmond has provided me with.

DD: In one article called "The Negro Woman in Literature," written in 1966, you said that "the writer has to remain at all times true to her personal vision, even though it might not be in fashion this season." And I think, considering that time, we pretty much know the kinds of things you were referring to. But I'd like to know what you see as the "fashionable" thing now that some writers might feel pressured to treat. Are we still concerned with "in" things in writing?

PM: Well, I said that, let's see, about twenty-five years ago, and I'm not too sure I knew just what my personal vision was back then, or maybe I was just trying to sound profound. Seriously, I probably meant that I wanted to remain true to those themes and concerns, some of which I've mentioned earlier, that excite and challenge my imagination and abilities as a writer of fiction—to continue writing, for instance, about people in relation to their communities and the struggle that one must wage to possess one's true-true name—the whole question of autonomy, not only personal and individual autonomy, but autonomy of cultures and countries. As an example of the kinds of pressures I've had to resist, I'm always being urged to write a novel that's set exclusively in the States. Some who read my work worry that using the West Indies as a setting, even if in part only, somehow goes against me. That it makes me less "folks," less African-American. Very interesting reaction. And these people really mean me well and even love me, some of them. But I'm afraid I really can't accommodate them because my way of seeing the world has been so profoundly shaped by my dual experience, those two communities, West Indian and African-American. Those two great traditions—they nurtured me, they inspired me, they formed me. I am fascinated by the interaction of the two cultures, which is really, as I see it, one tradition, one culture. But I'm repeating myself.

DD: You are, of course, one of the most highly regarded novelists of our day. Your work has been praised worldwide by critics as well as by other writers, and you have already exerted a major influence on your peers and younger writers. What goals do you set for yourself now? Does it continue to be just a matter of dedicating yourself to each novel? Is there any fear that you won't live up to the expectations that come as a result of the acclaim you've received thus far?

PM: Well, the doubt, the fear are always there. They go with the territory.

DD: It doesn't get worse as a result of success?

PM: Not really, because all of the hoopla, all of the praise and blame pretty much fade away once I sit to the desk and begin wrestling with the words, the sentences, the scenes, the plot, the characters, creating a fictional reality. What the world is thinking of me and the work and so on really does not have an impact on the writing itself once I'm truly immersed in it. But, of course, you always hope to go one better with the latest work. I mean that's the American way to be, isn't it? You always want to top that previous performance. And yes, to some degree I do feel the pressure, but not to the extent that I used to as a younger writer. Rather, I'm beginning to see each new work as another attempt on my part to communicate the world inside my head to the larger world around me, and my goals remain the same essentially: to create a body of work that will offer young black women, such as I was years and years ago, a more truthful image of themselves in literature. That's my ideal audience, although I invite and welcome *everyone* to read the work. I believe that literature that speaks to the truth of our lives is an empowering force. It gives us the sense of our right to "be" in the world, and once you have that sense of your right to be in the world, all positive things follow from that. The possibility of really beginning to salvage our communities will follow from that. As for myself, I simply write the book or the story. I try to get it as good as I can. I put it out there in that cutthroat public arena; I hope for the best . . . and go on to the next book. That's pretty much my life.

DD: I clearly recognize your concern about writing for young women and speaking rather directly to young black women, but a lot of your work obviously speaks to older black women, too.

PM: Yes, equally as important are black women of a certain age, my age. I tend to emphasize the young because of the fact that one of the things that I had to wrestle with growing up, as I came into consciousness and became a serious reader, was that I didn't see myself reflected anywhere. Certainly I didn't see myself reflected in the literature in any kind of truthful and complex way, and that was a very painful experience. There were no books back then that reflected my experience or reassured me that I had a right to be here, that there was much about my life that was of worth and value. That's why I stress the young black women, thinking back to that young woman I once was, searching for a sense of self.

DD: When did you discover black women writers?

PM: I discovered them, let's see, I was well into my teens, because although Zora Neale Hurston was being published during the years that I began seriously reading, I was never told about her, encouraged read her. Most of the books I read came out of the canon of European literature, and I do love the work and was very much taken with great sweeping eighteenth- and nineteenth-century novels: Thackeray's *Vanity Fair*, the work of Dickens, Thomas Hardy—I loved Thomas Hardy—and later, Joseph Conrad, Thomas Mann, all of that. Yet there was always, at a deeper level, a sense of lack. Something was missing—I couldn't quite define it. Couldn't really define it. I'm talking now about, oh around the age of thirteen, fourteen or so . . . until I came across a volume of Paul Laurence Dunbar's poems and was made aware that there *were* black writers and was given the courage by that collection of Dunbar's poems to go up to the white librarian at the library in my neighborhood and ask her to give me a list of books by and about black It was then, *slowly*, that I began educating myself.

DD: Do you recall whether there were any women writers those you read early?

PM: I think that the one who had the greatest impact, and who was critical later in the way I went about shaping the character of Selina in *Brown Girl*, was Gwendolyn Brooks and her poetic novel *Maud Martha*. Because what Gwen Brooks did in that book was to render her character from the inside out. We were privy to Maud's mind, to her thoughts. She was an *interior* being, someone with a consciousness, with thoughts; and I was very intrigued by that because so many of the black women that I came across in the literature, especially those written by whites—say, for instance, Roxy in *Pudd'nhead Wilson* and Dilsey—were reduced to mere surface and stereotype; done surface—with no life apart from the whites they served. But here, for the first in *Maud Martha*, was a complex rendering of a black woman— and that was exceedingly important for me.

DD: Yes, it seems to me, too, that the same situation obtained in the Caribbean—that people grow up not knowing Caribbean literature until they seek it out on their own—this situation is changing now. When were you first introduced to Caribbean literature?

PM: Much later on. Just shortly before I went to the West Indies as an adult. That was in the mid-fifties. By then I had read Lamming's *In the Castle of My Skin* and had begun my education in West Indian letters.

DD: I see. You mentioned once that Merle in *Chosen Place* was your favorite character . . .

PM: Merle is special to me. There's that big mouth of hers first of all. Also she represents a kind of idealized image for me. Merle's the kind of woman I would have loved to have been, someone who states in no uncertain terms what she's *thinking*, what she's *feeling*. Her commitments are very clear. She takes charge. Yet, at the same time, she has this vulnerable quality. She's an exceedingly important character in my work in that she sums up in her person and in the personal history I provided her with—what has happened to black people in this part of the world. She embodies an entire history. She is the child of the hemisphere.

DD: As in your other novels, there are in *Daughters* some memorable male figures, but here it seems that the women find their answers only when they are able to overcome the male, who is, to play on what becomes symbolic in the novel, blocking their view from the sun, and at that point, when the women begin to relate to each other—even to the keep-miss and the poorer sisters—they seem to blossom. Even with the historical figures, it's Congo Jane's love of something beautiful that stands out. Do you see this novel as being a more feminist statement about the need for the sisters to get together and work it out?

PM: I suspect that there's been a feminist—or to use Alice Walker's term—womanist perspective in my work from very early on. My very first story, written back in the early fifties, long before the feminist movement as such got underway in the seventies, was about a young mother and wife who insists on going back to college despite her husband's objections. He defeats her in the end and forces her to stop, but she briefly prevailed against him. Another early story of mine had to do with sexual harassment. The victim, a young black woman from the South, achieves a kind of strength—personal and political—as a result of resisting her white professor's attempts to seduce her. So there's always been that in my work.

From the time I started writing women have been central to my stories. There're a couple of reasons for this. One is that women were central to my world growing up. My mother and a group of her close friends were the principal people in my early life. They were women of great spirit, resourcefulness, and poetry—my mother most of all, before her life took its tragic turn. There's an African proverb that says, "It's woman's power on which a society ultimately depends." I sensed this particular power in that group of women long ago. Moreover, my mother and her friends constituted, I remember, a kind of community apart from the men in their lives. I learned an important lesson from that—something about the importance of friendship and support among women. And this theme was taken up in *Daughters*, the pivotal friendship between Ursa and Viney, as well as Astral Forde and her friend Malvern.

The other reason that women are central to my work is that they were seldom the principal characters in the books I read growing up—and they were almost never black. So that without being terribly conscious of it, I determined to make women—especially black women—important characters in my stories when I started writing. To make up for the neglect, the disregard, the distortions, and untruths. I wanted them to be center stage.

They're certainly at the center of the story in *Daughters*. And yes, the women in the novel do begin to find answers to the personal and moral problems they confront in the book once they overcome—to use your word—the powerful hold the PM exercises over their lives in one way or another. "There's no resisting him," Ursa says of her father. For the women in *Daughters* the PM possesses the magnetic properties of a polestar, so that for much of the novel these women, including Ursa, are like a constellation around him. In fact, I use that image in the novel.

When Ursa, at the behest of her mother, engineers the PM's loss at the polls, she not only achieves personal liberation, she also destroys the configuration of polestar and constellation that involves the other women in the novel. Let me point out, though, that the action taken by Ursa at Estelle's orders is designed, not to defeat the PM, but rather to restore him to his original commitment and values. To repeat the African proverb: "It's woman's power on which a society ultimately depends."

And another reminder: whatever feminist note is struck in the novel is not meant to obscure what I hope will be seen as a major theme in *Daughters*: the need for black men and women to come together in wholeness and unity. It is this which informs the novel at its deepest level.

* I am grateful to Mrs. Sonya Burke for her assistance in transcribing this interview.

Holding onto the Vision: Sylvia Baer Interviews Paule Marshall

Sylvia Baer/1991

From *Women's Review of Books* 8, no. 10 (1991): 24–26. Reprinted by permission.

SB: When I began my literature major in college, the writers that serious literature students were expected to emulate were all Eurocentric white males. And I assumed that my vision, as a woman born in South America, was not serious enough, and I ended up changing my major to psychology. I want to know how you were able to hold onto your vision and to your voice.

PM: I think credit for that has to be given to a group of women from my childhood, whom I talk about every opportunity I get—just four or five ordinary-looking immigrant women from a tiny island in the West Indies that nobody had ever heard of. They came to this country shortly after World War I and because they were black women without any particular skills the only work they could find was cleaning people's houses. And one of those women happened to be my mother.

The foundation stone for my development as a writer was established when I was a kid who was forced to be among these women. As a girl child, as they called me, I was with them around the kitchen table when they came back from their day's work out in Flatbush. I was there with my sister waiting on them, serving them cocoa and tea, or sitting over in the corner doing my homework, being seen but not heard.

The remarkable thing about them was that while they looked ordinary, they were actually poets; they did marvelous things with the English language that they had learned in the schools of Barbados, this tiny island from which they came. They transformed the King's English. They brought to bear the few African words and cadences that they remembered and they infused and enriched it with all manner of biblical quotes and metaphors and sayings drawn from their life as black women.

For these women who were immigrants and who always felt as if they were strangers in America, the language gave them a sense of home. They talked about everything under the sun—politics, Roosevelt, Marcus Garvey, the Second World War which was just beginning, the First World War when they were young girls still living in the West Indies waiting for the war to be over so they could immigrate to the United States. They talked about the 1935 invasion of Ethiopia by Italy. The political perspective that was so much a part of the way they thought and saw the world became my way of looking at the world. I am indebted to them for that.

I see myself as someone who is to serve as a vehicle for these marvelous women who never got a chance, on paper, to be the poets that they were. Especially in *Brown Girl, Brownstones*, my first novel, I see that I was impelled, forced, to write it, because once I got over my adolescent rebellion against family and community I was able to see the worth, validity, and sacredness of that community in which I grew up, and its women especially. I wanted to try to get it down on paper before it was lost. That's why I think it's been easy for me over the years to hold fast to the vision—because it's not me so much, it's because of them, these women whom I call the mother poets.

From very early on I had West Indian English—black English, West Indian style. Out on the streets I had black English, Afro-American style. As soon as I went outside to play with my friends I immediately switched into that vernacular. At school I learned standard English. I was trilingual. That's one of the things that informs what I try to do with language. It's to bring to bear those three forms, to play around with them and play them one against the other.

Another way I've held onto both vision and voice has to do with the reading I did at the Macon Street branch of the Brooklyn Public Library, around the corner from the house. That was the second phase of my education and preparation as a writer, because I moved from that great oral tradition which the mother poets represented, to the written tradition, and fell in love with that also. I was a voracious reader who read in a disorganized sprawling way from Jane Austen to Zane Grey without any order but loving all of it.

Although I readily identified with the characters of all the books that I read, and I especially liked the long, full-blown eighteenth- and nineteenth-century English novels, I sensed after a time that something was missing. Then one day while browsing in the poetry section of the library I came across a huge volume of poems, and to my amazement the photograph of the poet in the frontispiece was that of a black man, Paul Lawrence Dunbar. Of all the books I had read to that date, that my teachers suggested that I read, none were by black writers. That was a revelation to me. A number of the poems were in dialect, and I mother and her friends doing with their West Indian vernacular. Perhaps there was something worthwhile about that play with language, something interesting and valid about my own experience.

Dunbar also instilled in me the secret desire to some day write. That collection of poems gave me the courage to go up to the white librarian at the circulation desk and say to her, "Would you please give me a list of books by and about black writers?" And it was then, on my own, that I began my education.

SB: This was, in your early adolescence?

PM: Yes, around twelve or so. Then, as I began to fill in this gap in my education, some other people became important to me. One of them was the poet Gwendolyn Brooks. In her novel *Maud Martha*, the main character is a young woman with a husband and a child, living in an apartment in Chicago. She begins to wonder about her life: "Is this all there is to it?" Brooks makes us privy to the interior landscape of Maud Martha's life. And that was important to me because that was what I wanted to do if I ever wrote about these women in my community.

Ralph Ellison was important to me, not so much for *Invisible Man*, but for his collection of essays on the craft of writing called *Shadow and Act*. He talks about the responsibility of black writers to move beyond the sociology of our lives to deal with the individual, the interior person, to see us and to treat us as people rather than statistics.

SB: Do you mean rather than making a political statement?

PM: The political is always there in my work, but as subtext. I'm always seeking to treat my characters and their lives by writing about them as people rather than as representatives-of-whatever.

SB: Your writing has spanned four decades: What keeps you motivated? What keeps you writing? What keeps you going?

PM: First of all, it's my work. It's the thing that I do. It is what gives sense and order and a framework to my life. Writing is absolutely crucial. When I don't write I feel that the day is without shape.

And writing fiction is my way of answering questions I'm always putting to myself. For instance, *Praisesong for the Widow* began because I came across a tale about a place in the Sea Islands called Ibo Landing, with a group of slaves who, when they were brought over, decided after they took a long look around that they didn't want to stay because they knew what their history was going to be in this republic. So they left. They were in such a hurry to leave, so the folktale goes, they walked back across the Atlantic to home.

I couldn't get that story out of my head. It just took up residence in the back of my mind and gave me no peace. And I wondered to myself, "Why? Why did that story stay with me?" I came to understand that the Ibos spoke to something deep within me, a question that I'd always been putting to myself: "How do I, as a woman and a writer, a black woman and a black writer, live in a society that daily undercuts my sense of self?" As I began writing about the Ibos, they gave me the answer. In the same way that they put the physical distance of the Atlantic between this country and home, between themselves and this country, I had to put a psychological and spiritual distance between myself and what I perceived and knew to be some of the damaging aspects of American society. Its racism. Its sexism. Its class bias.

Now the woman in *Praisesong*, Avey Johnson, this middle-aged, middle-class black woman, has made it. In fact, she would be referred to in my day as a CTTR, a Credit To The Race. She has a wall-to-wall carpeted house in north White Plains, which is some of the most expensive real estate. She has annuities and bank accounts and stocks and bonds, left her by her late husband. And each year, now that her husband is dead, she goes to the West Indies with her two friends and her six pieces of matching luggage. Well, why did she come and take up residence in my head along with the Ibos? She too was answering questions that I had been putting to myself, perhaps unconsciously. She had to be a middle-aged woman because I was just moving into middle age, and I was asking myself, "How does one continue to grow in a society which is all about youth?"

Through Avey I was able to deal with the notion that one has women especially have—the absolute right to reconstitute their lives at no matter what age. And Avey does that. She takes a journey back over her life to see where she has, in her feverish climb up the ladder, disowned and rejected aspects of herself that would make her a more interesting and a more vital person. She's able to recapture that sense of self, that sense of history, which then permits her to move to another level in her life. To stage a private revolution and win it. And it's that capacity for change that I was trying to deal with in that novel.

I'm always putting these questions to myself. Writing offers me a way of answering them, through characters, through stories. What is so marvelous is that I find that they are questions that other people are asking themselves and sometimes some of them find the answers in the books.

SB: I think that's what makes your work so wonderful, the universality of it—we can all identify with it, we can all feel part of it.

PM: Yes, because I really think it operates on a couple of levels. Readers are not only emotionally involved with my characters and with the story lines, they're actually learning something about another people, another culture, another way of doing things, at the same time that they see their own concerns and questions being reflected in the work.

SB: It seems as if you're not influenced by literary trends—you write for yourself. Don't you ever feel the pressure of the literary establishment to change your writing?

PM: Not really. The publishing world is so capricious and so impossible to control, I remained with blinders on and kept my focus on what I'm about as a writer. I'm very gratified when people say to me that issues I dealt with some time ago are now being written about. Women questioning the roles assigned to them—that was there in my very very first story, "The Valley Between," which goes back to the early fifties. The characters all happened to be white because it was so personal that I felt I could hide what was going on in my own life behind these white characters. It had to do with a young woman who found herself married and with a child, but who longed to return to school, and the opposition she faced from her husband. That was before we thought about women demanding a right to have part of themselves to themselves. I'd like to see my work as pioneering, but I'm not thinking about that when I'm working. I'm writing out of what was going on with a whole generation of women like myself, women who were raised to find work that was important, were raised to have a sense of self, and yet at the same time were carefully programmed from the very beginning to go the established route, marriage, family, the lot.

Also, what has kept me from being too concerned about the literary establishment is that I've been pretty clear-sighted about what I'd like my work to do. If I can as a writer portray my community in all of its complexities and in a truthful way, I can accomplish a couple of things. I can provide an antidote to the unflattering and negative images of black women that have persisted in the literature and the society, and I can also offer young black women—such as myself at the earlier period, who had no models, who never saw herself reflected—a more authentic image of themselves. I see that as very overpowering, because once you see yourself reflected truthfully, and that means not a flattering portrait, but with the warts also, it permits you to feel that you have a right to "be" in the world. We begin building an internal strength within our communities, because we know who we are.

SB: Do you see a change in your style over the years, or do you use a particular style to match what you're trying to say within a novel? *Praisesong*, for example, was much more compact than your other two.

PM: What I'm always trying to do is to challenge myself as a writer. Coming up with a kind of style that best serves the story but also from time to time trying out different modes. *Brown Girl, Brownstones* and especially *Soul Clap Hands* were very literary. Because I was a very young writer, there was a desire to show that I was well-read, so there are a lot of allusions to predominantly Western literature because that was what I was subjected to—and I use the word subjected pointedly—in my education. The second novel, the big novel, *The Chosen Place, the Timeless People*, was a full-blown, somewhat self-indulgent one in terms of style and language. If there were five ways to describe something I would use all five. I decided to challenge myself with *Praisesong* and see if I could write in the lean, economical and distilled form, almost a poetic form, yet still create a resonance that would give fullness to the language.

SB: Now you have a novel coming out in October called *Daughters*. Tell me about the style of that.

PM: In *Daughters* I'm taking some other risks. It's a freer book in that I'm trying, in terms of point of view, to blend with the characters. If a character would describe something more colorfully or more interestingly than I would as narrator, I use the character's description.

I'm also trying redo some interesting things with time The entire novel takes place within the span of two months, and yet what I do with time is a weaving back and forth within those two months that takes us all the way back to slavery. The characters are all daughters who are in some way connected one with the other, back to the slave woman who figures as a symbol in the novel. One of the themes that informs my work is being not only connected with those mother poets who were my mentors and instructors but also with the women who created them. It's part of how we define ourselves as people. How do black women get a sense of self? How do we create an identity that will permit us to function?

SB: That's why it's so important for your characters to make that journey back.

PM: Yes—it's all about the creation of a more truthful and liberating identity. One of the principal characters in *Daughters* is dealing with, and I'm quoting T. S. Eliot here, what it means to come out from under the shadow of that red rock, that dependency that gets built in those early relationships. That's why the symbol of abortion, which I use in the novel, is so important, abortion meaning being able to cut away those dependencies that can be so crippling.

I had an absolute charmer of a father, a man who just had this gift of the gab. He was a poet, too. To wake us in the morning he would come into our room and say, "It's time to rise and shine and give God the glory." He was handsome. There was a photograph of him that used to sit on top of the piano, the old upright piano we had, wearing his spats and holding his cane, his hair parted in the middle.

But he was a man who had great difficulty as a black man dealing with a society that denied him a sense of himself. He was unskilled, not able to find the work that he felt was in keeping with what he was as a person. He eventually abdicated his responsibilities, abandoned us. He fled, and that was exceedingly difficult for me because I so loved him. In many of my relationships along the way there was almost a repeat of that early relationship, always looking for this father in the men that I became involved with, and always preparing myself for the end of that relationship. How long it took me to move away from that and to recover, to insist upon autonomy. This novel is about the subtle deferring to men that was so much a part of my childhood and the childhood of many women.

SB: You were talking about your father; how much of your fictional characters comes from real life? How much is the father in *Daughters* your father, how much is the father in *Brown Girl, Brownstones* someone you know?

PM: The fictional characters are not drawn totally or solely from people that I have known. They are creations. But a good deal of their emotional history is drawn from what I have experienced either personally or what I have seen in the community that shaped me. The father figure in *Daughters* is physically different from my father, or the work he does, or the places he lives. Yet in terms of his relationship with his daughter, that whole emotional nexus reflects feelings and emotions that I have had. Again, I certainly am not an Avey Johnson, but she permitted me to reflect upon what it means to be a middle-aged woman, a black woman in this society.

SB: Your women are the strong characters in the books: instead of having a patrilineal heritage, you have women carrying on the heritage. Do you do this on purpose?

PM: Initially it was not a conscious decision on my part to have women so central to the work. Yet who did I know growing up, who was I surrounded by? Even though my father was important to me, my day to day existence was lived among women, and their lives, what they expressed about themselves and their place in the world, what they sensed about their place in the world had its impact on me from very early. I was not privy to the world of men. Women were central.

When I moved from the kitchen to the library, one of the things that struck me was that women weren't very central in any of the books that I read. I don't mean to make this sound as if I sat down and spelled it out consciously on a piece of paper, no, these were currents and feelings circulating within me. Perhaps because of this lack, one of the things I wanted to do when I started writing was to make women principal characters in the work.

I don't see them as "strong" but rather as complex and central, and that's different for me. The other side of strong black women is so often weak black men, and I want to get away from that thinking, because it divides rather than unites. I don't see, for example, Silla, the mother in *Brown Girl, Brownstones*, as all that strong a woman. I see her as someone who has perhaps foolishly or unquestioningly bought the whole American materialistic ethic. And the price she pays for that is the death of love and the ruin of her family. I don't see that as being all that strong. I see some strength in the father. He insists upon American success on his own terms.

SB: If the Paule Marshall of the 1950s could talk to the Paule Marshall of today, what would she have to say to you?

PM: She would say, I think, congratulations on two counts. One of them having to do with the work. That I kept to the commitment I made to writing in the fifties, not to give up or be discouraged by what I would encounter. I was in for the long haul, and I knew that. I understood from very early on that it might not work out very well financially for me, that I was not going to hang myself up as a writer by becoming unduly concerned with making it big. I was very straightforward about that. Also the whole thing of trends and fashions within the publishing world was something that I wasn't going to be involved in. And I've been able, over the four decades, to stay true pretty much to that early commitment.

The other thing that the fifties Paule might feel good about is that I've been able, through a good deal of interior work, private work, to eliminate from my life a lot of emotional impediments and obstacles. A lot of the negative programming that went into those early years—I've been able to make my peace with it and achieved a kind of interior calm, self-acceptance and self-love. That's been important for me, and I hope that that personal liberation is evident in the work.

The *Booklist* Interview: Paule Marshall

Donna Seaman/1991

From *Booklist*, October 15, 1991. Copyright © American Library Association. Used with permission.

Booklist celebrated the release of Paule Marshall's new novel, *Daughters* [BKL Jl 91], by speaking with the author about her work. Marshall's fiction, including her three previous and highly acclaimed novels, *Brown Girl, Brownstones* (1959), *The Chosen Place, the Timeless People* (1969), and *Praisesong for the Widow* (1982), exhibits rare resonance and power. She is a major American novelist, but is not as well known among public library readers as she ought to be. Perhaps this interview will help to rectify that oversight.

BKL: In your novels, a sense of place seems linked to a sense of history. Many of your characters struggle to come to terms with the past, both personally and culturally, such as in the story of the rebels Congo Jane and Will Cudjoe in *Daughters*. Why do you feel that the past, understanding it and being aware of it, is so important?

Marshall: I think that it's due, in part, to a kind of longing, a desire to know my history. Not the kind of distorted, unflattering, and truncated version of black history that's offered in the texts and so on, but what it was really like. And even though I'm not a historian or a scholar, but a writer of fiction, I suspect, under the surface of nearly all my stories, I'm trying to set the record straight.

BKL: Your comments remind me of Ursa's rejected thesis in *Daughters*. She wanted to write about the relationships between men and women under slavery, how slavery brought them together.

Marshall: That's right, an area which I just found fascinating when I looked back at that history. That there was, under slavery, a kind of equality under the lash.

BKL: Equality of the sexes?
Marshall: Yes, and that, even though not much attention has been given to it, the slave woman played a very important role in the rebellion, in the uprising. The figure of Congo Jane is based on one of the great slave woman heroes in Jamaica, a woman by the name of Granny Nanny, who founded a town called Nanny Town. And, of course, in black American history, there are figures such as Sojourner Truth, Harriet Tubman, and a marvelous woman not given much play in the histories, Ellen Craft, who was so light-skinned that she and her husband sort of disguised themselves. Again, it's the concept of men and women working together that I find to be such a useful reference.
BKL: In your fiction, men and women seem to undermine each other; they don't seem to be able to offer help or support. Do you feel that a closeness, the sort of positive relationship you're talking about, has become more difficult to achieve?
Marshall: Yes, it has become more difficult, and part of it has been the aftermath of slavery. The larger society has, in a sense, encouraged that division, that dissension, because that's one of the ways, as I see it, of controlling the black community, of keeping it at its weakest.
BKL: Dividing the family?
Marshall: And making such a point of it, instead of balancing the picture of the black family. Society, selecting only what is grossly negative and projecting that as the only picture, undercuts the possibility of unity. That's been one of the concerns in my work.
BKL: In your novels, people try. For instance, Ursa's parents fight it . . .
Marshall: That's right.
BKL: . . . but they're forced apart.
Marshall: Yes, they are, and yet what I try to suggest, by the end of the novel, is the possibility of a coming together again. I'm always looking for, reaching for, that possibility. This is echoed in the character Robeson and his friend Dee Dee—the togetherness of those two children, male and female, how she's the one who guards him when he has the unhappy encounter with the police.
BKL: He's victimized by society's negative image of blacks: a nine-year-old boy playing an innocent game is perceived as a criminal, even dangerous, by the police.
Marshall: Yes, no one is spared. No blacks are spared, not even those who have "made it." Racism reaches out and touches blacks no matter what their social and economic phase is.

BKL: One aspect of your novels that intrigues me is their thematic continuity. From *Brown Girl, Brownstones* to *Daughters*, you have focused on the conflict between trying to beat the system by working within it, versus declaring yourself free of it, trying to be completely honest and independent, maybe even creative. In each of your novels, the central woman character has tried to find herself and define the world.

Marshall: In a way, I suppose Ursa could be seen as a sort of sequel to Selina. It certainly wasn't consciously done on my part, but because my principal themes and concerns as a writer were pretty much set in place in the earlier work, especially *Brown Girl*, they really have remained consistent over the years. My characters are always questioning the roles that are imposed upon them.

BKL: No matter how painful that questioning is?

Marshall: That's right. Always trying to come to terms with family, with community. Always trying—we're talking mainly about my woman characters here—always trying to rid themselves of that subtle deferring to men that's been bred into them and always seeking to overcome racism and sexism and class bias, the struggle to really establish, a West Indian writer puts it nicely, your "true-true name." So there are these areas of similarities between the two characters. I really see my work as one in which those initial themes and concerns are central. And not only the ones I just spoke about, but also the whole importance of the past in shaping the new self and the dangers of unbridled, unquestioning materialism, themes that run through *Brown Girl, Praisesong for the Widow* and *Daughters*. I'm also concerned about the impact of culture and history on the individual. All of these themes were set all the way back when I first started writing. And what I've been doing over the years is essentially reexamining them, looking at them again, exploring them in other ways. Trying to refine them, turning the prism so to speak, to look at them from another perspective.

BKL: It seems as though these concerns remain the same while the world becomes even more insidious. In *Brown Girl*, the prejudice Selina faces is overt and obvious, while in *Daughters*, Ursa is confronted with more subtle and frustrating corporate and academic resistance. Do you think this is indicative of the big picture?

Marshall: I think it is. Because what I do is look at the questions I'm putting to myself, look at the situation of my characters in terms of the world in which they find themselves. For Selina, those problems imposed upon her took on a different cast from those Ursa faces in the 1980s, but each character must contend with losing her sense of self. And so the work is reflective of its time even though the questions and situations I'm looking at are, unhappily, fairly constant. The struggle remains the same: how to achieve some measure of autonomy, some measure of sense of self in the face of all of these things that would work against that.

BKL: You've examined the conflict between emotional and spiritual needs and financial and material security. This seems to be a multi-dimensional conflict: racial, sexual, and cultural.

Marshall: Well, that really is one of the major concerns of my work. It stems from the fact that I come from a group [Marshall's parents immigrated to New York City from Barbados] that was consumed by the desire to acquire property. In many ways it was a very typical immigrant dream. Every group that has come here has been caught up in that same need to establish roots and by that to become part of the American ethic, which is about acquiring things.

BKL: And there's also a need for security, a desire we all share.

Marshall: That's one of the things I was exploring in *Brown Girl*. In *Praisesong*, again, I looked at that whole overweening desire to make it and make it big. In the process, Jay and Avey [the central characters in *Praisesong*] reject what was really special and unique and important about themselves. In *Daughters*, what I try to suggest is that there is certainly nothing wrong in taking from the society what is our due. When you look at our history, a good deal of the basis of American prosperity has to do with the slave labor in those cotton fields and in the cane fields of the West Indies. So a lot is owed us; the reparations that are due us are just endless, but the idea is to take what is due without relinquishing what has made you unique as a people. That's what Avey comes to understand. And that is what Ursa is seeking to celebrate and to acknowledge in her desire to write the story of Congo Jane and Will Cudjoe. To honor that past, to honor that history.

BKL: And to get back in touch with the spiritual aspects of life. You write about two cultures, American and West Indian, but your concerns are universal. How does fiction contribute to our awareness of these issues, to answers to these questions?

Marshall: I don't set myself up as someone answering questions. What I do, rather, below the surface of the story, is direct my desire to have the reader engage those issues, to reflect upon them, to think about them, to be made more, perhaps, acutely aware of them. So that, for instance, in the case of Ursa, how does she, this young woman, really cut out that kind of dependency from her life? How does she create this true-true name for herself? The same question—and again this is for readers reading at the deeper level—is reexamined in the larger context of culture and society. I'm talking about what goes on in the so-called developing countries, where people are still under the economic stranglehold of the West. They're seduced by Western cultural values and the sort of neocolonialism that still operates in so many instances. How do you really come out from "under the shadow," and I'm quoting T. S. Eliot here, "of that red rock?" That's really at the heart of my work. I'm eager for thoughtful readers to reflect on the way I think about these questions; by considering them, we can move closer to actually engaging in some form of action. I see the work as perhaps contributing to that.

BKL: You've written about your mother and her friends, the "poets of the kitchen," and their vivid conversations as being an influence on you as a writer. Did their conversations inspire them to take action?

Marshall: In part. What I sensed about the mother-poets is that they were using those conversations in several ways. First, to kind of deal with the very real situations they confronted each day. But also, to use language as a political force. They couldn't bear the sense of their invisibility, and they were far more invisible even than Ralph Ellison's *Invisible Man*. They had four strikes against them: they were women, they were black, they were foreigners, and they were poor. And they couldn't take that. They couldn't take that society didn't even know they existed except as a form of cheap labor. And so they fought back, they fought back at that verbal level. They had an opinion about everything going on in the world, and that was one of their ways of having a small sense of power. In an active way, a number of those women were very involved in the Marcus Garvey movement. They were members of his Nurses' Brigade, and they would march in their white nurses' uniforms up Seventh Avenue in Harlem.

And so there was this little girl, myself, locked-in, in a way, with those women, learning from them, having my sense of the world shaped by them. My whole involvement with the past really comes out of the fact that they talked a lot about the past in terms of the places they came from and the things that happened in their childhoods. I think that when I started to write, all of this was there in my consciousness.

BKL: As a black writer, and as a woman, do you feel that there's an extra moral imperative, a responsibility to address racial, sexual, or political issues? Does that happen very naturally, or are you aware of it?

Marshall: I don't really spell it out in terms of responsibility or what is required of me as a writer, as a black woman who's a writer. Rather, I ask: what interests impel, inspire, challenge, excite me, obsess me, as a writer. And I find that the themes we've discussed, those concerns, questions, those conundrums, are the things that fulfill all of those requirements. It's not only my experience, when I talk about "my" or "I," I'm really talking about the collective "I." These themes and concerns really come out of the things that speak to something very deeply in me, and I'm writing out of that. So I don't really see it in terms of responsibility as such, but I do have, in a way, a kind of ideal reader. I sometimes ask myself who am I writing for, and I see her in my mind's eye. She's a young woman who vaguely resembles myself when I was in my late adolescence and early twenties. A young woman trying to understand herself, come to terms with her family, her community, seeking a way to protect herself against the racism and the sexism, that she's just become conscious of. She comes to a shelf, in a library or a bookstore, comes across a book by someone called Paule Marshall. And to her surprise, this author is black. And she opens the book and starts reading out of curiosity, and she finds that there's some things in the story that touch upon her life and her feelings, and it gives this young woman a sense, at that very deepest level of her being, of her right to be in the world.

BKL: That seems so basic, and yet I think many people don't feel it; they don't have that sense, and it hasn't been nurtured.

Marshall: Yes, and certainly when you're black there is the attempt on the part of the larger society to chop away, to cut away at that sense of self. And so once that's in place, all positive things follow like the possibility of really joining with black men to rescue our community. So I really see fiction as performing a very valuable role in that way. It's really about creating a body of work that will offer black women—the young ones, as I was years ago, the older ones as I am now—a chance to see ourselves reflected truthfully in fiction, as a people with force and style and beauty, but with shortcomings, also, a complex portrait. And then these women are joined by a host of other readers, other young women, who don't look like them.

Out of the specifics of my life and experience, and again, I'm talking collectively, has come work that has a kind of universal meaning and makes connections for other people and that has been very rewarding, really rewarding.

Meditations on Language and the Self: A Conversation with Paule Marshall

Melody Graulich and Lisa Sisco/1992

From *NWSA Journal* 4.3 (Fall 1992): 282–302. Reprinted by permission of Indiana University Press.

In a series of remarkable novels, *Brown Girl, Brownstones* (1959), *The Chosen Place, the Timeless People* (1969), *Praisesong for the Widow* (1984), and now *Daughters* (1991), Paule Marshall has given us portraits of black women looking back into history and creating themselves. For her powerful and original work, she was awarded a MacArthur Grant in the spring of 1992. The daughter of Caribbean immigrants, Marshall creates characters and plots that wander back and forth—literally or imaginatively—between the States and the islands, attending to the distant echoes of Africa. Her characters possess a dual citizenship that feeds their imaginations and inflects their speech, while her interest in the intersections of African, Caribbean, and Afro-American cultures enriches her work. Her fiction redefines "America," questioning American myths and values, locating the United States in the larger North American community, acutely exploring the political realities of colonialism and materialism. Yet Marshall's characters are always fully human individuals who realize themselves within the historical, political, and cultural backgrounds of her fiction. In *The Chosen Place, the Timeless People*, Saul Amron draws the kind of parallels between personal and collective history Marshall's novels explore so richly: he talks of the importance of going back and understanding, of coming "to terms with the things that have happened in your life . . . And that's not only true for people—individuals," he adds, "but nations as well. Sometimes they need to stop and take a long hard look back. [The United States], for example. It's never honestly faced up to its past, never told the story straight . . ." (359). Marshall has devoted her career to telling the story straight, to facing up honestly to personal and cultural pasts.

During the interview Lisa Sisco and I conducted with Marshall on 10 April 1992, she talked candidly about self-creation, voice, and work; about her major themes and the evolution of her work; about the influence of the women she called "the poets in the kitchen" and the importance of reading Afro-American writers; about her use of historical materials and her understanding of what it means to be a political writer; about sexual harassment and Anita Hill, Richard Wright and Zora Neale Hurston; about the problems between Afro-American women and men and how they can sometimes be transcended in what she calls the "free zone," in sexual intimacy; about Afro-American culture and her sense that "double consciousness" or seeing double is empowering rather than handicapping; and about her work in progress.

Most particularly she talked about *Daughters*, the new novel that one critic has called "flawless in its sense of place and character, remarkable in its understanding of human nature, . . . a triumph in every way" (Schaeffer 29). Filled with references to Afro-American and Caribbean history and cultural traditions, the novel offers the kind of "thick description" of cultural practices anthropologists attempt (Geertz 3); in fact, in the interview, Marshall describes *Praisesong for the Widow* as originating in an anthropological study of the Sea Islands, *Drums and Shadows* (Georgia Writers Project). *Daughters* begins with an epigraph to an Alvin Ailey dance: "Little girl of all the daughters, you ain' no more slave, you's a woman now." The "little girl" who breaks her personal and familial bondage and grows into a woman is Ursa/Bea Mackenzie, named for her two grandmothers. Ursa, who thinks of her life as a "series of double exposures," possesses dual citizenship: her charming father, Primus, known as the P.M., is an elected representative on Triunion, one of Marshall's fictional Caribbean islands, while her mother Estelle, is from the United States and encourages her daughter to return there to go to school and work. By moving back and forth from Triunion to the States, the novel's plot points out parallels and intersections between the politics and histories of the West Indies and the United States. Divided into four parts, "Little Girl of All the Daughters," "Constellation," "Polestar," and "Tin Cans and Graveyard Bones," the novel is told in the voices of a constellation of women who are all, in one way or another, in bondage to Primus, the polestar: Ursa, Estelle, Primus's mistress, Astral Forde, and his longtime servant, Celestine. These characters, according to Ursa's friend Viney, a single mother with rural southern roots, comprise "Ursa's tin cans and graveyard bones": "You remind me of a cat with a string of tin cans and some bones from a graveyard tied to its tail when it comes to your folks. And I don't mean your parents but Celestine and especially Miss Stone-face [Astral Forde]. . . . The cans and bones keep up such a racket you can't hear your own self, your own voice trying to tell you which way to go, what to do with your life." *Daughters* explores Ursa's efforts to learn to listen to her own voice, to "create a self," but it also reveals the influence and importance of other voices, especially those of the "daughters" who mothered her. Ursa must understand the significance of those voices in her life, those of her folks in Triunion and also those from the States: Viney; her son Robeson; Ursa's mentor, Mae Ryland, a community activist; her lover, Lowell Carruthers, whom she meet in the "free zone"; and Sandy Lawson, the mayor of "Midland City," who, like Primus, began as a reformer but compromised his values and lost touch with his community.

When the novel opens, Ursa has just had an abortion, partially because she cannot decide whether she can make a commitment to Lowell. Her unresolved feelings about the abortion, about her relationship with Lowell and about her work echo her unresolved feelings about her folks. She is struggling to write a M.A. thesis she's been working on for years, a thesis that originated in a childhood moment when her mother held her up to touch the feet of a statue of Triunion's two heroes, Congo Jane and Will Cudjoe, "coleaders [of a slave revolt], coconspirators, consorts, lovers, and friends" (14). Although discouraged by an advisor who finds her topic "highly doubtful," Ursa still hopes to examine "the relatively egalitarian, mutually supportive relations that existed between the bondmen and women" that allowed them to resist slavery together; she has read an article by Angela Davis about the subject but can find no models in her own life (11). Only when she faces the tin cans and bones of her past in the final section, rids herself of her father's dominance, and feels the pain of her abortion can Ursa actually begin to write her thesis, to recognize the power in her ability to "see double," to find the "*real* work" Mae Ryland envisions for her, to discover how, in Viney's words, to "be useful" in the larger struggle for political and economic equality for all.

Much like Selina in *Brown Girl, Brownstones* and Avey Johnson in *Praisesong for the Widow*, Ursa begins the process of self-creation at the end of the novel by understanding her history; like Merle Kinbona of *The Chosen Place, the Timeless People*, she is "still trying [when the book ends] to come

to terms with her life and history as a black woman, still seeking to reconcile all the conflicting elements to form a viable self. And she continues to search . . . for the kind of work, for a role in life, that will put to use her tremendous energies and talent" (from Marshall's introduction to the novella, *Merle*, in *Reena and Other Stories* 109). In the interview, Marshall expresses confidence that Ursa can now write the story of the "relatively egalitarian, mutually supportive" relations between men and women. But on this and other matters, Marshall speaks most eloquently for herself.
—Melody Graulich

Melody: We want to begin by asking you about the idea of "real work." Mae Ryland suggests to Ursa that she would like to give her some "real work" to do. That seems to be a theme you've raised elsewhere, in the introduction to "Reena," for instance, where you say the struggle to find meaningful work is important to women of your generation. Could you talk a little about that struggle and the importance of work?

Paule: It's been a theme and a concern that has preoccupied me from the very beginning. I wasn't able in *Brown Girl, Brownstones* to define it clearly enough for myself so that I could write about it in any depth. When I have Selina at the end of the novel going off to become a dancer on a cruise ship to the Caribbean, part of that journey is about discovering the West Indian aspect of herself, to get a sense of that world out of which her parents came, but it's also about her need to find work, to do something, which is in keeping with her particular spirited self. She knew when she rejected the West Indian community's demands to be the lawyer, the doctor . . .

Melody: And to marry.

Paule: And to marry, oh yes, yes, those two strains. Selina knew that's not what she wanted. That was not her kind of work and she was going to discover, through the dance perhaps, the thing that she most wanted to do. So it's always been there, that need for my characters to find real work. I think it springs from my own need and a question I'm always putting to myself: "Is what I'm doing truly meaningful?" This business of sitting alone writing for six, seven hours a day and having the arrogance to feel that what is going on in my head is of interest to anyone else. Is that really meaningful work? So many of my novels grow out of questions I'm putting to myself. I think I've been able to answer this particular question over the years. And in the affirmative. To say, "Yes, what I do is meaningful; it is real work." Because I've managed to put on the literary map the dual community, West Indian and African-American, that nurtured me. And to celebrate women, especially a group of West Indian women, my mother included, who were my mentors and teachers early on. To put them on the page. That was important work for me. These women, the "mother poets" as I call them, never had the opportunity to be recognized, published poets. They were invisible, both as poets and women. Talk about Ralph Ellison's *Invisible Man*! These women were invisible on four counts: they were black, women, immigrants, and working-class. They had all of those strikes against them.

They fought against that invisibility and their means was the spoken word. They took the King's English taught them in the islands and made it into an idiom that expressed their special quality. Language as creative expression, and as a way of making sense of the world. In fact they talked about world affairs, about economics, politics, along with the stories they told. In discussing these weighty matters, I suspect they felt they were in some measure in control of their lives. So that language was also a kind of weapon for them. In fact they referred to it as such. They would say to each other "Soully-gal, you gotta take you mouth and make a gun in this white man world." They were always using language as a weapon, as a strategy for survival. So, the meaningful work for me, was, in some small way, and it's only been in a *small* way, to get down on paper something of the quality and force and strength and humor and contrariness of those women.

Melody: Do you feel liberated when you get to a moment as in *Daughters* when you use that language you're talking about, as perhaps in Astral's voice?

Paule: Oh yes, very much so. In fact, *Daughters* is in many ways a meditation on language. Because I was finally able in the novel to honor all the voices and the different variations on the English language I heard growing up in Brooklyn. There was the West Indian black English, as I call it, the voice of my mother and her friends, the mother poets, which is of course Astral Forde's voice in *Daughters*. Then there was the African-American voice of my spiritual mother long ago, a woman from the Deep South. Her name was Mrs. Jackson. She was the local hairdresser. Whenever I went to get my hair done she would tell me stories about growing up in the South. She was, for me, the emblem of unconditional love. There was no tug of war between us, as in my relationship with my mother. There she was, this woman who was totally accepting of me.

Melody: And she has that role in *Brown Girl, Brownstones.*

Paule: Very much so. In fact, she appears in all of the novels. In *Chosen Place, Timeless People*, she and my maternal grandmother are very much part of the character Leesy. In *Praisesong for the Widow* she's Great Aunt

Cuney. She's there in all of the books. I'm always acknowledging the importance of Mrs. Jackson in my life. In *Daughters* she is Mae Ryland, that down-home, southern, African-American voice and presence. I also try in the novel to celebrate the Creole talk from Haiti that is part of my experience. My second husband was Haitian and I spent over ten years going back and forth to Haiti. And although I don't speak Creole aside from a few words, I absorbed a sense of the language, its power. And so the Creole expressions I use in Celestine's chapter are my attempt to convey something of that speech. Then of course there's the urban home-girl talk of Viney and Ursa living in New York. For the first time I got a chance to bring all the voices together. That was very important to me.
Melody: What about Estelle's voice?
Paule: Estelle's is largely black American, urban, northern, northeastern, which of course is another one of the voices that shaped me.
Lisa: Would you say that the stories Estelle tells about Will Cudjoe and Congo Jane constitute another voice, the voice of history? I'm interested in the way you constantly look backward and tell stories about slaves and other black history, the story about Ned Cuffee in *Chosen Place, Timeless People*, for instance.
Paule: Yes. One of the things I discovered in doing the research for *Chosen Place, Timeless People* was how exciting and important, technically and emotionally, was the wealth of historical material I began uncovering. History—that long look back—is central to nearly all of my characters and this is reflective of my own life, my need to define, to create a self. The fact that so many unflattering and fraudulent images of black women have been projected in the literature, I see as a positive challenge: to create a true-true self. It's what I've been about in my life and in the work. And part of that process is looking back into history and taking from it what one needs in this creation. That's one of the reasons that history is so important for me. My struggle has been to make it a natural, organic part of the fiction. I work long and hard at this. For example, in *Daughters*, instead of immediately offering up the story of Will Cudjoe and Congo Jane, I simply signal their importance in the first chapter, by Estelle having Ursa touch their statue. It's only later in the novel that we discover they serve as models for what black men and women need. As Ursa's lover tells her at one point; "You know that's what we [black women and men] really have to get back to if we're ever going to make it." Congo Jane and Will Cudjoe stand as historical referents. One of the marvelous things I learned in doing the research for *Daughters*, was that slave women, both in the United States and in the Caribbean were

very much involved in the rebellions and the uprisings. We only hear about Nat Turner and Denmark Vesey, Toussaint Louverture and Gabriel Prosser and the like. We're seldom made aware of the role women played in the resistance to enslavement. For example, my Congo Jane is based largely on Nanny of the Maroons, one of the great slave heroines of the West Indies. I also learned an important fact about the relationship of the bondsmen and women. Because slave women were subjected to the same—if not worse—treatment as the men, being forced to work in the fields, the beatings, rapes, etc., it is said there developed a great sense of cooperation, closeness, and equality between black men and women. There was a greater ability to resist together. "What we have to get back to if we're going to make it," as Ursa's lover says. And there it was historically documented. In fact, there's a term used to describe the nature of the relationship between slave men and women during that period. Angela Davis, in an article in *The Black Scholar* some years ago refers to it as "equality under the lash." The West Indian historian and present ambassador from Jamaica to the United Nations, Dr. Lucille Mair, has also written about this concept in her book on Nanny, the Jamaican slave heroine. I kept unearthing this mother lode of historical material that was never made available to me as a young woman in the schools of New York City. I had to dig it out for myself and make it central to the fictional worlds I create, an integral part of the story. This was true not only in *Daughters* but in *Chosen Place, Timeless People,* and of course *Praisesong for the Widow.* I'm so pleased that Julie Dash was able to use some of the material from *Praisesong* in her movie *Daughters of the Dust.* The scene where Ula says "It was here that they brought them. They took them out of the boats right here where we standin'" is taken directly from *Praisesong.*

Lisa: One of the things you've said about your own writing is that sometimes you've felt you weren't able to capture the oral artistry. Did you feel that *Daughters of the Dust* was able to do that? One of the things that fascinated me about the movie was that the language was so beautiful.

Paule: Well, for myself, I think I finally managed to capture [the oral artistry] in *Daughters.* I had been struggling with it for a number of years and was finally able in that novel to bring together all of the voices in my head in a way that worked. The first time I saw *Daughters of the Dust,* I found it so visually stunning I missed much of the dialogue. Then, too, I saw it in a very small theater where the sound system wasn't particularly good. When I went back a second time and I wasn't so totally caught up in the visual, I was more able to more closely attend to the dialogue. Then, it became a much greater experience for me.

Melody: I had that same experience last night seeing Endesha Ida Mae Holland's play, *Down in the Mississippi Delta*. It took a while to feel as if we could distinguish the different voices and just listen.

Paule: Yes, yes.

Melody: You talked about all the voices in *Daughters*. What about Primus's voice? It's largely absent in the novel.

Paule: Yes, because the book is primarily about the daughters, the women. Maybe I can get to Primus by talking a little bit about how *Daughters* came about. I was hard at work on *Praisesong for the Widow* when I became aware of a group of maybe four or five women milling around backstage in my mind. I really couldn't make out their faces right off; it was very shadowy. I knew though that one of them was a young woman I had been wanting to write about ever since I was her age, in my mid-thirties and for a number of reasons I had never gotten around to her. But I couldn't see the other women clearly, and among these women backstage in my mind, there was one man, a kind of polestar figure around whom the women were situated like stars in a constellation. In fact, I used "Constellation" as the title of a section of the novel. That's all I had for the longest time: these women and this one man milling around in my head like Pirandello's "Six Characters in Search of an Author." Well, they had their author but the author didn't have a story for them. And so when I finished *Praisesong*, I tried out several ideas on them and nothing worked. And when I said I tried out several ideas I mean I wrote reams and reams of pages, any number of drafts, and they just weren't right. And then one Saturday evening, about eight years ago, I was at City Center Theater on West 55th Street here in New York, waiting for the lights to dim and the curtain to go up on a performance of the Alvin Ailey dance company, and I was leafing through the program, when I came across this epigraph to one of the dances that was going to be performed that evening. And the epigraph read, "Little girl of all the daughters, you ain' no more slave, you's a woman now." I didn't know at the time that it's an old saying among southern black folks. But it struck me with the force of a revelation. Because "Little girl of all the daughters, you ain' no more slave, you's a woman now" suggested to me—other, more contemporary forms of bondage: familial, social, political, personal, the bondage of the mind and the heart, and the long struggle (which is Ursa's struggle in the novel) to overcome those kinds of dependencies and domination and achieve a truly independent self. For the first time, I had a clear sense of what I wanted to do with these characters. And I knew right off that the novel would be called *Daughters*. Usually my titles are the last thing that come to me. The book is done, it's at the publisher's, and I still don't have a title. That was not the case this time. I also knew that the daughters of the title would be those women circulating around in my head. And the little girl of the daughters would be the young woman I'd been trying to write about for the longest time. And there at their center would be the P.M., the polestar, and symbol of domination and emotional seduction. When Ursa moves against him at the end of the novel, she not only frees herself, she also frees him. As important, she destroys the constellation and its inherent inequality.

Lisa: So does she also destroy the model of Will Cudjoe and Congo Jane?

Paule: No, she doesn't. In fact, once she comes out from under the shadow of the P.M. and his aspirations for her, and the seductive nature of their relationship, the fact that he's this charming person she really can't resist, and continues to love even as she struggles against him . . .

Melody: And who has so much sexual presence . . .

Paule: That's right, oh absolutely, which is one of the things Lowell points out to her in their confrontation scene, and forces her to acknowledge. Once she breaks up the constellation and moves away from that domination and dependency the P.M. represents in her life, she will be able to write the story of Congo Jane and Will Cudjoe. Somebody asked me the other day, "Well, what happens to Ursa?" And I said, "I really can't tell you," but I know she's going to be her own person. At the end she puts her limbs one by one on the bed and finally puts to rest on the pillow the oversized forehead that she inherited from the P.M.

Melody: And it's almost as if she gives birth to herself at the end of the novel as opposed to the abortion at the beginning of the novel.

Paule: Yes, but the abortion is completed at the end of the novel because she aborts the P.M. When she feels those waves of pain when she falls on the beach—pain which she did not feel in chapter 1—she has finally, finally let him go, cut him away, while continuing to love him.

Lisa: What about the other women? Will they be able to break that connection with the P.M.?

Paule: Yes, I think so. It's suggested in Ursa's final scene with Astral Forde. Ursa assures her that she will never take the hotel from her. Ursa understands that the hotel is central to Astral's life, it's her meaningful work, to go back to your first question. As Estelle says, "She's been married to that hotel." In essence, Ursa says to Astral, "Yes, you can have it. You don't have to fear that I'm going to come and take over." She gives her that. Which is a way of breaking the constellation of lesser stars around the P.M. For Estelle, when she puts everyone out of the house at the end, tells them to "go on home, there's nothing more you can do! What's done is done," there is a possibility that she and the P.M. can perhaps recapture something of their early relationship, when they worked together as a team, and she shared his high ideals. Because the P.M. genuinely wanted to do something progressive and meaningful for his district and was not only frustrated by the political situation and the almighty presence of the United States that periodically sent the gunboats, but also by his own imperfections. I've been accused of black man bashing but I don't really accept that; I was just trying to create a complex and interesting, a credible character in the P.M. I mean how many of us aren't seduced from the high ideals we set out with? This doesn't make him weak; this doesn't make him negative; this makes him human.

Melody: I was struck by Mae Ryland saying of Sandy Lawson, who's in the same position, ". . . I'm [not] all that angry with him. I'm disappointed in him. I'm disgusted with him. . . . But I don't know as I'm ready to give up on him yet." That really echoed to me at the end that you weren't ready to give up on the P.M. yet.

Paule: Absolutely. Yes, because that's one of the things the novel's about: the need to find in those who can effect change what is positive and good and try to work with that. Because we're all needed in the struggle.

Melody: To find what is "useful," as Viney's grandfather says in the novel.

Paule: Useful, yes. Viney's grandfather says, "The woods are on fire out here and everybody who can tote a bucket of water has to come running." That's about being useful. You might say that's at the heart of the novel: being useful to something larger than the self.

Melody: Do you think of your own work in those terms? Do you think of yourself as a political writer or an activist? Is your mouth a gun, so to speak?

Paule: I don't sit down to my P.C. thinking about myself in those terms. I'm too busy struggling to find the right words and to shape the sentences. I'm not there debating with myself whether I'm a feminist writer, a political writer, a black American writer, an Afro-Caribbean writer. I don't have time for that stuff. When I'm forced to define myself and what I'm trying to do in the work, I usually start talking about the Macon Street branch of the Brooklyn Public Library. I spent an awful lot of time there as a kid, hiding out from my family, my community, and the rages of adolescence. And I was a voracious and disorganized reader; everything that came along. Zane Grey, Jane Austen, *Little House on the Prairie*, *Great Expectations*. All of it. I identified with all those characters. But after a time, I sensed something missing. I couldn't quite define what it was, until one day I came across the work of the black poet Paul Laurence Dunbar. And it came to me: I never saw myself or anyone in my community or my community reflected in any of these books that I read and loved. I was not present. I'm not talking about myself, but about the collective me. I was simply not present in the literature. And so when people ask me, "What do you see yourself doing; what is the work all about?," I answer them this way: "If someone like myself, as I was way back then—some young woman in her mid-teens, late teens, early twenties, searching for clarity and definition, some sense of herself, who she is—can go to the library or bookstore and can find herself and her life reflected in a truthful and complex way in a book of mine, I will have done my job. I will be part of an empowering act. Because I believe that once you see yourself in the literature in this complex and truthful way, it gives you, at a level beyond words, a sense of your right to be in the world. And with that, other things of a positive nature follow. You can begin moving toward clarity and definition—making demands of what you want to do and be. Moreover, you can then begin joining together with others to salvage our community, because that is the ultimate task. So if my work can give some young man or woman a sense of their right to be in the world, it is a political act, it is meaningful work, it's all the things that I set out to do, even though I could not have articulated it years ago.

Melody: Do you still feel that need today, that need that you felt as a small child, to find those books? Do you still actively seek to read Afro-American writers?

Paule: Yes, especially the works of younger writers coming along, who are so talented, many of them. But I still basically read all over the place. Last summer, for example, I read Lorene Cary's *Black Ice*; I went back and read *Ake*, a wonderful autobiography by Wole Soyinka, the Nobel Laureate from Nigeria. I read E. L. Doctorow's *World's Fair*, about growing up Jewish in the Bronx. It's a beautifully done book. Just all over the ball park. And I read not only for enjoyment, but for instruction. I'm always learning. I'm always looking to see what I can steal (and transform, of course) for my own uses.

Lisa: When you teach writing, do you do that for your students, encourage them to find readings that "give them a sense of their right to be in the world"?

Paule: Oh, absolutely. First of all I encourage them to read all the time. Because you can't hope to write fiction well if you can't analyze fiction. It also helps you increase your powers as an editor of your own work, because as you read all over the ball park as I do, you find yourself developing a greater critical sense, which you then bring to the writing. I also encourage them to initially even imitate the style of a writer whom they admire. Sometimes that helps in the process of developing their own voice and style. In the writing classes I teach we don't get to the students' work immediately. We spend a few sessions analyzing the work of the established writers, a Flannery O'Connor, for instance, who's a master of the short story. We'll just take the work apart, line by line, to see how the writers achieve their effects, how it's all been very deliberately done. That's essentially my approach to teaching. It's about helping my students to master the basics of the craft, that is, to create interesting, credible, and complex characters. And to provide them with situations, events, scenes that reveal them to the reader and also propel the story forward. Plot, in other words. There are certain mechanical aspects that make writing work. It's fine to be talented and have something to say, but the two pillars of fiction are people and plot, which is where I can be of help. So that while I encourage them to take chances, to be wild and way out, I also remind them of the verities of the craft. It's working with them on those two levels.

Melody: It seems as if you've said that your works usually begin with character, with people, and then the plot follows. Is that so?

Paule: It varies from book to book; it really does. With *Daughters* it began with the characters in my head. *Praisesong for the Widow* started with a place. I came across this place called Ibo Landing in a book entitled *Drums and Shadows*, which was a series of interviews with some very old people who lived on the Sea Islands, off the coast of Georgia and South Carolina. Nearly everyone spoke of a place on one of the islands called Ibo Landing. According to a story handed down over the years, a group of Ibo slaves decided they didn't like the looks of America as soon as they were brought ashore and turned around and walked back home across the Atlantic Ocean. That's how *Praisesong* began, with that folktale.

Melody: The way you talk about historical background, the Cuffee Ned or Congo Jane or Ibo Landing sections, reminds me of Toni Morrison and Shirley Ann Williams, who based *Beloved* and *Dessa Rose* on historical fragments they had discovered about slave women.

Paule: As I said before, I'm also very taken with historical material. I don't go about gathering it in any sort of scholarly way but through casual reading. For example, right now I'm reading Karen Brown's *Mama Lola: A Voodoo Priestess in Brooklyn* about her initiation into Haitian Vodun. I'm finding all kinds of interesting historical material there. History is important to me on two counts: the personal quest for a truer definition of self, and for the richness, texture, and resonance it lends to the work.

Melody: I really felt that texture in *Daughters* with Paul Robeson and Jackie Robinson and Alvin Ailey and all of those figures coming in.

Paule: That's how I treat not only the past history, but fairly recent history as well: weaving it into the fabric of the novel, paying homage to it even if it's just by way of naming a little boy after Paul Robeson.

Melody: Or mentioning the dancer and choreographer Judith Jameson, just in passing, there she is.

Paule: Yes, that's right, there she is, there she is. What joins writers like Toni Morrison, Shirley Ann Williams, and myself is that we've discovered this rich vein of material that was not considered worthy and we've been mining it. For example in Toni Morrison's *Song of Solomon*, her slaves were flying. Now that's an old folk story that goes way back in African-American cultural history.

Melody: And the little girl in Faith Ringgold's recent children's book, *Tar Beach*, also flies.

Lisa: You remind me of Zora Neale Hurston and what she was doing with her folklore studies. But she was severely criticized for bringing black culture into her fiction and celebrating it. The well-known conflict between her and Richard Wright was because he believed that African-American writers should write to uplift the race. How has she affected what you're trying to do? And what do you think of the conflict between those two writers?

Paule: I have the utmost admiration for them both. I can understand, in a way, Wright's opposition to Hurston's work. He was so embittered and outraged by racism, poverty, and prejudice he experienced as a boy in Mississippi, that he committed himself as a writer to protesting the treatment of black Americans in as searing a fashion as possible. So he created these larger than life heroes like Bigger Thomas in *Native Son* who has been criticized by Jimmy Baldwin and Ralph Ellison as lacking in complexity and depth.

Melody: Overwhelmingly tragic figures.

Paule: That's right. For Wright, stark, exaggerated creations highlight what happens to blacks because of racism, the brutalization. He wrote out of the way he perceived the world to be, in the Protest Tradition of the '40s and '50s. That was his vision.

Melody: I'm thinking while you're talking of the moment in *Daughters* where Robeson is grabbed by the cop and then Ursa wishes to see again his unmarred eyes. And it's as if a way of looking at the world is changed forever.

Paule: Because of that experience, absolutely. And so, Wright, having had experiences like that, heaped one upon the other, from the time he was a little boy, came to that vision. And came to it with formidable creative abilities. He was a very fine writer. There's a poem of his called "Between the World and Me" in which he describes a lynching. It's in those same stark terms, uncompromising, harrowing. He talks about the cigarette butts red from the lipstick of the women watching, lying on the ground under the body hanging from the tree. He forced us to see the horror of it. And by seeing it, to make the necessary changes. He was committed to art-as-a-weapon. So that he considered Hurston's work a kind of romanticized, folksy rendering of black experience, one he couldn't tolerate. Each artist sees the world differently. It's the same world but they perceive it as a Rashomon experience. Zora was not unaware of the horror that Wright depicted, but she was also concerned with the ways and means that we as a people have managed to deal with that, to survive it . . .

Melody: To not be tragic figures.

Paule: That's right.

Melody: To be something more.

Paule: That's right, to be something more. This was where her emphasis and her vision were. She was determined to show the world the marvelous ways in which black people through language—again language, that crucial area of creative expression—managed to assert their humanity. That was her focus. How in the face of oppression they managed to remain feeling, creative, interesting, vital human beings. And she does that through the stories told on Joe Stark's front porch in *Their Eyes Were Watching God*, by the men who were the great storytellers. Hers were the "father poets"; mine the "mother poets." Unfortunately, I came to Zora quite late in my life, years after I was out of college. In my day there were no black literature courses.

Melody: Alice Walker describes the same experience in "Zora Neale Hurston: A Cautionary Tale and a Partisan View."

Paule: That's right. I wish I had known her work earlier. I think I would have been more certain of what I wanted to do with the voices, with the language earlier on and wouldn't have had to wait till *Daughters* before it all finally came together for me.

Melody: I'm thinking of Hurston's Eatonville Anthology written with polyphonic voices, with several different voices, which is similar to what you were describing in *Daughters*.

Paule: Yes, yes. She's been a great resource for me, a great resource. Her style, her daring, the fact that she was able to be this Renaissance woman, to be all these many things . . .

Melody: To create the self.

Paule: That's right, creating the self. To be an anthropologist, ethnographer, novelist, playwright—a multi-talent. And she was great, they say, to have at a party. If you wanted to make it a real party, ask Zora.

Melody: She reminds me of another question that I wanted to ask you. Both your work and hers richly explore female sexuality. I mentioned that I always read the scene between Clive and Selina in the park aloud to my classes when I'm teaching *Brown Girl, Brownstones* because it's such a wonderful scene. Could you talk a little about that theme in your work?

Paule: One of the things women in my stories are always questioning is the role family and community impose upon them. Certainly this is true of Selina as a sexual being. As for myself as a young girl growing up in that mixed African-American and West Indian community of Brooklyn. No one talked about it. It was an issue that was thoroughly repressed. No one talked about it. You were certainly never instructed as to how one went about becoming a sexual person.

Melody: You remind me of the scene with Selina and Beryl in the park where they are trying to share information. They don't have enough to share.

Paule: Right, they don't have the vocabulary; it has not been given to them. But Selina, in many ways my idealized image in that first novel, the kind of young woman I longed to be back then, took charge of her life. She stood up to her mother and at the age of seventeen took a lover. (Something I never would have dreamed of doing!) She expresses what all the little repressed West Indian American girls of my generation could not express. It's interesting that a number of people have said that I really write these very steamy love scenes.

Melody: I would agree with that.

Paule: They come completely out of my head. [Laughs.] I think I write about sexuality, people coming together sexually, as the place, the time in our lives when we can sometimes set aside tensions and animosities and conflict that beset us, a place where, for just a short while, we come together, embrace, and sometimes truly communicate. Sometimes I use it as a metaphor for the kind of bonding that is needed between black men and women. In *Daughters* I created a "free zone" between Ursa and her lover in the early days of their relationship.

Melody: That pattern seems to imply that a harmonious relationship is a natural relationship, and in some way the conflicts are often socially constructed.

Paule: That's right. That's why Congo Jane and Will Cudjoe are so important in the novel. They are the model, the historical fact. And we—the present-day black men and women—have moved away from that kind of solidarity and equality.

Melody: Can you envision that? I mean you said you thought that Ursa could write the master's paper on Will Cudjoe and Congo Jane, on "the relatively egalitarian, mutually supportive relations that existed between the bondmen and women" (*Daughters* 11). We were wondering whether you would write that in the present tense, a mutual relationship of coleaders and coconspirators like that. Can you envision that kind of a relationship? It doesn't happen in *Daughters*.

Paule: No, it doesn't. I was looking at, dealing with, writing about our situation today. And that, to a large degree, is fraught with conflict and division. I mean, I'm not going to romanticize it. This is where we are at the moment, and it's regrettable, even tragic, but perhaps acknowledging the sorry place we've come to is the first step toward change. And I believe that change is even more possible, more likely if we are made aware that there was another period when we *did* have a greater closeness and equality and sense of cooperation and unity. So, that's all there in *Daughters*.

Melody: The historical details or myths like Ibo Landing are so liberating. They provide such models for contemporary action for your characters.

Paule: Yes. And that's where I really stop. People get impatient with me because they say I end my books at the beginning. And in a sense that's true. I'm a writer of fiction. I don't offer solutions. Rather, I suggest, I imply, the possibility of action.

Melody: Your characters need to get back in touch with that larger cultural or historical past but they also have to break with their familial past, to get rid of what Viney calls the "tin cans and bones" of their personal past, all at the same time. Two things are going on in your work at once.

Paule: Yes, because at one level, and usually the most accessible, I'm dealing with the character working out his or her personal destiny. So that, for example, *Daughters*, can simply be read as the story of one young woman trying to come out from under the shadow of a father whose love and aspirations for her have clouded both her personal and professional life.

Melody: As he does when she's swimming. *He* stands between her and the sun.

Paule: That's right. His shoulders in the way of the sun. Her personal struggle is to free herself of that particular domination and dependency. The book can be read at that level. But what I'm also trying to suggest in *Daughters* is that Ursa's struggle with the P.M. reflects the larger struggle of the Third World to free itself of the domination of the West and America. That's why the political backdrop is so important in the novel, the fact that a place like Triunion, a place like Midland City, are still under the domination of the powers that be. They are also struggling to come out from under the shadow of the forces in control of their lives. So the political is always present in the work. On the surface the stories are personal, about people. I'm a storyteller after all. But my people are defined by the world they live in, which is basically a political world, so there is always that link between the personal and the political in the work.

Melody: That seems to me to be one of the greatest strengths in your writing—your ability to create such concrete real characters, but also explore the larger cultural context.

Paule: And the political. After *Brown Girl, Brownstones*, I wrote a story called "Brooklyn" in which I had a young woman character who helped me move toward the political in my work. It was a story about sexual harassment. When the young woman, a student, resists her professor's attempts to seduce her, she begins to understand her own power; it's suggested she can now live in a way that's useful to more than just herself, a life that has a political dimension. I got a clue with that character as to where I wanted to move as a writer. It was no longer enough for me to be concerned solely with my character's personal emancipation. I had to link that to the larger context of landscape which had to do with culture, politics, with the social world these characters inhabited. With "Brooklyn" I was able to make that important breakthrough.

Melody: I wonder if you wrote that story to rid yourself of the anger that you felt.

Paule: That's right. Because the story was based on an experience I had as an undergraduate.

Melody: Did it work? And is that a connected issue to what you just said? Are you still ridding yourself of the anger?

Paule: No, I'm no longer angry; no, not at all. In fact, his country place where he always wanted to take me for the weekend is close to some very good friends of mine, so that years ago I would occasionally see him there. And we'd chat. I've forgiven him because I was able to exorcise that rage through the story.

Melody: He was useful.

Paule: That's it, he was useful, I put him to use. But for a long time after it happened, I wasn't able to write that story.

Melody: Did you watch the Clarence Thomas/Anita Hill hearings?

Paule: I did. I wrote to Anita Hill, just a brief note that said, "Thank you and bless you," because she reminded me of my own experience with the professor and I knew what she was undergoing, the brutalization, the insult and disregard.

Melody: I had the same sense. I wrote her a letter too, thinking that it was going to be hardest two or three weeks later, that she would really need some support when she got back to her regular life.

Paule: Yes, she's going to be at Hunter College I think next week and it's already sold out.

Melody: I'd like to ask you a question about one of the things I find most interesting in your work, what I think of as "ceremonies of reconciliation," a phrase which is used in the epigraph to *Chosen Place, Timeless People*. Your work is filled with characters who reconcile. Susan Willis has said that you're a writer whose task has been "to articulate the difficulties of being in two worlds at once" (53). Would you use the word "difficulties"?

Paule: No, I wouldn't. I don't agree with that at all. What I find difficult is the public's inability to understand that it's *not* difficult. Some people get very uncomfortable when they're asked to describe me as a writer. Some say, "Well, she's, you know, an African-American writer." Others say, "No, no, she's Caribbean, she's a West Indian writer." Or, "She's a feminist writer." Then again, "No, she's a black feminist woman writer." I have this long laundry list of descriptions thrown at me. And I think it's because there's a need in this country to place people in categories, especially if you're an artist. America is a society that is suspicious of the arts and artists, because the artist is essentially a questioner, a naysayer. My work, for example, continually questions the ethics of a society that is based on acquiring things. Our rampant materialism is a major theme in the work. Americans need categories for the artist so they can perhaps better understand and thus control you. In my case there's often a refusal to accept the fact that I am both African-American and West Indian. A writer who comes out of a dual tradition and who tries to honor both in her work. I have an enormous amount of trouble convincing people of that. Because I'm always trying to answer questions that I'm putting to myself through the work, I have Ursa in *Daughters* embody the theme of reconciliation. She is someone like myself, solidly American through her mother, yet part West Indian through the P.M. She's also a kind of antihero. I mean physically, she's not very heroic. She's short and small with a rather large forehead . . .

Melody: She feels squat.

Paule: That's right.

Melody: I like the way she blames her mother for the body she inherited.

Paule: Right. Astral Forde describes her as "the little waterhead child." So she's this antihero at the same time that she's Everywoman. I use her to bring together, to reconcile, the two great traditions that have gone into making me, the African American and the West Indian.

Melody: Do you think your interest in that theme originated with your fascination with the word "beautiful/ugly" that your mother used?'

Paule: Perhaps, because the concept of dualism, of each thing containing its opposite, was crucial to the way the mother poets saw themselves and the world. There was never the strict division between opposites you find in Western thought. There was always for them this complexity, this duality, this sense of the beautiful/ugly. The world as a complex creation. It's a very very African view of reality and perhaps my life reflects this principle: I'm this person who is of these two cultures, of two very complex traditions.

Melody: It reminds me of the Alice Walker line, "Folks what can look at things in more than one way has done got rare," which I often put at the top of my syllabi to encourage students to see the world as a "complex creation" (*The Third Life of Grange Copeland* 129). Your treatment of your dual cultural background is liberating.

Lisa: And that's a lot different from W. E. B. Dubois's ideas of double consciousness because for him it's a debilitating thing.

Paule: Yes, that terrible tension we live with as black Americans, being Americans and yet not accepted and treated as full citizens, can be crippling and debilitating. It can undercut our powers and make our lives unnecessarily arduous and frustrating. It's the cause of the outrage Richard Wright felt so deeply and wrote about at times with such eloquence.

Melody: Your most powerful characters are always reconcilers, beginning with the story about your grandmother, "To Da-Duh," where you admired so much her ability to bring into relation opposites rather than being somebody fragmented in opposite directions (*Reena and Other Stories*). You also dedicated *Praisesong* to her.

Paule: Yes, although in "To Da-Duh," what finally kills her is that she recognizes her world, which has to do with the earth and land and growing things, is being threatened by the world of technology that the child represents. Da-Duh senses the destructive power of the machine age, and dies.

Melody: Machines enter into your work in a lot of places, the cars, and the factories.

Paule: Absolutely. One of the major themes in the work is America's excessive preoccupation with materialism and the impact of that on its citizens and the rest of the world. I saw the community in which I grew up overtaken by that overweening need to acquire things. And for me, this overemphasis on materialism in many ways meant the death of love. That's what *Brown Girl, Brownstones* is about, the death of love. The mother acquires the house, chases out the old tenants, turns the place into a high-priced rooming house; she now has a coat with a huge fur collar and so on, but she's alienated her children. One daughter escapes into a lackluster marriage. Selina, the heroine, is gone, and her husband is no longer. So what does she have? That's the irony. The same dramatic irony is true in the case of Avey Johnson in *Praisesong*. She finds herself with the pearl necklaces, the white gloves, the trip to the Caribbean with her six pieces of matching luggage, but . . .

Lisa: She lost her spirituality.

Paule: That's it, the richness that she and that young husband had when they staged their Saturday make-believe ballroom dances at home; when they listened to the blues, the richness of the culture, they have disavowed that. And as a result, they have died in a way.

Melody: Do you think of yourself as writing about marriage? Is that one of your themes or is that something that is part of the landscape?

Paule: Part of the landscape, part of the landscape. It certainly is one of the things I'm always puzzling over in the work, as I've puzzled over it in my life.

Melody: Marriage really is an important theme in American literature that nobody talks about in the way they talk about the wilderness or the sea.

Paule: Not really dealt with, yes.

Melody: But your works seem to me to have very rich treatments of marriage.

Paule: Yes, that's true of all the novels, especially *Praisesong for the Widow*. I received a lot of positive fan letters from black males with *Praisesong*. They considered Jerome Johnson a positive image, the fact that he chose not to abandon his family, but stayed, gritted his teeth, worked hard and succeeded.

Melody: And it costs, you're so clear on what it costs him.

Paule: Yes, a kind of spiritual and emotional death. In *Daughters* I tried to suggest that marriage is a partnership—that was certainly true of the P.M. and Estelle in the early years; and Estelle insists at the end that it is going to be that again.

Melody: One last question: do you want to talk about what you're working on now or is that something you don't like to talk about?

Paule: I'm not really ready . . . I haven't written a word. I've only been thinking about it. To give you a sense of how a book comes to be, in my case, the idea for this new one goes back to my childhood, and to a photograph. When I was a kid we lived in this brownstone house we were leasing on Hancock Street. We had the first two floors, the basement, and the parlor floor. A very formal, seldom-used living room with an old upright piano was on the parlor floor. And on top of the piano was a photograph of a little boy of about three or four wearing a Lord Fauntleroy suit and holding a ball. It's the classic photograph of a kid that the family takes. He was our first cousin, Sonny, we were told. But we never got to meet him because of a dispute between the two families. And when West Indians don't speak, it lasts for a lifetime. But for whatever reason, the photograph of Sonny remained on the piano. And I used to wonder endlessly about him because we don't have a large family. From time to time over the years we would get news of him. We learned that he became a jazz musician who played the baritone sax.

Melody: Sonny's blues.

Paule: That's right. And that he went into the army and there it seems he developed some illness and died at the age of twenty-three or so. That's it, that's all I know about my cousin Sonny. And so I've been thinking I'd like to invent a life for him based on the few facts I have. As I said, I don't as yet have a word on paper, although I've started doing some research, talking to people in Brooklyn who knew him, just to get a sense of where I might take it. That's all I've got. But there is that photograph of this little boy that I so wanted to know and maybe I can get to know him by recreating him in this novel that is yet to be.

Lisa: So the work's not done yet.

Paule: No, no, far from it, far from it.

To Be in the World: An Interview with Paule Marshall

Angela Elam/1996

"To Be in the World: An Interview with Paule Marshall" in *New Letters* by Angela Elam, published in volume 62, number 4, 1996, pages 96–105. It is included here with the permission of *New Letters* and the Curators of the University of Missouri–Kansas City.

New Letters: I've read much good criticism about *Brown Girl, Brownstones*, published originally in 1959. But it really didn't catch fire with the public at first. It's such a vivid portrayal of a certain time and place, the 1930s and '40s, in—how do you refer to it?
Paule Marshall: Bajan (Ba-jen), in Brooklyn. Bajan is the shortened version of Barbardos or Barbadian, yes.
NL: Do you think the book was ahead of its time, that maybe the public wasn't ready for a young, black heroine?
Marshall: There were a number of factors. There wasn't the kind of climate within the literary community to be open and receptive to a book like *Brown Girl, Brownstones* at that time. Books by and about women were not taken seriously. That was part of it. Random House, its publisher, didn't really do the kind of promotion and publicity for the book that would have, perhaps, launched it to the public. And again, I think it was, and I don't know how conscious this was on their part, but a feeling that, well, books by women, first novels, and by black writers—they're not going to sell. There was this real feeling in a great part of the publishing world, that the black community did not support its writers, did not buy books. So, it was a critical success; it was not a commercial success.
NL: It must have made you feel good when a publisher decided to reprint it in 1981.

Marshall: I remember Florence Howe, the head of the Feminist Press, said to me: "You know, I'm always having people ask me, What happened to *Brown Girl, Brownstones*? Why don't you bring it out?" And it was a wonderful kind of relationship that was set in place between The Feminist Press and myself. I agreed to them bringing out a new edition of *Brown Girl, Brownstones*, and the book became so popular that it was one of the books that kept the doors of the press open. So it was a wonderful trade-off between my book and The Feminist Press.

NL: One of the things that struck me in this particular book—also in *Daughters*, your most recent novel—is that your dialogue is so alive, so rich.

Marshall: One of the things that I've wanted to do as a writer is to try to get down on the page some of the language that I heard coming along. I lived in this wonderful polyglot world in Brooklyn, in the '30s and '40s and early '50s, where you had all these various immigrant groups coming together. There I was, this kid growing up in a language wonderland, so to speak. There were the Italians, who were a fairly new immigrant group, who would come through the neighborhood selling vegetables on their horse-drawn carts. They were there, struggling with the English language. There were the Jews who owned the little mom and pop stores in the neighborhood. There they were, with their version of the English language. There were the Southern blacks, just up from the South, that great migration north; there they were, speaking their own brand of black English. And there also was my family, which had come to America in the early '20s, another immigrant group from the West Indies. They had their own spin on the English language. They spoke this wonderful West Indian vernacular. I heard this talk around me all of the time. As soon as I would enter that brownstone house where we lived, it was almost as if I had been transplanted to the islands—my mother and her friends kept that West Indian culture so completely intact. So one of the things I wanted to do—this was in no way conscious as I started writing—but I had the sense that that almost miraculous thing they were doing with language was passing off the scene, and I wanted to capture some of it on paper.

NL: Silla, in *Brownstones*, is such a strong woman. Her daughter Selina admires her, and at the same time is almost horrified by her, because her strength almost makes Silla seem cruel, sometimes.

Marshall: For Selina in the novel, and I think in part for myself, growing up in Bajan Brooklyn, the women who are so central to my world always seemed like these larger-than-life figures. When I began writing, I wanted to bring them center stage because they were so pivotal. They were the figures that held up the world for me.

I remember once, as a kid, I took a ride on the Fifth Avenue bus, all the way from Washington Square Park up Fifth Avenue to the Cloisters. As we passed Rockefeller Center, and that wonderful bronze statue of Atlas holding the world on his shoulders, I immediately thought of my mother. She was this figure that held up the world. She was that central to my existence. In *Brownstones*, I was trying to suggest how powerful these women were in my world. Yet, of course, they were absolutely powerless in real life. That dislocation, that sense of the difference between who they were to me and to other young women like myself, and the way they were seen by the world, was something I wanted to explore in the work.

NL: You capture that well when Selina goes off to college. She's reminded of the put-downs that are made toward her people; you get the sense of how powerless these women are in the outer world, but they do have that power on the inside.

Marshall: That's why language was such an important art form for them. It was the most readily available form, and these were women who had a tremendous need for creative expression. They used language not only to express themselves artistically, but also to have a sense of controlling the world, controlling their world. In the novel, not only do they talk about buying houses, they talk about their husbands and their children, and so on; they talk about the price of things in the stores, and they talk about politics; they also talk about what that work life of theirs is like. They use language as a means, as a kind of weapon. In fact, one of the characters, Florrie Trotman (they're sort of discussing world affairs and politics and so on), remarks that "In this white-man world, you got to take yuh mouth and make a gun."

NL: Did you feel that way when you were young, that you didn't have that power?

Marshall: As a girl child—that was the way all little girls were referred to— as girl child, I was sort of locked in, a lot of times, with these women in the kitchen, while they held forth in their coffee klatches. They didn't drink coffee, but those were coffee klatches, nonetheless. They drank cocoa and they drank tea, and my sister and I would have to keep them supplied, and be there, visible but not heard. I suspect that at a deep level, not conscious at all, there was a measure of envy on my part, a realization that I would never have that particular gift. These women were able to handle language with such ease, and to tell these wonderful stories and just sort of toss them off; and the next day they would tell another series of just absolutely excellent stories and just toss them away. I would never have that particular gift. To create on the spot, and each time to do it so brilliantly. So there was this envy of that. The ability to stand on one's feet and hold forth with eloquence. So when I began to write, it was with the realization that I would have to resort to pencil and paper.

NL: I was about to say that's probably what drove you to be a writer.

Marshall: That was one of the factors. In the novel, the young heroine, Selina, who is not Paule Marshall, but a compilation of any number of young women I knew at that time, also had this need for creative expression. This is why she becomes a dancer.

NL: I want to talk a little bit about the father, Deighton. Deighton is always dapper, dressed in great clothes, and very much involved with his shoes. I couldn't help but see that come up again in *Daughters*, where Viney's one-time boyfriend is also like that—an artist, though—and dapper, and he was into those shoes; he was obsessed with those shoes.

Marshall: I must have a thing about shoes; I didn't even make that connection. What I was trying to do with the father in *Brown Girl, Brownstones* was to suggest that he was a man with a great artistic and poetic sensibility. I mean, he does notice wonderful things—he's out there on his sun porch, you know, and that light comes in, the sun and so on. He notices and he appreciates; he offers Selina images of what the island was like, and he describes to her the foliage. I mean, he's got a poet's approach to life.

What I wanted to suggest was that this immigrant community could not afford a Deighton Boyce. In a sense, they drive him out. Their focus is so narrow and so sharply placed on acquiring a foothold in what they call "this man country"—which is how they refer to the United States. They never say America; they never say the States. It's always "this man country." They're always keeping America at a distance. Still, they're determined to establish themselves here. Because of the amount of energy that's involved in establishing those roots in this new place—the energy is so great—they can't afford anyone who is not pulling his load. That's the reason for that whole scene at the wedding when they sing to him—"Small Island, go back where you come from . . ." when they really banish him.

I mean if you want to talk about themes—the book really is about the death of love—the mother's overweening ambition to establish the family in this new place. The price she pays for that is tremendous. And that price is the alienation of her children, because both Selina and her sister leave at the end of the novel, and, as we said, the wreckage of her marriage. And so there she is, the mother, this larger-than-life figure at the end of the novel, left with her house—she finally has acquired it—and she's thrown out all of the long-standing tenants who were in the house so she can convert it into a kind of rooming house, which will permit her to make more money. So she has, in a sense, succeeded to the American dream.

NL: The death of love is something that you also discuss in *Daughters*, which moves back and forth in time and place. You'll have a scene in America and suddenly you're in Triunion, one of the islands, and in that way it is very cinematic, yet you have these characters who are struggling with the same problems. You have the couple who seem so much in love, the mother and father, again, Estelle and PM—Primus MacKenzie is the character's name. They have a different struggle and yet it's the same kind of thing.

Marshall: In my most recent book, the couple has a better chance, perhaps, of succeeding. Because it's out of love on Estelle's part that she sees to it that her husband loses the election. She's convinced that only by losing the election can he, perhaps, come back to his basic political commitment. She calls upon the main character, her daughter, Ursa, to engineer PM's defeat at the polls. She's really doing it out of a deep and abiding love for him.

NL: The interesting thing is that you have Primus on the island, a politician trying to do good for his people, and he gets caught up in all this development stuff that we have to deal with constantly here in the United States; and he loses sight of what's really good for the people.

Marshall: In most of my fiction since *Brown Girl, Brownstones*, I'm concerned on the one hand about the individual, realizing self; there's always that sort of quest for an identity that really reflects, expresses, one's true, true self. It really is about individual empowerment. Most of my women, most of my major characters, are caught up in that quest. That's a fairly standard theme in the literature.

But I realized after a time that that was not enough, that the individual struggle had to be matched with the struggle of communities to realize themselves, as well, to achieve empowerment. So I'm constantly examining both the individual and what it means to define oneself. How do you heal yourself? How do you reconcile conflicting aspects of your history? That cannot be done in isolation. It has to be done within the context of the community that shapes you, to which you belong.

That certainly is true in *Daughters*. Ursa's struggle to, in a sense, come out from under the shadow of her father, who has all of these ambitions for her, is used, essentially, as a kind of metaphor for the struggle of the larger community, not only of this island called Triunion, but also in the communities of black America. There's that ongoing struggle to achieve the vitality and independence of the community.

NL: How have you found that reflected in your own life? I know you've moved around a lot, freelancing as a writer. Did you find yourself becoming involved in the community in Richmond, Virginia, let's say, because you were there for twelve years?

Marshall: Oh, yes, it's spelled out in my own life, in practical and public ways. During the '60s, I was involved in any number of organizations and movements, and the movement in general. Living in Richmond for the past twelve years, not only does one want to contribute to various causes and organizations and advocacy groups, but I wanted to do something that was hands-on. I became a member of Habitat for Humanity, where you go out and actually build houses for people who have never known what it is to own their own house.

But, also, I see the work—writing—as a way of contributing to that larger struggle. It's the hope that because I've tried to portray characters who are complex, credible, and fully developed that offsets and rectifies that whole one-dimensional stereotyped picture of blacks in literature that's been so standard over the years. Perhaps, a young black woman, a young black man, who is searching for self will come across one of my books, and see himself or herself and perhaps even their world, reflected in a truthful and complex way. I believe that seeing oneself reflected truthfully in the literature is a kind of empowering act. It not only gives you a sense of your right to be in the world—this is one of the fantastic things that literature can do—but it also gives you, then, the power to move to the next phase. From your own personal empowerment, you can begin to mobilize, to really bring about the liberation of your community. This is the way I see the work having a direct connection with the ongoing struggle.

The Art and Politics of Paule Marshall: An Interview

James Hall and Heather Hathaway/2001

Previously unpublished. Printed by permission of James Hall and Heather Hathaway.

HH: We would like to focus today primarily on *The Fisher King* since it is the most recent of your novels. We find interesting the use of a male protagonist and, more specifically, that of a child. Why did you choose a child narrator in this instance?

PM: If you look at some of the other work, children are important to the stories. Certainly there's Selina in *Brown Girl, Brownstones* whom we meet when she is seven or so. There's also Robeson, the little boy in *Daughters*, as well as Marion in *Praisesong for the Widow*, the daughter who forces her mother to start examining her life. So children do matter in the work. When I started thinking about a novel that would deal with a jazz musician who, although he is a background figure, is central to all of the action, I was faced with the question of how I would portray him and his world. I'm not a musician, I don't play an instrument, I certainly couldn't deal with jazz in a technical way. So how was I going to manage this?

The story of the novel is based on the memory of the formal photograph of my boy cousin that sat on top of the upright piano at home. Although I never met him, I did know that he became a jazz musician who played the baritone saxophone. I knew I could not write with authority about that boy, as the jazz musician he becomes, as the dissident, the artist, who goes against the values and mores of his community. But perhaps I could speak to his life through his grandson, Sonny Payne. The grandson might serve me best because he could bring a wonderfully innocent presence in the novel, given all of the rivalries, the conflicts, the suspicious and doubtful motives of the adults around him. He could also, this little boy, serve as a link of all the generations. Four generations are dealt with in *The Fisher King*, and little Sonny takes the novel into the twenty first century, he brings it up to date. Moreover, he possesses the capacity to reconcile Florence Varina and Ulene, those two embittered old women who are his great-grandmothers. Because of their love for the child, they are able finally to say something kind about each other. Only fleetingly, they don't relent—Ulene does not relent and attend the memorial concert, for example—but she has a kind word to say about Florence Varina and vice versa. So the child serves as a reconciling element in the novel.

Sonny also embodies another important theme in *The Fisher King*, which is the need for unity in the black world. In his person, the boy embodies all the wings of the black diaspora. He's African through his father, the deported vendeur on the steps of *Sacre Coeur*. He is also both African American and West Indian through his mother—what does Florence Varina say to him?—"You got some of *all* of us in you, dontcha? What you gonna do with all of that colored from all over creation, you got in you? Better be somethin' good." And it's the possibility of *good* coming out of this little boy that has to do with his innocence, with the role he plays in reconciliation, as a healer. Even though I dealt with children in my other work, this is the first time I think that I've worked with a child character in a larger, more thematic way.

HH: Yes, and significantly he needs to *stay* a child in order for him to work, in comparison to Ursa, for instance, to whose childhood we only return through memory, or Selina, who grows up throughout the course of the novel. I was struck by how, in showing us the story through his own innocent eyes, you were able to temper any skepticism readers might have about the various relationships in the novel. Sonny's vision and intentions are pure; think of when he takes part of Florence Varina's tree into Ulene's home and then leaves it there. Then he even brings it to Hattie's, doesn't he?

PM: Yes, "where are you going with that thing?," she asks him. It's an alm of peace, symbolic of his efforts to bring about forgiveness and reconciliation.

HH: In addition to a new type of narrator, you also experiment with a different narrative frame in this work. Can you tell us about that?

PM: One of the courses I've been teaching recently is called "The Craft of Short Fiction: The Short Story," and I've fallen in love with the form. I can't *write* short stories, but one of the things that I've come to love about the form is how its brevity, its compression, allows for so much implication and suggestion. That's one of the things I was experimenting with in *The Fisher King*. "Can I possibly write a more compressed, tight, pared-down kind of

novel and yet still have it retain the focus and complexity of a full-blown work of fiction? This was indeed a challenge because there is a lot of the Victorian novelist in me, you know! I like those books that go on and on!
JH: There's also a cycle of short, long, short, long in your works.
PM: That's right, yes. And now I've gone to shorter, shorter! I tried the shorter form with *Praisesong* and people had any amount of trouble with that. I can't tell you the trouble they're having with *The Fisher King*! [laughter]
HH: I've found that, regardless of the length, I'm incapable of reading your work quickly because there's so much to digest. So much is suggested that I constantly find myself reading, pausing, thinking, going back to an earlier section. So while the form might be shorter now, there's nothing lost, there's nothing left out.
PM: That's right, even the short books are not a fast read. I wanted to challenge readers also in *The Fisher King*. I wanted readers to be involved in the book with the same intensity that I was. I wanted them not just to deal with surface story but to unearth the themes and concerns below the surface. The reader of *The Fisher King* is going to have to work almost as hard as I did. True, there are some who feel that it's a surface book that is a quick read. Yet even they say, "I really have to go back and read this again," which suggests to me they sensed there was more to the surface story, and they are intrigued and interested in probing more deeply to find out.

One of the themes that has escaped nearly everyone has to do with the nature of love. This child comes along and all of these people fall in love with him, but the way they love him also forces us to question the nature of love. All of the people in the novel bring their own essentially selfish agendas to their love for little Sonny. You know, some readers have terrible problems accepting the ending of the book. When it is suggested, and only suggested—it's not stated flat out (I would shoot myself if I ever did that as a writer!)—that Hattie allow Sonny to remain in America, readers cry, "How could you take him away from Hattie?" Well, I was simply trying to force them to examine that love. "Just *look* at this love they all *profess* for this little boy." But the love they profess is really about addressing their *own* needs.
JH: Their own needs and different parts of the child's needs too; no single person can bring everything that he needs. One of the reasons why I found myself having to make my way slowly through the book is because of the historical references in the novel. Not only am I engaged by the emotional depths of the family drama, but the historical resonances are so powerful that I can't read the book and not think about James Baldwin and Sonny Rollins and Bud Powell and Mary Lou Williams . . .

PM: And John Coltrane. Yes, because of that nightclub in Paris that has his portrait—it's still there. I used that as the model for the whole sense of Sonny Rhett Payne's portrait that hangs outside. It's all there—what happened to jazz musicians in Paris over that period.

JH: One story in particular that I couldn't get out of my head was Baldwin's "Sonny's Blues" in which two brothers, one of whom, like Everett, committed himself to the possibilities that might be found in his music while the other brother struggles to make sense of that choice, and in some ways, never comes to terms with it. I was wondering why you consciously decided to go back to that moment in the fifties now. Heather and I were discussing, for instance, how the image of the brownstones marching in goosestep in *The Fisher King* uses language almost identical to that in *Brown Girl, Brownstones*. Was there something about that moment you wanted to return to or did you have a desire to go back to think through some historical course in Brooklyn?

PM: Well, in a sense it was a kind of return to Brooklyn—which for me is essentially the beloved country, the source of who I am as a woman and a writer. I wanted to more fully develop one of the themes that was not given its full weight in *Brown Girl, Brownstones*: namely, Selina's whole struggle to be an artist. The fact that I kept the photograph of my boy cousin on top of the piano in my head over the years indicates that it spoke to me in some profound and deep way. This cousin of mine that I never met who became a jazz musician, this Sonny, was so much a part of my life as a little girl. I wondered about him, wanted to play with him, but never met him. Then I learned later on that he had become a jazz musician, which was an extraordinarily brave thing for him to do given our community—it was extraordinarily brave to go against the grain of that community of strivers, both from the West Indies and the deep South.

HH: Extraordinarily brave—not unlike becoming a writer! [laughter]

PM: Well, that's it! That's why I held on to it for so long in my consciousness because I sensed that it was going to permit me, if I could ever get around to writing the story, to deal with my own struggles with that community. I needed to go back to those houses, to that world that was both West Indian and African American, my dual heritage, and *The Fisher King* permitted me to do that.

HH: It's interesting to think of *The Fisher King* in relation to *Brown Girl, Brownstones* because so many of the themes, as you just mentioned, are suggested with Selina but not developed. Do these connections extend perhaps, even to small details, like the photo? The picture of the little boy on the piano makes me think of the photo on the mantle of Selina's family—the photo that included her brother but not Selina because it was taken before she was born. She is curious about the brother that she didn't know, the one who was there before she was and then gone. Was that another piece working in the back of your mind?

PM: No, I didn't make that type of clear-cut connection in creating this work.

HH: [Laughter] No, of course not! That's what *we* (as literary critics) always do! Impose . . .

PM: Yes, you impose what you impose! There is a lot resonating in the writer; we don't consciously take material out of the reservoir and place it on the table and say, "This is the way the connections work." No. No.

HH: Well, as a matter of fact, in preparing for this interview, Jim and I talked about the troublesome role of the scholar or critic—about how our compulsion is to uncover patterns, imagine order, create connections when the author may neither have seen nor intended for any of those patterns to exist.

PM: Well, I think that's the tendency of the non-writer. I can see how it's done. You could take the character of Selina from *Brown Girl, Brownstones* and say, "Well, you know, Merle, in a sense, is a grown-up Selina, who is demanding to be heard." You could take Marian, in *Praisesong for the Widow*, this daughter who insists that her mother become a more emancipated kind of woman, and say, "Look, there's that Selina again." But I think it's a dangerous enterprise. Nevertheless, it's done and that's what putting a book out there in the public domain is all about. It often becomes to others something altogether different from what it means to the writer. It's just open to all of that. It is exciting, in a way, that you can see all of these patterns and order. But for me, *The Fisher King* was simply a book through which I discovered some things I wanted to say and I created characters who could help me say them.

HH: I'm intrigued by how the music itself functions as a character who commands a "presence" in the book without us ever hearing a sound or even seeing a note transcribed. That's another element that slows us down as readers because it insists upon our attention to auditory aesthetics. The concert scene, for example, leaves me imagining the sounds of the songs and wondering, "What is Jojo's song like?" Again, it's the mere suggestion of the sound that is so powerful because of the freedom and responsibility it gives the reader to create the sound in his or her mind.

PM: Yes, that's exactly what I was trying to do with this novel; implication and suggestion are what *The Fisher King* is really all about. It does demand that the reader fill in, imagine what the song "Basically Bach" must have been like because we know this was a boy who was forced to play Bach and yet was driven to play jazz. How did he bring the two together? My goal was just to put it there; that's why the book is so indebted to the short story form. That's also why, perhaps, readers who like my other work have problems with *The Fisher King*—because it doesn't give them as much. In the past I would have written—and agonized over for months!—a paragraph that would have spelled out in great detail what the song to JoJo was all about—you know, using more than five adjectives to describe a single certain thing! I decided to pull back with this book to see if I couldn't do it in a tight, economical way.

PM: Yes, it was hard for me to do because I am a writer who is in love with language. I just love to go on and on! I have also been committed for so many years to making sure that the reader sees as I see, which means I have got to go into a lot of description. I am, as someone said, "a picture writer." I don't know whether that was a compliment or an insult! But in *The Fisher King* I decided, "Let's see if I can't do it another way." I think you really you have to, at some point, challenge yourself in these ways as a writer.

JH: Was Hattie's speech at the concert one way to do that—to force yourself to stop by using the structural limitation of her speaking to an audience in a confined space of time? Did you think, "I can't let her go on forever because she has to get off stage now."

PM: Yes. That did serve me well. I wanted to do some filling in, I wanted to give some sense of the unconventional yet very committed life that those three young people had together over the years, but I needed to do it without pulling away from Sonny and the ongoing narrative. How was I going to give that information? The concert served my purpose.

HH: I wonder how many people get frustrated with or don't like the book it because of its troubling ending. It is troubling to think of Edgar's motivations and whether it was appropriate for him to spy on Hattie. There's a lot of unresolved pain at the end of that novel and, especially as Americans, we really want the happy ending.

PM: Yes, I experienced that type of reaction at Black Oaks Bookstore in Berkeley, which is a wonderful place that has invited me to give a reading with each of my books. But they weren't so happy to have me this time! A woman said to me, "Well, I loved *The Fisher King*, but that ending! I can't forgive you for that ending because I'm a grandmother and I know about grandchildren." The readers got so involved emotionally! Well, of course, on one hand a writer wants this because a book that has some merit to it is an emotional as well as an intellectual experience. But it seems that this ending, *this* ending—even the *New York Times* said, "Oh, the ending is a fright!"—they also wanted a happy ending. Well, the book is not about happiness, for god's sake, it's about the way we are as humans! With all of our mixed motives! Here is Edgar, seducing this little boy—seducing him—over and over. It was very skillfully done, but it was still seduction. On Edgar's soul rest the burdens of, first of all, not understanding his brother and second, not coming to his brother's rescue when he reached out to him. How was he going to make up for that? All that he accomplished in his life couldn't make up for his sense of betrayal and failure, so he used this child to help assuage that pain. And Hattie! Her love is not pure. I mean, why not permit that little boy to have a sense of family?

HH: It's all about ownership, so much of the time.

PM: Ownership, yes, because Sonny, the child, embodies for Hattie the only true family she ever had. He embodies those three people who were so central to her life—Sonny Rhett, Cherisse, and JoJo—to whom she was truly mother. She was using this little boy, as much as she loves him, for her own selfish reasons. I was trying to say, "This is the way we are," and not to pass judgment on any of them. Those two great grandmothers, how they alienated the children they profoundly loved by demanding they be other than what they were! It really is a book that looks at the whole nature of love.

JH: I was actually worried, as the book was working toward its conclusion, that there would be a happy ending.

PM: Now you know I wouldn't disappoint you like that! Not Paule Marshall!

JH: I had a hard time understanding Hattie's attachment to Paris. She never learns the language, she never really makes it "home," and yet she can't leave it. It's clearly a love-hate relationship.

PM: Yes, very much so. Her commitment is to those two people who were the center of her life. You know, when she sees the nightclub scene of the debut, she sees that triangle, the three of them. She's the base and she will never leave. She goes to the cemetery all the time to visit their graves. For Hattie, the "City child," a foster care child, they were her family.

JH: How difficult was it to write about that triangle because it's obviously something that could be exoticized?

PM: Right. I decided to give it a fairly deft touch, not to linger with it, not to spell it out. I just tried to suggest that there was a kind of internal harmony to it. At one point they all are celebrating the first birthday of JoJo. At another they make an accommodation to the fact that Hattie and Sonny

Rhett would be involved sexually when they were on the road, and when they would come back to Paris they would still have their little threesome family. This was simply how they lived. This is why Paris was so important in the novel, of course, because it was a city that would tolerate and accept that kind of unconventional life. I didn't want to go into great depth because it would move me away from what I saw as the essential theme of the novel.

HH: Handling it deftly also emphasizes the authenticity or sincerity of their love for one another. Despite the unconventionality of their relationship, regardless of where individual readers stand on that, you make clear that these people loved each other. That's the bottom line.

JH: It's functionality, compared to other triangles in the book, is what's striking.

HH: Yes, and in its functionality it really calls into question a different kind of love. What is marriage? Is marriage an artificial institution?

PM: Absolutely.

HH: By not being more detailed about the sexuality and sensuality in the novel, their love almost rises to a level of transcendence. Is that what their love is supposed to be about?

PM: That's certainly what I was striving for. I knew that I had to give some details in order to set it up, so that's why it was very important to have that latent period between Cherisse and Hattie during their adolescence. It very clearly establishes their sexuality. It's important that Cherisse is the one in Paris who writes and says to Hattie, "It's just not the same without you." Cherisse was very much a part of that triangle.

HH: Yes, she's the one who says, "We share," *partager*.

PM: Doing it in that once-over-lightly way has a greater impact than if I'd gone through that whole business, which I could do, of spelling it out gesture by gesture, touch by touch, graphically.

HH: I have a question about that. Does JoJo leave because she sees Hattie and Cherisse being intimate? Is that really what drives her away?

PM: Yes, and this is where perhaps I could have done just a tad more with JoJo to show the trauma of the sudden breakdown of her life—the wonderful life she knew in the 5th Arondissement, her school, her being dressed neatly, her having her own room, three people adoring her. This suddenly came to an abrupt end. I wanted to say very lightly, very quickly, that when they moved to rue Sauffroy she becomes a very different person. The thing that, for JoJo, very clearly spells the end of the life she once had was the revelation of the sexual love between her two mothers. She is a girl who is going through all of this. I've never thought of a sequel before, but if I can do it, I might explore that in some way; yes, that's worth some thought.

JH: Explore the repulsion, or the shock? Or JoJo's life? Where she is now?

PM: Yes, where she went, how she went, what happens. People say, "But what happened to JoJo?" She is in the book in such a minor way yet there is for some, I think, a sense—and this is what details will do for you in a novel—a sense of those pictures torn and left on the floor, including even the baby pictures. Somehow that image stays with readers. They want to know about JoJo.

JH: From the very beginning JoJo is interesting. It is disorienting from the start how she is related to these three people: Hattie tells Sonny Rhett when they are in bed that he needs to have a baby with Cherisse because "everything will be perfect then."

PM: That's the unconventional nature of their love, of their relationship. You know, that really hasn't been dealt with yet by the critics. I think there is a sort of stand-offness.

JH: Well, even with the power of that triangle, both Hattie and Sonny have their *medicaments*. It is not dwelled upon, you touch on it two or three times in a way that is not moralistic. It is just the suggestion that, even as powerful as that triangle is, these folks have had other lives with other difficulties. You get the sense that they have their own struggles to continue with, however satisfying, however comforting, their collective relationship might be.

HH: If I think about where the real connection is in that threesome, it's between Hattie and Sonny because Cherisse, in some ways, is not capable of that kind of love. That's part of the point, isn't it? Sonny Rhett says to Hattie about Cherisse, "We both know that she wants to be admired."

PM: Certainly admired more than loved! There are people like that—they want to be admired, not loved so much. Cherisse, who is fragile in the sense that she understands her limitations, has been able to create a life for herself that will be satisfying. I mean she becomes *Français*!

JH: But she can't sing.

PM: But she cannot sing, yes, she cannot sing. That's right. Like Ursa in *Daughters*, she has come out from under the shadow of that red rock. This is why her rejection of her mother and the States is so complete—all of that reminds her of her limitations, her fragility, her failings. These are all people who have their own particular pain in the novel, and yet together they have managed to come up with a life that brings some pleasure and joy. We really have to find little areas in life that bring a measure of satisfaction, of pleasure, and they've done it, while they're suffering. Some people see only suffering and pain in the novel, unfortunately. But I hope that it is more complex than that.

JH: Part of the painful irony that moves their relationship ahead is what happens in the history of jazz and the decline in the interest in the music that Sonny plays.

PM: Yes, along with the emerging racism in France. All of that is backdrop. But that is part of the world they are in. The novel deals with the very real history of the decline in the adulation of the black musician that took place around that time.

HH: Did you ever live in Paris?

PM: I have been to Paris a lot and I have lived there for a couple of months. I had an apartment over near the *bois de boulogne*, which is really a working-class neighborhood. When I am in Paris, I spend a lot of time on the metro; I am a great metro person. I might be staying at a hotel in the Latin Quarter or the 5th Arondissement, but I am on the metro all the time going out to the other Paris. In the novel, I wanted to get away from that whole romantic image of Paris—which is why the book is having so much trouble being translated into French! I was just over there recently to give a talk at the Pompideau Center and I thought I would try to see if I could get some publishers interested in bringing out a French edition of the book. I remember one translator saying to me: "But you know, there are some *nice* places in that Arondissement!" It was clear she was so insulted! So they are very sensitive, and then of course there is the figure of Madame Molineaux! But that is the reality of Paris today that I want to touch on.

JH: What makes them uncomfortable with that particular portrayal of Madame Molineaux?

PM: Well, that she is an alcoholic. They are also very sensitive about their own feelings towards the Algerians. There is a lot of discomfort about accepting that, and to have someone—especially an outsider—writing about it with a fair amount of truth is disturbing because they know that that is what those neighborhoods are like.

JH: I also see Madame Molineaux somewhat lovingly in her alcoholically charged moments playing Monopoly with this little boy. Again, there is this odd intimacy that is created out of necessity on both their parts.

PM: Yes, that's right. People form relationships that help to sustain them. Here is this old woman whose neighborhood is changing, the great love of her life is gone, but there's the little boy whom she can accept even though he is an intruder. She can accept him! But she can't accept the Algerians. All the complexity that goes into the relationships we form and what we seek in those relationships is part and parcel of what the novel is about.

HH: Complexity, yes, but there is as much beauty in the relationships that are not so complex. I am thinking of the innocence and honesty that characterizes Sonny's relationship with the three older women in the novel. He accepts both his great grandmothers and Madame in a way that is unconditional. He just loves them. It does not matter whose hand is shaking or whose head is nodding, and that unconditional love provides a corrective for us when we read it.

PM: Yes, one of the reasons technically I had to introduce Madame Molineaux early on was to prepare us to accept that Sonny can accept these two great grandmothers so easily because he has already had an experience of living around old people. Edgar asks him, "You're around old people a lot, aren't you?"

HH: How painful is it for you to go through the emotions in the depth required to write about them well?

PM: It is painful, but it is what the writer really has to accept about the art. Ralph Ellison has been very helpful to me in this instance. He really insists upon the pleasure and the pain that is so much a part of writing fiction. I accept that. I cannot tell you what goes on in that room in which I write! The gnashing of teeth, the tearing of hair! No, I would not inflict that upon readers! They don't want to hear it by the way; they want to think that there's a muse who comes along, places his or her hand gently on your shoulder, and then it all flows. Or they'll say, "Why does it take you so long?" as though it somehow just magically happens. It is just hard drudgery, work, work, work. But it is work that brings a satisfaction when it comes out right that you just cannot describe—you cannot describe the pleasure of it. I try not to convey so much the pain, but rather those moments of joy. When Ulene turns to that little boy and says, "You've given me an easement," there's a moment there that, in a sense, tempers all of the pain that you can feel about her situation beforehand. Or when Florence Varina sees him as her escort, this gentleman from Paris, France! Those are moments where the pain of life is softened, tempered. I regret that more of that isn't seen in the novel.

HH: I think it is seen. I personally don't find this a dark or depressing novel. Your portrayal of Hattie, for example, is so real that we come to "know" her, and with that kinship comes a deep sense of compassion for the emptiness that led her, after these deaths, to need to cling to Sonny so much. Their relationship is wonderful and joyful at times, but the parts that hurt are those that force us to recognize, through Hattie, the ways in which we, like her, are all too human.

PM: Yes, that's it—and that is the key word—the essence of human nature.

JH: The parts that hurt are not necessarily the moments of extreme pathos. There is something about recognizing and connecting with the most basic struggle and the ways in which, in that recognition, your attention moves on to how you suppress that struggle in your own life. Right? The boy, Sonny, in his own desire to return again "tomorrow and the day after the day after the day after that forever" is also obviously heading toward a disappointment as much as he is toward the reconstruction of something that has been absent for him for long time. You can't return tomorrow and tomorrow and tomorrow. Again, the powerful tension for me is between, on the one hand, the way Hattie insists to Edgar that families look like a lot of things—

PM: Right. There are all kinds of families and blood's got nothing to do with it.

JH: —but on the other hand, the way we are hardwired to need to know certain things. As we were saying before: who is JoJo, and where is she, and what has happened to her? I find myself interested in the obsession in this country with genealogy and being able to trace back so far, as if that clarifies somehow who we are. As someone pointed out to me, the farther you go back, the further you get from who you are! The ancestor you find five or six generations back is someone you actually share with hundreds of people. So you haven't found out anything more about yourself; instead, the past shows less and less of who you are in a way. You are who you are at the moment and that consists in part of the network you create around you that works.

HH: So you're saying that family is primarily culturally constructed. That's one element, but there is some significance to the notion that blood is thicker than water. Sonny's never seen his cousins, he's never met his uncle, he doesn't know his great grandmothers and yet he feels an almost intuitive love for them.

PM: Yes, because as deeply attached as he is to Hattie—seeing her as father, mother, sister, and brother, seeing her as the one who really, in a sense, stands between him and all of the hurt in the world—what does he long for? To be grown up so that one day he can take the train and go down to Toulon and try to find that mother, so that he can climb up to the *Sacre Coeur* and ask if anyone has ever known his father. He is reminded of his father by the guys with the hard hats who are renovating the old houses along Macon Street. He's acutely aware that an element is missing in his life and that he can talk about it only with those cousins of his, people who will be able to understand because they are in the same situation.

HH: Yes, my favorite image in the novel reveals just how attached Sonny is to Hattie. When Edgar suggests that Hattie is "old," Sonny panics a bit. At the thought that she might be old, that he might lose her, Sonny is described as feeling that "balloon in his chest begin to fill again, ready to stifle his breathing, his heart, and to bring on the floodgate." That's such a beautiful description; I know exactly how that feels.

PM: This is one of the reasons that all the blood, sweat, and tears, and tearing of the hair goes on for a writer. How do you find the images that would be in keeping with an eight year old? You struggle a lot to convey his feelings in terms that might seem simplistic to the reader but are in keeping with the way the child would describe it to himself. Part of why the book is so compressed is because I had to work hard to hone the language so that it would be in keeping with Sonny's point of view, Sonny's perspective. But it is not a cute book. That was one of the things I was in dread of! Because I was dealing primarily with a perspective of an eight year old, I was worried that it would come off as cute. So I had to do a lot of restraining, a lot of holding back, to state things simply but truthfully in his terms. It's a wonderful challenge to pare down the language.

HH: Well, you do a great job of it; Sonny's emotional life is as deep as anyone's in the novel. Despite the limited perspective he has as an eight year old, he possesses as sophisticated a sense of connection and confusion as everybody else.

PM: I had to really go back in time to accomplish that. What was that little boy in the photograph on top of the upright piano really like? Who was the little girl looking up at him, wanting to know and play with him? What was happening in their heads, in their feelings? One of the nice things about being a writer is that you really have to be close to that sense of wonder, of curiosity, and the feelings of a child. I depended a lot on that in this book. I think I was prepared for it by Robeson. Some people say that the character they love most in *Daughters* is Robeson. Creating him helped me try to bring off this little boy in a way that would make him a real little boy, with depth and complexity. Also, in having him be a boy, I could really use that whole Arthurian legend in a way that would make sense because Sonny is the knight Percival who comes along and rescues the wounded king and protects his kingdom. With a girl it would be different, it would be hard to have the image really work. I get a lot of problems with the title too: "Who is the Fisher King? That was a movie, wasn't it?" [laughter] So the book evokes all kinds of questions, complaints, praise and damning and so on . . . it's interesting, a book that's only 225 pages, the shortest book I've ever done!

HH: Did it start big and then did you cut and cut and cut? Or did you know all along that it would be shorter than all the others?

PM: No, it didn't start big; of course, I went through any number of drafts. But I knew at the very outset that I wanted to try my hand at a lean book that would really get away from the literary language. One of my great struggles involves overstating things, and I've really worked on that over the years. It's not as literary as say, as *Soul Clap Hands and Sing* which is very decorative. In *The Fisher King* I tried to get away from that excess and I saw that I might be able to do it if one of the principal characters was a child. I wanted to see if I couldn't use the child as a way of imposing a kind of surface simplicity in the book. He is an important character and is also the point of reference for the reader, because all is revealed through him. We learn about what's been happening in these two families, what happened to his grandparents and so on, as it is revealed to him.

HH: Tell us about his two great-grandmothers.

PM: One of the ongoing themes in the work has been the immigration/migration part of our history. The fact that one great-grandmother is from the West Indies and one is from the Deep South permits me to introduce that important element in the novel. It also permits me to talk about community conflict. Again, in a very subtle way, I wanted to make the point of how dangerous it is and how the black community, made up of these two major elements, cannot afford that kind of conflict. It goes back to the personal because someone like myself who was West Indian through my parents, but also very much African American, was caught in that dilemma. I would hear African Americans say the unflattering things that came out of the mouth of Florence Varina when I was a child. I would hear the equally unflattering things that West Indians said about African Americans. Of course it all had to do—the tension, the conflict—with the scramble over the few crumbs from America's economic table. But it was a very painful thing for me because, as I saw it, I was both! I was both! So I resist when critics try to make me solely a Caribbean writer and, grudgingly sometimes, an African American writer. The only one who has really captured where I stand as a writer, the only one who has been able to articulate it for me, is Toni Cade Bambara. We were once at a conference at Dartmouth College speaking with a group of black students. The first question thrown at me by a young black student—one who definitely had an "attitude"—was "where do you think you belong, you know, your work." Well, I was ready to get an attitude also, and Toni came to my rescue! She said, "You know, for years when I taught Paule Marshall's work at Rutgers, I always taught her as a writer of the diaspora who is really addressing the great wings of our journey." To get that into the work, to have people recognize it and to relate to it in some way, has been a real struggle for me. This again is why a Sonny is so crucial in that novel.

HH: Yes, and in comparison to something like *Brown Girl, Brownstones* where Selina is "biologically" West Indian but culturally diasporic, Sonny is the literal and figurative union of those great wings.

PM: Absolutely.

HH: It's interesting that you say people want to make you more of a Caribbean writer because when I first was introduced to your work as a student in the early 1980s, we were in the midst of an explosion of "black women writers"—you, Bambara, Toni Morrison, Alice Walker, Jamaica Kincaid, Gloria Naylor, Gayl Jones—and all of you were known as just that, by this generic label of "black woman writers," whatever that meant. What actually led to my own scholarship on your writing was my concern that readers were overlooking the diasporic side. That generic label, or even the slightly more specific "African American woman writer" just didn't make sense to me—not for anyone, but especially not for you.

PM: There you are. There you are. My feeling is I could be placed anywhere. I dislike the categorization. I dislike the pigeonholing. But of course, that's so American. Americans can't deal with complexity. They need to have a hole for you.

JH: Was all the media and other attention that was directed to your writing and that of other black women writers in the mid-1980s a cause for optimism, or was it a cause for suspicion, nervousness?

PM: I dealt with it in terms of how movements come and go. America is great for that—there's always something flowering up, getting a little attention for a time, and then fading off the scene. So even though I was very pleased that attention was being paid—that we weren't seeing our literature only in terms of Baldwin, Wright, and Ellison—I was also aware that it would fade off the scene gradually, which it has to a large degree. But I was pleased by the fact that some people realized that I had struck the note early on, in the very first thing that was published of mine, "The Valley Between." There this young woman was already wrestling with the question of her right to some kind of self-definition, to a life and work that was her own.

JH: I get the sense from occasional pieces you were doing at the time that you were perceptibly uncomfortable about how intercommunity gender dramas were being played out in not necessarily productive ways.

HH: You mean like *Reckless Eyeballing* [by Ishmael Reed]?

JH: Yes, well that would be one example! [laughter] But more generally, with the ways in which folks egged Reed on and encouraged him to satirize various things.

PM: Such as the denigration of women and so on? I was teaching one semester in the early 1980s at UC-Berkeley where Ishmael was already installed, and I can't tell you how disrespectful he was of Alice [Walker]. I gave a party and Alice called me and said, "Is Ishmael going to be there," and when I said "Yes," she just didn't come. It was all about scrambling for the few crumbs yet again.

JH: Part of the cost of simplistic national or gendered categories is what they leave out, and one of the categories in which I've always felt strongly that you belong is that of political writer.

PM: Absolutely! The only critic that has really appreciated that, but stated it in a negative way, was Christopher Lehman Haupt, who reviewed *The Chosen Place, the Timeless People* for the *New York Times*. He understood the politics of the novel and yet chided me for writing politics. That novel really is about the West and the rest of us. But again, always, even when the political and social concerns are at the center of the story, I'm committed so profoundly to being a storyteller. The surface story has to work. At the same time, what makes writing interesting for me is being able to locate below the surface all of these truly important themes and concerns.

JH: And sometimes just to say, in the most direct way, what is wrong with the social order as it is.

PM: Yes, I can create a Merle who will just say it out front.

HH: Tell us about Florence Varina. She's about as different from a Merle as you can get! I'm interested especially in the "beauty queen" side of her and your purpose in creating that.

PM: Florence Varina is like a lot of people growing old but not being able to accept that fact. I see it all the time in older women who wear too much make-up and have various cosmetic operations. This is so much her struggle. She was always this person who dressed well and she holds on to that as part of her definition. That is who she is. It cost her her marriage, but she had to be stylish. She had to have a house that was, as Sonny puts, like a *palais royale*. He'd never been inside one, but he was sure that's the way it must have looked! Again, in trying always to see things through his eyes, I had to do a lot of homework. How is he going to react to that living room? He had to react in terms of who he was, where he came from, and as a little kid.

JH: Florence Varina is a wonderful character to caution against the speed with which we might judge behaviors, because at one moment her concern with style can seem an imitation of an upper middle-class ideal, but then when she comes outside with Sonny in her "final performance," it has to do with elevating a moment for him. He picks up on how ill she seems to be, and that she would put herself together for him in response to him being well dressed humbles us as readers because we know we were judging her or uncomfortable with her at an earlier moment.

PM: But even before, when we first meet her in the novel—and yes, she is this pretentious, snobbish, impossible creature, full of prejudice—when she says, "Been holding in too much, too long," you know the depth of her pain. It's always about suggesting the whole complex picture.

HH: You provide through her an interesting commentary on how so many women, Cherisse being another one, identify themselves based solely on only external perceptions. "If *you see* me this way then *I am* this way." But they lack a core knowledge, a reverence for the central person they are underneath all that. This is something the other grandmother, Ulene, seems to have all along. While we don't get the whole picture of her life, we do understand that she is a woman who is certain about certain things—namely, who she is and what she wants for her children. For Florence Varina, on the other hand, the bus has to keep coming by so that she can do the "performance"; it seems that so much of her identity is bound up in performance. But that, to me, is another element that makes her so profoundly human.

PM: Yes, but that performance also permits her to retain her house and her life. Again, it's not just because she needs to act out of this construct; no, it's a very practical business. This is why Ulene, at the end, is able to say she knew better how to cut and contrive than even I. Then there is the irony in how Cherisse is so much her mother's child, the irony of it! Her whole concern with clothes and appearance, and so on—she's Florence Varina all over, the mother she despises.

HH: How about one last question before we take a break? Why did you set *The Fisher King* in 1984, as opposed to the time in which you were actually writing it?

PM: I wanted to avoid the nineties and a lot of the cultural stuff that was going on then because I felt that using that as a time frame would intrude on the story and distract the reader. By setting it in the eighties, I could just hint at the whole nineties scene and what would happen to kids culturally during that decade—such as when the cousins do the slap together in the car. I wanted to direct the narrative to that less complicated period of the eighties, the "neutral" eighties, so the setting didn't interfere with the story.

BREAK

JH: I would like to shift our discussion to your history as a writer. A graduate student of mine is working on a dissertation that compares you and Ann Petry and Dorothy West. She wants to examine the kinds of networks that you participated in to support yourself as writers at a historical moment when, not only for women, it was a tough time to be a writer at all. I am interested in how you came upon writing as a career. I know you went to Hunter for a couple of years; was there a job that you were thinking about at the end of that?

PM: Well, I started out as a social work major at Brooklyn College and I think that had to do with the fact that there were really only a couple of options available for women going to college at that time: one, of course, was to teach and the other was social work. For some reason, I knew I didn't want to teach. Never say never! [laughter] Life! So I chose social work. Then after those two years I became very ill [with tuberculosis] and had to leave school for a time, and during that period I really had to deal with the fact that I was majoring in something I really did not want to do. So when I returned to school, I became an English major—but I held fast to the decision not to teach. Even when my faculty advisor called me in and said, "You know, you have to graduate and I'm really pleading with you to take your education courses," I held out.

JH: That was 1954?

PM: Yes, I graduated and I got a job with a clone of *Ebony* that was called *Our World*. Even though it was not a particularly satisfying work experience—I had to churn out *Ebony*-like stories about entertainers and their lifestyles, how many swimming pools they had, how many hundreds of pairs of shoes in their closets, that kind of thing—it helped me because I became fearful that I would end up a hack writer for a third-rate magazine. So in an act of desperation one day, I went home and started writing *Brown Girl, Brownstones*. I had flirted around with the whole idea of writing fiction but it was such a terrifying prospect. I had been a member of writers' groups, talked about writing fiction a lot, engaged in any number of debates about realism and naturalism and so on, but I didn't really write seriously. But I think after the shock of working for a magazine that was always on the verge of going out of business—which it finally did—I decided to dive in.

JH: At one point, *Our World* did send you out into the world, though, right?

PM: Yes they did. To Brazil, the West Indies . . . and *Soul Clap Hands and Sing* came out of that Brazilian experience. It wasn't all negative, working at that magazine, it wasn't all negative at all.

JH: There is an amazing photograph of you in *Our World*. You were getting off the plane in Trinidad, perhaps, and your expression just seemed to say, "Joy!"

PM: Oh really? Ohhhh! I don't remember . . .

JH: Well, I'm probably the only person who has ever read all of *Our World*! But I was searching out your presence. One of the things I was paying attention to was the moment you finally made an appearance on the masthead, which I suspect was a struggle.

PM: Yes, it was indeed—even though my rise to the masthead was really swift because they were going out of business. They brought me in as a researcher and in two months time I was promoted to Food and Fashion Editor, and after that, I was a Featured Writer! [laughter]

JH: Was John Davis [the editor of *Our World*] supportive of you wanting to be a writer? Did he know that you had literary ambitions?

PM: No, not really. He was just willing to take a chance when I came into his office off the street with my Smith College white gloves on and said, "I have been looking for a job for almost a year and I haven't been able to get one." He said, "What can you do? What experience do you have?" I said, "Well, I'm trying to get a job so I can get some experience!" [laughter]

JH: I am fairly certain that *Our World*'s John Davis was the same John Davis who was on the masthead of the magazine *Fire!!* that Zora Neale Hurston, Langston Hughes, and Wallace Thurman edited during the Harlem Renaissance.

PM: Yes, I think you're correct; he was someone who was always interested in writing and publishing. He was a book publisher who was willing to take chances on young writers, but I think it was a miserable disappointment. I can't tell you how cruel the magazine business is! He just didn't know how to handle the business aspect of it and couldn't get a partner who did, so eventually he had to sell the whole thing to *Ebony*. The name *Our World* will never be in existence again because *Ebony* magazine owns it.

JH: You said you participated in writers' groups?

PM: Yes, the Harlem Writer's Guild.

JH: What was the experience like there?

PM: Well, it was wonderful to be in the company of peers, people like myself who were all taking on this terrifying business of trying to be writers. There were even one or two of them, such as John Killens, who had already been published. It offered a community of writers that I desperately needed when I was working on *Brown Girl, Brownstones*. Now, in terms of their criticism of my work, that's another thing that we won't go into! I didn't have much patience with their comments! But I needed that group to know there were others out there with this absolutely insane notion of being a fiction writer.

JH: Were there many women in the group? Was Hansberry in it?

PM: No, Hansberry wasn't, but I think most of them were women. It would vary from time to time. Rosa Guy was in the group initially, and Sarah Wright and Brenda Wilkinson . . . you know, people were coming and going. It was really John Oliver (Killens) and Rosa's workshop. They were the two leading stars, certainly while I was a member.

HH: How long did you work with them?

PM: *Brown Girl, Brownstones* was published in 1959. I don't recall being involved with them very much after that. I just needed it in that early period to shore me up.

JH: Were there points in the late fifties, early sixties that networks of women in particular were important to you? Were there opportunities for you to step back and think, either individually or collectively, about your roles specifically as women within the civil rights movement?

PM: Yes, but it was almost in a negative way. There was the sense that it was almost a disservice to the movement for women to be demanding attention and liberation *as women* because there was this larger reality of civil rights that we had to address. I remember Abbey Lincoln, a wonderful singer, who was living at the time with Max Roach, really felt she had to stay a few paces behind, defer to him, because black men had to be supported and encouraged.

JH: At the same time, she got together the Congress of Women of African Heritage. It must have been very difficult ground to negotiate.

PM: Yes, it was very difficult because on one hand, we felt a need and desire to embrace the whole larger struggle and perhaps, as some argued, even to grant primacy to the men. At the same time, we were women who felt a tremendous need to fulfill self. A lot of marriages went on the rocks because of that, certainly one of mine did. It was a very difficult time because there was always the need to have your own sense of self, to be respectful of that, to express that. How were you going to do it and at the same time defer? That, of course, has been the dilemma of any number of women writers.

JH: I am interested in the tendency to see silence as the alleged response to such dilemmas. I stumbled upon accounts of the protest that Abby Lincoln,

Sarah Wright, and Rosa Guy organized at the United Nations around the assassination of Patrice Lumumba and I am surprised that none of the stories we tell our students now deal with that at all. As you are describing all the strands of conversation that were taking place, what was in the air, the personal and existential dilemmas you were dealing with, I find it hard to understand how can we not know that these artists were organizing themselves, in different ways, in response?

PM: That is due to historical omissions. The record is just not there. Think of all the protests and demonstrations that Louise Meriwether organized in Hollywood when there was talk of making a movie of William Styron's book on Nat Turner [*The Confessions of Nat Turner*]. This should be part of the history but it is not! If it is not in the archives there in the Schomburg [library in New York], then it is not known. This is how history is controlled. When history is described as a truthful assessment of an era, that is not necessarily true.

JH: How did you finally push the manuscript of *Brown Girl, Brownstones* out the door?

PM: I had no idea how to go about it in the orthodox way, which meant even then getting yourself an agent who would shop it around for you and know what publishers might be interested in your type of manuscript. So, not knowing any of that I simply went to the Yellow Pages of the New York telephone book, then to "Publishers." There were no publishers under A, but there was one under B, Bobbs-Merrill, so I sent it to Bobbs-Merrill, which was a very reputable publishing house at that time. Bobbs-Merrill kept it for close to six months and I was really in a dilemma: Do I call and ask them what they are doing with my manuscript? Might this damage its possibilities? Or was it just languishing on somebody's desk and they had forgotten to send it back to me? So I just sat there waiting and waiting until I learned that yes, Bucklin Moon, who was one of the great editors at the time, had very much liked the book. But editors played musical chairs and he had gone off or had been urged to go off somewhere else and left the manuscript behind, so they sent it back to me. But in the interim, while I was sort of dancing attendant on Bobbs-Merrill, I had heard that the editor-in-chief at Random House was interested in young writers. He had just discovered William Styron's *Lie Down in Darkness* and brought that out. So I said, "Interested in young writers? Okay!" I packed up my manuscript, sent it off, and they took it. I was extraordinarily lucky. But I was unlucky too because, since I did not have an agent when the book came out, there was nothing done by way of promotion and publicity. Even though it got excellent reviews, because it was a first novel, there was no publicity or marketing done. Bennett Cerf was the publisher of Random House at the time. It was only when the Feminist Press came along in 1981 that the book was resurrected.

HH: So you had to go through a good long time of never seeing it loved in the way that it is now loved? It was not until 1981 that people were really aware of it?

PM: Absolutely. It had just disappeared off the scene in 1959.

JH: How did you pay the bills during that period?

PM: Well, because it was so well received critically, I got a Guggenheim the year after it was published. Then I got an American Academy of Arts and Letters Award. Then along came the National Endowment for the Arts, I got a couple of awards from them, and I got a Ford Foundation. Oh, I was very good at writing the applications! They supported me for a long time. Then when the grants ran out, that was sometime in the seventies, I started teaching. At that time there was a lot of pressure on university campuses to diversify and at Yale the students were threatening to pull a Cornell on them with the guns at the door and so on! I got hired there and stayed for about three years, and I have been teaching at various places ever since.

HH: In the interim, how did you respond to the critical acclaim but lack of public awareness of *Brown Girl, Brownstones*? Did it affect your writing?

PM: The critics liked it and there was a modest readership, but my salvation as a writer, from very early on, has been my commitment to staying the course, no matter what. It is harder for writers to do that now, when pop culture is so valued. It is hard to think about loving your work to the extent where, even if it is not noticed, you continue doing it. For me, after *Brown Girl, Brownstones*, I was so eager to grow, to test myself as a writer. I was so committed to the art because I had found the thing I wanted to do. I would love—after all, my ego is just as overblown as anybody else's!—to have the world at my door, reading my work, but you have to deal with the reality that this might not happen. So, you find a way of making a living while continuing with your work. That was very possible for me in those days because of the grants I received. The reason I was in Grenada was because I got a Guggenheim. I tucked my son under my arm and went down there. I could afford a house that had a sort of outer house which I made into my study. I had a nursemaid, I had a housekeeper, there was a beautiful beach nearby. Was I complaining?! [laughter] So you see, I found a way to support myself and to do the work. I hoped, yes, that there would be a larger readership, but I also knew that might not happen.

HH: What did you feel like in 1981 when *Brown Girl, Brownstones* was flying off the shelves?

PM: Well, in 1981 it was a book that I had done a couple of decades ago. I was eager to have people read the book that came out in 1969 which was *The Chosen Place, the Timeless People*. Oh, talk about the work that book took! I was eager for people to be reading that and I was also involved in trying to write *Praisesong for the Widow*. So even though I am very pleased that *Brown Girl, Brownstones* has become a sort of American classic, I sometimes get a little irritated at all the people who say, "Oh, I love *Brown Girl, Brownstones*!" Okay, but there are some other things out there too! [laughter]

JH: In lots of ways, the appearance of *Brown Girl, Brownstones* in the 1980s distorted people's perception of who you had been over the last twenty years. The ways in which that coming-of-age story was talked about tended to make you into the person you were when writing your first novel.

PM: Yes, there are readers who know me only through *Brown Girl, Brownstones* and that is why they become unsettled and annoyed when they come across a book like *The Fisher King* or *The Chosen Place, the Timeless People*. That is the way it goes. How do you address that? How do you get a closer look at the later work? I don't know because these later works are not in the popular genre, they are not easily accessible, they are not easy reads. As I said earlier, I demand a lot from the reader. The politics of the publishing marketplace are also involved and they are fierce. You have to cultivate connections and if you are not skilled at that, it can take away from your work receiving that special kind of attention. But the way that you deal with that as a writer is through the whole commitment to staying the course. You write for a readership that can appreciate it. It might not be sizeable in terms of millions, but a respectable readership out there sustains you. As one young scholar said to me, "Your work has given us a future." Wonderful, wonderful! So you take something like that and you let it sustain you because that's what it's about.

JH: Did marketplace politics come into play with *Praisesong*? Did publishers expect you to do another book that looked exactly like *The Chosen Place, the Timeless People*? Was there resistance to a novel about an older woman?

PM: No, not really. I had gotten a handsome advance for *The Chosen Place, the Timeless People*; it was expected that the book would go big so they gave me a large advance. It took me a long, long time to research and write, but the success just didn't happen because it came out at the wrong time. It was vilified; a book that dealt with an interracial relationship, oh my, people got negative! Larry Neal! All they saw through their very narrow lens was this one relationship in the novel. And yet that book is still being taught. But there was a resistance that was brought on by the time—certainly by the black intelligentsia. That there was an interracial relationship in the book was just insupportable to them, so they didn't even deal with the real meaning of the novel.

JH: Part of the resistance also might have had to do with how little attention had been given at that point to how the novel as a form might be transformed by the history taking place. Most of the theorizing centered on poetry and the use of the vernacular, for example, and lots of attention was being paid to the direction of drama at the moment, but rarely did people focus on the novel.

PM: Yes, maybe the reception also had to do with it being a novel, and even sort of a classical novel at that. You are right, there was a feeling at the time that you had to come up with new ways of writing—radicalized poetry and so on. I suppose it is possible that they might have just seen it as "just another conventional novel" and dismissed it as such. Anyway, that was something of a blow because I thought that, within the black intelligentsia and writers, it would have gotten a fair hearing. But not at all, not at all.

HH: Do you think it has since?

PM: By some, but many thought that the whole novel should have been written in the vernacular.

JH: During the time that you were thinking about and beginning to write *The Chosen Place, the Timeless People*, were you thinking about what it would mean for you to be a writer in the midst of the ways in which the civil rights movement was transforming itself? Did you think about being out in the world in the ways in which people were debating Ellison's absence and other folk's presence?

PM: I had to deal with it in a couple of ways, first of all by being as much out in the world politically as I could be, so I was a member of the Association of Artists for Freedom and all of the other groups out marching and demonstrating. I did not go South, but in the North there was a sizeable movement also and I was a part of that. But there was not a separation of writing and politics; it was just always clear for me as a writer that the political was inseparable, inseparable, from what I felt I needed to say—what I was impelled to say—in the world. I could not avoid the political. I would always, yes, be primarily a storyteller, but a storyteller who is always telling about the social, the political, the racial, because they are my reality. How could I write and not deal with the subjects, areas and concerns that were at the very core of my being? I had no conflict with that. I had no conflict with being able to be active politically. I remember once I said to Malcolm [X] (he would call me every once in a while when he just needed to talk), "I have been wrestling with whether it isn't indulgent and self-centered of me to be here sitting writing?" He really made it clear to me that the struggle is fought in many ways, on many fronts, and literature is certainly one of those fronts.

JH: That must have been a pretty amazing affirmation.

PM: Absolutely, because then I could feel a kind of comfort in doing what I really wanted to do and know that I was making a contribution. Certainly *The Chosen Place, the Timeless People* was my contribution in that period.

JH: How did you come to meet Malcolm X?

PM: Gosh, it goes back so far. It was part of that community of people who were becoming politically aware, radicalized and involved in the movement. Malcolm and I just had an easygoing kind of relationship in which he knew that sometimes, to just get away from the pressure, he could get on the phone and just talk to me. I remember the last time I saw him: I threw a New Year's Eve party and he came. I had called him because I knew the pressure he was under, and I knew that the powers that be had decided that he had to go. So, I just called him and said, "I'm doing this disgraceful thing of having a New Year's Eve party," which I very seldom do because I can't stand the way people drop in and drop out! "I'd love for you and Betty to come." And he said, "You know, we really need to." So they came and I made sure that, because in African American culture a lot of pig is eaten at New Year's, I had lamb for them. I remember he stood for the whole night with his back against the wall; the inevitable was very close at hand. But he did come. I think he was a little disappointed with the party because of the amount of pig! [laughter] But people were just so pleased to see him—that was one party where you didn't get people flowing out! They stayed, they went over, even though he stood in that one spot, and talked to him. It was wonderful. That was the last time I saw him. [pause] So I was involved, but at the same time I saw writing as part of the involvement.

HH: Certainly you can see literature as a powerful and lasting political tool in addition to more immediate forms of activism?

PM: I think there is a place for each. But you do get the feeling from time to time that you are somewhat ensconced in your study while, as Maya [Angelou] would say, "the woods are on fire." *The woods are on fire.* So I had to wrestle with that until Malcolm really helped me to see that I, too, was making a contribution in my way.

JH: Your comments in "Shaping the World of My Art" are still resonant in this regard for me when you discuss how, in the same paragraph, both Ellison and Fanon are important to you. That's the most straightforward message about the many ways to be engaged in the struggle. You talk about how people need to find what is powerful for them, what works for them, what provides them with a way of making sense of the world.

PM: Yes, I am someone who really looks to all kinds of sources for direction and enlightenment, so I can go from a Fanon to an Ellison, who might seem very different from one another. For me, Ellison was so important, not so much *Invisible Man* but his collection of essays called *Shadow and Act* in which he talks about the black writer's responsibility to really deal with the *complexity* of our lives.

JH: Everybody's responsibility.

PM: Yes, yes, right. But it is even more so the black writer's responsibility not to take a segregated aspect of our experience and make that seem to be the totality of it. It is something that I have found invaluable.

JH: Was your family background enough to make you diasporan in perspective, or was it due more to the radicalizing that was taking place at the moment?

PM: That sense of a larger political world goes all the way back to my childhood. My parents, especially my mother and her friends, were very involved with the Marcus Garvey movement. Even though there was the "back to Africa" movement and even though my mother's group contributed to the Black Star Line, they would never have gone to Africa. But they talked a great deal about Garvey, about his embracing and promotion of the black world. That had a tremendous effect on me. It gave me the clear sense that my world was not solely defined by Bed-Stuy Brooklyn, but that there was this larger world of peoples of color. The talk among the women was about Africa and the West Indies, so I always had the sense of a larger world than the one in which I was confined. And that world was defined politically, yes, defined politically. That background was helpful when the civil rights movement came about in the sixties because I'd had that earlier preparation. I was ready to deal with a world that was larger than self, larger than that little constricted community I was in. For me, the *reality* of the black experience was that larger world. Most of my characters come out of that feeling on my part, with the most recent one of course, being Sonny.

JH: What politicized you in such a way? Obviously the continuity with your mother's perspective is clear but there were some differences too in that, by choosing to become a writer as opposed to a social worker or a nurse or a teacher, the roles that were publicly held out to you, you broke from the pattern. Was it simply about vocation or was there a sense that you weren't going to be a striver in the same way that, perhaps, other members of your Bajan community were?

PM: I can't answer that. I mean, my mother and her friends were really responsible for my secret desire to try my hand at writing because they were such phenomenal talkers. They were remarkable in their ability to use language, and even though I certainly wasn't conscious of it, there was a part of me that wanted to see, to discover, whether I had something—I wanted something—of that power with language that I sensed they had. They were all, what they called, "mout' kings." Brilliant talkers. It was their use of language, the joy, the authority they found in language, the way that language served them as a political weapon, that I sensed. I could not have articulated, could not have described it, but I sensed at a deep level that I wanted some small part of that. I think I knew early on I could not have it the way they did—being able to, on the spot, each day create the marvelous and magical. I knew I would have to do it in a harder way, by putting it down on paper. But I wanted something of that gift of language, of being able to manipulate words and to hold others spellbound. It was there that the base, the foundation, was laid.

What added to it was when I discovered literature and found there the same use of language, that same power with the Word. The word in capital "W"! I just knew this was what I wanted to do, even though there were tremendous pressures from the community to be the social worker, the school teacher—and even greater pressure in Bajan families far better off than mine to be the doctor or the lawyer. My mother, with whom I had a difficult relationship, offered me no encouragement. "College, what?! They just started hiring colored at the telephone company! You best go and beg them for a job!" But I had made up my mind. I was the valedictorian in my junior high school, salutatorian in my high school, and so it seemed to me, "Well, why *wouldn't* I go to college?" I had this tremendous drive to go to college. But that meant I had to work two jobs to pay my way, which is why I got sick after those first two years at Hunter College.

HH: I don't know when your mother died. How much of your work did she get to read?

PM: Nothing. She died before *Brown Girl, Brownstones* was published. But her Bajan friends in Brooklyn had a very interesting reaction to *Brown Girl, Brownstones* when it came out. They praised it, but then to show their latent disapproval, they said, "But why that wuthless girl have to tell the truth?"

They wanted a happy ending—like all readers! I'm sure she would have had pretty much the same opinion.

HH: Was your mother aware of her own gift with language?

PM: For her it was as natural as breathing. Children of her generation in the West Indies were raised to be confident on their feet. They had what were called "tea meetings," a very British custom, where they had to recite long memorized passages from the classics, even though they might not understand a word! But this gave them confidence and self-assurance. There was none of the hesitation that you get in American speakers where there is the hemming and hawing that I find so irritating—and that's of course, why I write every word down! I was exposed to her gift from early on. If you went to a West Indian wedding it was like being in a majestic forum. When they addressed the bride and groom, the whole ritual of marriage, they *held forth in eloquence*! Men and women alike.

JH: Obviously one of the ways in which *The Chosen Place, the Timeless People* will be remembered is as a pioneering postcolonial novel. You point to the continuity from your mother's relationship with the Garvey movement, but what other things moved you along to a different type of analysis and openness?

PM: Well, of course, there was the whole movement of the sixties: embracing of one's blackness, reaching out to Africa. There was a willingness to identify and to be associated with Africa. So I was writing not only out of the early instruction and exposure of my childhood, but also out of what was happening at the very present moment.

JH: Had you met any African or Caribbean writers at that time? You were living in Grenada during part of writing that, right?

PM: Yes, but I had met a number of key people before that. I had traveled some in the West Indies and met writers such as Derek Walcott and George Lamming, Earl Lovelace and Eddie Brathwaite—sorry! He's no longer Eddie but Kamau Brathwaite. I had also met Chinua Achebe, as well as Wole Soyinka, at FESTAC [Black and African Festival of Arts and Culture] in 1977.

HH: Jim referred to *The Chosen Place, the Timeless People* as a pioneering postcolonial novel. I would be interested in hearing your view of how critics and the academy have defined the concepts of postcolonial and postmodern, and of postcolonial and postmodern writing more specifically.

PM: Well, I think I can talk with a little bit more certainty about postcolonial because it does have to do with a very real thing—with the breakup of an empire and what was going to happen to these little fledgling nations now that the metropolitan powers had withdrawn. That interested me endlessly because I began to see that even though the powers had withdrawn, they had left their imprint on these islands and countries. There was still very much a colonial mentality operating in these places. I would go into the primary schools in Barbados to give a talk and there was the queen, sitting right there on the walls. You ask yourself, "Is this truly independence?" I began questioning the whole *notion* of independence. I saw the political leadership continuing the old policies, the old attitudes. As I thought about and reflected on all of this I knew that, in order for me to answer the questions that I had *put to myself* about it, I would have to write. When you write, it's not spelled out in a kind of orderly way. It is all percolating—nagging questions, observations that are troubling—before you begin even thinking about writing about it.

HH: When you begin to write, how much do you know what you are going to write about?

PM: I have a kind of outline, very rough, of where I think I may want to take a novel. Regarding *The Chosen Place, the Timeless People*, I was in Barbados in the fifties overhauling *Brown Girl, Brownstones* when a group of anthropologists who were having their first fieldwork experience came to town. Observing their interaction with the indigenous population both interested and troubled me. But I didn't give very much thought to it until the sixties when the civil rights movement began; then I began to see the possibilities of a story about those people that I had met all those years ago. I began to see how I could use the experience in a story that would reflect what was going on politically. But it was only when I got the book underway that slowly, over time—and I cannot emphasize that enough—over time, things began to be revealed to me. It really has to do with the fact that writing literature, fiction, is both a conscious and unconscious experience. I began writing the book in a very conscious way, trying to define my characters, trying to convey a sense of place and so on, concentrating on all of the technical problems. I was also at the same time creating the kind of energy that released information, direction, and ideas from that deeper level. It's all there at that deeper level. But for me, and each writer has his or her own way of accessing that material—Virginia Woolf wrote a lot about trusting the unconscious, so did Flannery O'Connor—I find a way of accessing it by forging ahead and writing stuff that I know is not going to remain. I call it "throw-away writing," which, for me, generates the type of involvement with the work, the kind of energy I need, to open up that deeper level.

HH: Are the "throw-away writings" actual elements of the story, or are they pieces of background writing, character biography, scene setting?

PM: The "throw-away writing" is related to the story, but it is material that

I sense will be supplanted as more information comes to light from that deeper place within myself. As a writer, you understand what you want to do with the novel as you actually get the process underway. This is why I encourage my students who are working on novels not to feel they have to have the whole thing absolutely clear in mind at the start, because one of the marvels of writing is that you come into greater understanding once the actual work is underway. That's exciting, that really is exciting.

HH: Tell me a bit about how things revealed themselves when writing *Daughters*. I am particularly interested in the way that novel provides a critique of tourism and neocolonialism.

PM: I was really trying to accomplish a couple of things that had to do with both the personal, with Ursa, and with the political, with Triunion. Ursa is coming out from under the shadow of patriarchy, becoming able to make a break with her father who was so attractive, so irresistible, but who also cramped her, did not permit her to flower. At the same time, the novel also deals with the patriarchy that is neocolonialism, the imposition of the larger powers, and how nations, societies come out from under *that* red rock. It's about the long struggle that is involved with finding self—whether it's personal self, or community self, or national self. *Daughters* essentially engages how to stand on your own two feet. For Ursa, that means being able to love the PM but also to make the break from him. For a country like Triunion—it's perhaps a struggle that's not going to be successful—but it's about at least being aware of how they are still under the heavy patriarchal hand of the outside powers, whether they are expressed in terms of tourism—the whole economy of some of these fragile little islands is tourism—or whether it's something else. You have got to talk about that in political terms. The book really tries to address both personal and political emancipation.

HH: Is there a novel that you found more difficult to write than any of the others?

PM: They all have their own type of difficulty so I would not compare, say, the difficulty of *The Chosen Place, the Timeless People* with the difficulty of *The Fisher King* or *Daughters*. They all exist for me in their own universe. I have been with them in their particular universes and lived with them through all the pain and the pleasure. I can't say I suffered more with one than with another—each of them presented its own kind of travail. I don't merge or confuse them with each other.

JH: What was *Praisesong*'s particular difficulty?

PM: How to incorporate the folktale of the band of enslaved Africans walking across the Atlantic back to Africa. I sensed that tale had something of great importance to this middle-aged, middle-class black woman who is the protagonist. What was this message? That question fired me to take on the book because I had to answer it. And how, then, in terms of craft and technique was I going to make it happen? I wrestled in that novel with trying to render in fictional terms what was being said by those Africans to this well-heeled African American woman.

HH: I know we have been talking for a long time, but I am wondering whether we might talk more about *Soul Clap Hands and Sing* for just a few minutes? The resonance of that text seems to be rooted in the poignancy of the human mistakes we make in just trying to love ourselves and love one another. Can you comment on that?

PM: Well, on one level my motivation for writing that book was very practical. When *Brown Girl, Brownstones* came out it was very positively reviewed. The only criticism as such was that the men—the father, Deighton Boyce, in particular—weren't dealt with in a very sympathetic way. I seemed more capable, according to some, of writing about women than men. Well, I knew at the time that the second novel was going to be a long haul, and since they were criticizing my ability to write about men, I decided to write a book of four novellas in which all of the principal characters would be men. Three of the novellas in *Soul Clap Hands and Sing* came directly from time in South America and the West Indies as a reporter for *Our World*. It was, as I saw it, a sort of quickie book but again, I was really trying to look at the impact of colonialism—certainly in the British Guiana story and even, in part, in the Brazil story. The one that is most anthologized, though, is "Barbados." Why is that? I do think it is partly because a woman takes a stand, she comes into her own, in that story. It is a book of love and what happens when you don't extend yourself. It continues a theme at the heart of *Brown Girl, Brownstones*—how acquiring property and the quest of the American dream often brings about the death of love within the family.

HH: How did "Brooklyn" end up being in there?

PM: Thanks to my trials and tribulations with a professor at Brooklyn College! [Laughter] I saw that same imposition of people in authority, the people of nations in authority, on those that they consider the other, on those that they consider fragile.

JH: I would say it also rehearses some things that come up in *The Chosen Place, the Timeless People* in connecting together different kinds of persecution. Even with this professor, this objectionable harasser, there is also this level of sympathy for him as being persecuted under a type of McCarthyism.

PM: Absolutely. I don't create villains. My characters have fatal flaws, but with some redeeming qualities as well.

HH: I am surprised to hear that people find your portrayal of Deighton unsympathetic. If anything, I would say the portrayal of Silla is less sympathetic. Deighton's character is, for me, one of the most moving and painful in all your books. He is such a flawed, at times tragic, beautiful-ugly man. Maybe that is what people resist, the fact that you actually create real people as opposed to the stereotype of a man that society keeps trying to make men into. Primus, from *Daughters*, strikes me in much the same way—as just a handful of beautiful-tragic contradictions.

JH: Yes, one of the things that I thought was moving about *The Fisher King* was that Sonny's struggle did not revolve around stereotypical notions of manhood. Even his signature was not about defending.

PM: Yes, both Sonny-Rhett in *The Fisher King* and Deighton in *Brown Girl, Brownstones* represent aspects of my community that I am always trying to explore, to examine, in the work. They are both artists. True, Deighton couldn't play the trumpet, but he had an artistic temperament. He was the one who made Selina aware of nature and of values apart from the material. These two are liabilities in the eyes of their community. Society can't afford them! For example, in the wedding scene in *Brown Girl, Brownstones* when the guests sing "small island, go back where you come from!" they are really rejecting Deighton, the artist. They can't afford the threat he represents to their notion of the American dream. He is the sacrificial lamb to that dream. That's really one of the major themes of that first novel and of most of my work.

HH: Well, with that we have come almost full circle so why don't we close. You have given us so much to think about as we approach your existing and future writing! Thank you so much for both your work and the time you have given us today to talk about it.

Richmond, Virginia
September 21, 2001

Paule Marshall on Race and Memory

Dawn Raffel/2009

From More (more.com), April 23, 2009. Reprinted by permission of Dawn Raffel.

Paule Marshall, the hugely influential African American novelist, short story writer and essayist (her many books include *Brown Girl, Brownstones*; *Soul Clap Hands and Sing*; and *Praisesong for the Widow*) turns 80 this spring. She is going strong, with a stunning memoir, *Triangular Road*, just out from Basic Civitas. I recently spoke with Ms. Marshall:

Q: I read several of your novels when I was a young woman; for me, this book felt like a gift not only of itself but because it brought me back to your earlier work, which I want to re-read. Your new book, *Triangular Road*, is a memoir with a wide-angle lens, spanning continents and cultures. What was the impetus for writing it?

A: It was essentially a desire to look back over my life and identify some of the people and some of the situations that were so fundamental to my writing. Of course, family was very much a part of that. Also, community. First, there is Brooklyn, where I was born and grew up. Then there's the fact that my parents came from Barbados, which sort of sits off by itself like a shy lily, away from the string of islands that make up the Caribbean. And then there was curiosity on my part about the colossus of Africa. That's why the memoir is called *Triangular Road*.

Q: What is the road? Is it water? Is it a road of blood? Of time?

A: It's a road of time. It's a road of connections. It's a road of identification of the factors that not only created me as a person but also deeply influenced my writing.

Q: You talk a lot about the poet Langston Hughes.

A: Mr. Hughes had a profound impact on me. One of the most astonishing things was that when I finally managed to finish my first book [*Brown*

Girl, Brownstones] and was given a reading at a small storefront in Harlem [in 1959], who should walk in but the poet laureate of Black America? He became a kind of mentor, a friend. He would suggest places where I should apply for grants and would recommend my book to funding organizations. The State Department used to send him around the world as a cultural ambassador. For one of those trips, which was to Europe, Mr. Hughes told the State Department that he wanted to take two young writers with him, and he chose me as one of those. His taking a junior writer gives you a sense of what a kind and thoughtful person he was.

Q: In your book, you describe the Atlantic as an entire ocean sitting Shiva. Can you talk about that?

A: Yes. I used to stretch whatever grant money I got by going to live in the West Indies, especially Barbados. And one of the things that struck me there was the awesome presence of the sea. I would take long walks along the beach and hear the waves crashing on the shore. There was almost a kind of distraught, mournful, angering sound to it. In the Jewish religion there is the ritual at death that's called sitting Shiva. The cries of loss, the tearing of the clothes are very dramatic expressions of distress. And it just struck me as a wonderful way to describe the Atlantic as it came in from Africa.

Q: As if it had a memory of the dead.

A: Yes. Weeping for all of the black people turned into slaves. Barbados was the first island the slave ships reached. That was landfall.

Q: You also write about the island of Carriacou and witnessing a ring/shout—a ritual of song and dance, which inspired your novel *Praisesong for the Widow*. Why is it so important for us to connect to our deep past?

A: It gives us a deeper sense of self. History tells us in a very dramatic way where we've come from, what we've had to endure and how we have overcome it. Also—and especially with Carriacou—our cultural strength and inheritance, those songs, those dances, those rituals, were part of a whole survival system.

Q: You write about your futile attempts to trace your missing father's roots in Barbados: "Everything about Sam Burke was also hidden behind God's back and remained so." A few lines later, you describe yourself as, "again, furious with the father I continue hopelessly to love"—which I found so moving and so universal. I think many people have that fury and that love even after the loss of a parent. Your parents died fairly young. Do you feel that your relationship with them continues?

A: It doesn't continue in a formal way, but it is so much a part of my sense of being, who I am and how I came about to be the writer Paule Marshall.

My mother was a great storyteller and she and her women friends would sit around the table in the brownstone house and recall their lives as girls growing up in Barbados. I call them the poets in the kitchen.

Q: The way you've recorded them, their language was very melodious. It had its own cadence that's just beautiful to read.

A: Yes, they did. This was their way of sort of diluting that stiff British education they had been given in Barbados, so the language expressed their special way of looking at the world.

Q: Although your first novel, *Brown Girl, Brownstones*, was a coming of age novel, you've said that writing it was a way of moving forward. *Triangular Road* looks back on five decades, but I was wondering whether in some way the writing of it is also a way of moving forward.

A: *Brown Girl, Brownstones* was an attempt to be daring enough to see if I could translate onto the page some of the impressions and experiences and relationships that made up my world growing up. I thought that if I remembered the poetry and drama I heard in the voices in my neighborhood, if I really tried to understand what their whole need was, in coming to America and purchasing houses and so on—if I could understand the sociology of their lives, I would maybe be able to make it real for the reader.

Q: I think you did! *Triangular Road* is a record made much later in life, but do you also feel that it moves you forward? Is there another project now?

A: I think there might be. The last chapter in *Triangular Road* describes a conference I attended in Nigeria. That was my first time in Africa, so that was the other leg of the triangle. There was Brooklyn, there was Barbados, there was Africa-at-last; the colossus from which we all came. If I can convey some of my impressions from after this conference, when I was able to travel in East Africa, I will be writing about that.

Q: I hope there are many more books.

A: Well, that might be the last one, but anyway, it's always nice to want to move on to something else after you finished one book, at least for me.

Index

Achebe, Chinua, 184
Ake, 140
American Academy of Arts and Letters, 178
American Youth for Democracy, 54
Angelou, Maya, 181
Association of Artists for Freedom, 51, 54, 69, 180
Austen, Jane, 60, 117, 139

Baldwin, James, 41, 52, 65, 68, 69, 142, 159–60, 171
Bambara, Toni Cade, 66, 170–71
Baraka, Amiri, 52
Beloved, 141
"Between the World and Me," 143
Black Ice, 140
Black Star Line, 62, 182
Black Women Novelists, 79
Brathwaite, Edward Kamau, 37, 109, 184
Brent, Linda, 57
Brooklyn, New York, 36, 41, 54, 59, 70, 73, 78–79, 84, 144, 152, 160
Brooklyn College, 54, 174, 187
Brooklyn Public Library, 87, 95, 117, 139
Brooks, Gwendolyn, viii, 40, 60, 66, 77, 93, 113, 118
Brown, Karen, 141
Brown Girl, Brownstones, viii, ix, xii, xiii, 39–40, 43–45, 48, 50, 54–56, 59–65, 67–69, 74–76, 77, 79–80, 83, 84–88, 90, 93–94, 102–4, 110, 113, 117, 121–23, 126–27, 130, 132, 133–34, 144, 146, 149, 151–55, 157–58, 160–61, 171, 174, 176–79, 183, 185, 187–88, 189–90, 191
Buddenbrooks, 31, 87

Cary, Lorene, 140
CBS Television Workshop, 50
Cerf, Bennett, 74, 93, 178
China, 25, 38, 46
Chosen Place, the Timeless People, The, x–xii, 32–36, 46–50, 54, 58, 69, 75, 77, 81, 88, 90, 100, 102, 104, 109, 113–14, 121, 130, 132, 133, 134–36, 147, 172, 179–81, 184–88
Christian, Barbara, 79, 86
Clifton, Lucille, 52
Coltrane, John, 160
Columbia University, 51, 75, 77
Congress of Women of African Heritage, 176
Conrad, Joseph, 34, 39, 52, 60, 113
Craft, Ellen, 125
Crisis of the Negro Intellectual, The, 109
Cruse, Harold, 109
Cuba, 17–18

Dash, Julie, 136
Daughters, xi–xii, 94, 96–110, 114–15, 121–22, 124–27, 130–39, 141–49, 152, 154–55, 157–58, 165, 169, 186, 188
Daughters of the Dust, 136
Davis, Angela, 83, 101, 136
Davis, John P., 43, 175
Davis, Ossie, 51, 69
Death in Venice, 32, 52
Dee, Ruby, 51, 69
Dessa Rose, 141
Dickens, Charles, 113
Doctorow, E. L., 140
Douglass, Frederick, 39
Down in the Mississippi Delta, 137
Drums and Shadows, 131, 141
Du Bois, W. E. B., 39, 48, 90, 148
Dunbar, Paul Laurence, viii, 34, 52, 73–74, 113, 118, 140

Eliot, T. S., 94, 99, 121–22, 128
Ellison, Ralph, 33–34, 41, 52–53, 65, 98–99, 118, 128, 134, 142, 167, 171, 180, 182

Fanon, Frantz, 182
Fauset, Jessie, 59
Feminist Press, 93–94, 152, 178
FESTAC, xiii, xiv, 31, 184
Fire!!, 175
Fisher King, The, vii, xii, 157–70, 172–73, 179, 186, 188
Ford Foundation, 50, 178
Friedan, Betty, 70–71

Garvey, Marcus, 42, 62–63, 117, 128, 182
Granny Nanny, 101, 125, 136
Great Expectations, 139
Grey, Zane, 52, 117, 139

Guggenheim Fellowship, 178
Guy, Rosa, 40, 176–77
Hansberry, Lorraine, 65, 69, 176
Hardy, Thomas, 113
Harlem Writers' Guild, 69, 175–76
Haupt, Christopher Lehman, 172
Haydn, Hiram, vii, 74
Hearne, John, 37
Heart of Darkness, 34
Hill, Anita, 131, 144–45
Holland, Endesha Ida Mae, 137
Howe, Florence, 93, 152
Hughes, Langston, ix, xiii, 87, 175, 189–90
Hunter College, 43, 183
Hurston, Zora Neale, 44, 48, 52, 59, 66, 77, 87, 93, 113, 131, 142–44, 175

In the Castle of My Skin, 113
Incidents in the Life of a Slave Girl, 57
Invisible Man, 33, 52, 93, 118, 128, 134, 182

Jones, Gayl, 171
Jonson, Ben, 11–12
Joyce, James, 39

Kelly, William Melvin, xiii
Killens, John O., 41, 51, 176
Kincaid, Jamaica, 171

Lamming, George, 37, 113, 184
Larsen, Nella, 66, 71, 87
Lincoln, Abbey, 176–77
Little House on the Prairie, 139
Living Is Easy, The, 52
Lovelace, Earl, 184
Lumumba, Patrice, 177

MacArthur Grant, 130
Magic Mountain, The, 31–32, 88–89
Mair, Lucille, 101, 136
Malcolm X, 181
Malraux, Andre, 25
Mama Lola, A Voodoo Priestess in Brooklyn, 141
Mann, Thomas, 31–32, 39, 52, 60, 87–88, 113
Man's Fate, 25
Maud Martha, viii, 60, 71, 77, 93, 113, 118
Meriwether, Louise, 177
Morrison, Toni, 66, 77, 141–42, 171

Naipaul, V. S., 37
Nanny Town, 101, 125
National Endowment for the Arts, 50, 52, 178
Native Son, 142
Naylor, Gloria, 171
Neal, Larry, 92, 180
"New Renaissance," 41
Nurses Brigade, 42, 128

O'Connor, Flannery, 105, 141, 185
Our World Magazine, 43, 86, 174–75, 187

Paris, France, 163–64, 166
Payne, Sonny Rhett, 160
Petry, Ann, 40, 65, 174
"Poets of the Kitchen Table," 77
Powell, Bud, 159
Praisesong for the Widow, xi, 54, 58, 75, 77, 80, 93–94, 99, 102, 104, 110, 118–19, 121, 126–27, 130, 131, 132, 134–37, 141, 148–49, 157, 159, 161, 179, 186–87, 190

Pudd'nhead Wilson, 113

Raisin in the Sun, A, 65
Reckless Eyeballing, 172
Reed, Ishmael, 172
Reena and Other Stories, 72, 77, 133, 148
"Return of the Native," ix
Rhys, Jean, 102
Richmond, Virginia, 110–11, 156
Ringgold, Faith, 142
Roach, Max, 176
Rollins, Sonny, 159
"Romance in the Dark," 67

Sartre, Jean-Paul, 34
Selvon, Sam, 37
Shadow and Act, 33, 52, 118, 182
"Shaping the World of My Art," vii, 55, 182
"Some Get Wasted," ix–x
Song of Solomon, 142
"Sonny's Blues," 160
Soul Clap Hands and Sing, ix, 30, 45–46, 54, 75, 77, 88–89, 121, 170, 175, 187
Soyinka, Wole, 140, 184
Stepto, Robert B., 62
Street, The, 65
Stuyvesant Heights (Bedford-Stuyvesant), New York, 41
Styron, William, 29, 177

Tar Beach, 142
Thackeray, William Makepeace, 113
Their Eyes Were Watching God, 44, 77, 143
Third Life of Grange Copeland, The, 148
Thurman, Wallace, 175
"To Da-duh, In Memoriam," ix, 102, 148

Triangular Road, A Memoir, ix–x, xiii–xv, 189–91
Truth, Sojourner, 125
Tubman, Harriet, 125
Tutuola, Amos, 36

University of Iowa Writer's Workshop, 75, 77
Updike, John, 34

"Valley Between, The," 72, 120, 171
Vanity Fair, 113
Virginia Commonwealth University, 77, 96

Walcott, Derek, 184
Walker, Alice, 171–72
Washington, Mary Helen, 68
West, Dorothy, 48, 52, 174
Wide Sargasso Sea, 102
Wilkinson, Brenda, 176
Williams, Mary Lou, 159
Williams, Shirley Ann, 141–42
Woolf, Virginia, 185
World's Fair, 140
Wright, Richard, 39, 41, 52, 62, 87, 131, 142–43, 148, 171
Wright, Sarah, 176–77

Yale University, 39, 51, 75, 77

Zola, Emile, 52

PS
3563
.A7223
Z46
2010